HE SPARED HIMSELF IN NOTHING

ESSAYS ON
THE LIFE AND THOUGHT OF
ST. JOHN NEPOMUCENE NEUMANN, C.Ss.R.

HE SPARED HIMSELF IN NOTHING

ESSAYS ON
THE LIFE AND THOUGHT OF
ST. JOHN NEPOMUCENE NEUMANN, C.SS.R.

EDITED BY
JOSEPH F. CHORPENNING, O.S.F.S.

SAINT JOSEPH'S UNIVERSITY PRESS
PHILADELPHIA

m·real

The plates in this book are printed on Mega Gloss paper.
M-Real Paper Co. is a financial supporter of Saint Joseph's University Press.

Library of Congress Cataloging-in-Publication Data

He spared himself in nothing : essays on the life and thought of John
Nepomucene Neumann / [compiled by Joseph F. Chorpenning].
    p. cm.
Includes bibliographical references.
  ISBN 0-916101-44-4 (alk. paper)
 1. Neumann, John, Saint, 1811-1860. I. Neumann, John, Saint,
1811-1860. II. Chorpenning, Joseph F.
  BX4700.N4H4 2003
  282'.092--dc22

                                    2003017313

Published by Saint Joseph's University Press
5600 City Avenue
Philadelphia, Pennsylvania 19131-1395
www.sju.edu/sjupress/

Saint Joseph's University Press is a member
of the Association of Jesuit University Presses

TABLE OF CONTENTS

PART I
THEOLOGICAL AND SPIRITUAL FORMATION

PART II
MINISTRY

Part III
Theology and Spirituality

LIST OF ILLUSTRATIONS

LIST OF ILLUSTRATIONS

INTRODUCTION

JOSEPH F. CHORPENNING, O.S.F.S.

The year 2002 marked a double anniversary for one of Philadelphia's own, St. John N. Neumann, C.Ss.R.: the twenty-fifth anniversary of his canonization, and the sesquicentennial of his episcopal ordination as fourth bishop of Philadelphia. To commemorate these dual historic occasions, Saint Joseph's University Press has prepared this volume of essays on Neumann's life, ministry, and thought. This book also aims to foster a renewed understanding and appreciation of, as well as stimulate further research on, the first United States citizen to be declared a saint by the Roman Catholic Church. Four of the essays in this collection were originally published in scholarly journals around the time of either Neumann's beatification (1963) or canonization (1977). They have stood the test of time well, although today they are not readily accessible; hence, it was thought worthwhile to reprint them.[1] To these, five new original essays have been added that bring to light previously unexplored aspects of Neumann's formation, ministry, and theology and spirituality.

Neumann's biography and writings are among the principal threads running through the essays in this volume. Before proceeding to introduce these essays, therefore, the reader may find it helpful to have at the outset a sketch of Neumann's life and writings.

JOHN NEPOMUCENE NEUMANN (1811-60)[2]

Named in honor of the patron saint of his native Bohemia, Neumann lived just forty-nine years. Almost half of these years (twenty-four) were spent in the United States: from 29 May 1836, the day he arrived in New York City, to the day of his death, 5 January 1860. Born to exemplary Catholic parents, on 28 March 1811 in Prachatitz, Bohemia, a German-speaking mountain village in the Austro-Hungarian empire, Neumann also received his elementary education there. He subsequently attended the gymnasium or secondary school staffed by the Piarist Fathers, a religious congregation founded in the early seventeenth century by St. Joseph Calasanz (1556-1648),[3] in the neighboring but larger provincial capital of Budweis. Afterward Neumann continued his studies for two years (1829-31) at the Budweis Institute of Philosophy conducted by the Cistercian monks.

When he completed his course of study in philosophy, Neumann had to make a decision as to whether he would study theology or law or medicine. He had a strong interest in the natural sciences and felt an attraction to medicine. Neumann's hesitancy about studying theology was due to the fact that out of eighty or ninety applicants for theology, only twenty would be accepted. While his father was not opposed to Neumann studying medicine in Prague, his mother convinced him to apply for theology, and shortly thereafter he was accepted into the Budweis Theological Seminary, but as an extern student due to lack of space in the seminary.

In November 1831, Neumann began studies for the priesthood at the diocesan seminary in Budweis. His final two years of preparation for ordination (1833-35) were spent at the archdiocesan seminary associated with the theology faculty at the University of Prague. During this time he considered becoming a Jesuit or Dominican. Toward the end of his final term of study, Neumann learned to his dismay that his bishop had decided not to ordain any more priests since the diocese already had many more than it needed. This forced Neumann to turn to his long-cherished ambition, inspired by St. Paul's missionary journeys and the ministry of the Slovenian priest Frederic Baraga (1797-1868; from 1853, bishop of the Vicariate of Upper Michigan, later bishop of Sault Sainte-Marie and Marquette) among the Ottawa and Chippewa Indians, of becoming a missionary in the United States.[4]

Neumann was ordained a priest for the Diocese of New York on 25 June 1836. For the next four years, he carried on a zealous, but lonely, pastoral ministry among the smaller German congregations in the Buffalo-Rochester area. Inspired by the strong devotional fervor fostered by the Redemptorists at St. Joseph's church in Rochester and desiring the life of a religious in a community, Neumann joined the Redemptorists in 1840. He made his religious profession on 16 January 1842, becoming the first Redemptorist to be professed in the United States. Thereafter he served German communities in the Baltimore and Pittsburgh areas, and also rose to positions of responsibility within the Redemptorists as rector, vicegerent, and vice provincial. On 1 February 1852, Neumann was named fourth bishop of Philadelphia, succeeding Francis Patrick Kenrick (1797-1863), who, after twenty-one years of episcopal ministry in Philadelphia, had been named sixth archbishop of Baltimore. Consecrated on Passion Sunday, 28 March 1852, Neumann served Philadelphia as an exemplary pastor until his untimely death eight years later.

Neumann's body was buried in the lower chapel of the Redemptorist church of St. Peter the Apostle, where it lies today. A series of stained-glass windows in the chapel portray Neumann's life and many accomplishments. Neumann's cause for canonization was the first process instituted for a person from the United States. Pope Benedict XV signed the decree on the heroicity of Neumann's virtues in 1921. In the history of sanctity, this document was a watershed because it maintained that heroic virtue does not call for the spectacular because, in the pope's words, "the most simple of works, if carried out with constant perfection in the midst of inevitable difficulties, can bring every Servant of God to the attainment of a heroic degree of virtue."[5] Thus, Neumann's charism was that he did ordinary things in an extraordinary manner, and, indeed, this "ordinariness" is undoubtedly the source of his enduring attractiveness. Neumann was declared Blessed by Bl. Pope John XXIII, although the

actual solemn ceremony of beatification on 13 October 1963, during
the second session of the Second Vatican Council, was celebrated by
Pope Paul VI, who also canonized Neumann on 19 June 1977.

NEUMANN'S WRITINGS

From childhood, Neumann was a voracious reader. He says that
he acquired "a decided passion for reading" from his father, who was
"a great lover of books." His mother nicknamed him "the little
Bookworm." While other children spent time "in sports or bird
catching, I spent in reading all the books I could get hold of."[6] This
was but the beginning of a lifelong appreciation and love of books
and reading. Indeed, love of books is a constant theme in the brief
autobiographical sketch that Neumann wrote, *ex obedientia*, and
dated 27 March 1852, the eve of his ordination as bishop.[7]

Complementing this facet of Neumann was his "talent for
writing" and gift for evangelizing by the ministry of the spoken and
the printed word. Neumann prepared for this ministry from his
seminary days in Prague by compiling 2,000 pages of manuscript
notes—handwritten in his characteristic neat Gothic script—on
theology as "an arsenal of theological lore for his own instruction
and, in all probability, for future publication."[8] Divided into ninety-
one treatises covering dogmatic, moral, and ascetical theology, and
meticulously arranged under the general divisions employed by
St. Thomas Aquinas in his *Summa Theologica*, these notes reveal
Neumann's close reading of—or rather immersion in—the writings
of Augustine, Aquinas, Bellarmine, Canisius, Alphonsus Ligouri, and
many other standard authorities, as well as of the great spiritual
masters Teresa of Ávila, Louis of Granada, Francis de Sales, and
Vincent de Paul. Although Neumann never published a book based
on these notes, they assisted him in preparing sermons and some of
his later published works.

Neumann's most well-known works were written in German, in
connection with his pastoral ministry in Pittsburgh and Baltimore,
and were used extensively in German-speaking communities in the
United States during the mid- and late 1800s: two catechisms, one

for children and another for adults (first published in Pittsburgh, probably in 1842, with many editions thereafter), and his *Bible History* (first published in Pittsburgh in 1844, with many subsequent editions). As bishop of Philadelphia, Neumann published several important pastoral letters on timely topics, such as Catholic education and the dogma of the Immaculate Conception, the solemn definition of which, by Bl. Pope Pius IX on 8 December 1854 at St. Peter's Basilica in Rome, he was privileged to attend.

Of no less importance are Neumann's writings that were not written with a view to publication but were first published at the time of his beatification and canonization. For example, his *Autobiography* was first made available in a critical German edition in 1963, followed by two English translations, one by Alfred C. Rush, C.Ss.R., in 1977, and the other by Raymond H. Schmandt in 1978.[9] Neumann's *Spiritual Journal* (*Mon Journal*) was begun in 1834 during the final year of his theological studies at Prague, and continued almost until he became a Redemptorist novice in 1840. To be precise, there are actually two diaries: one in German (Neumann's native language), which begins with 22 March 1835 and ends with 27 November 1839, and another in French (a language that Neumann was learning), which begins with 1 October 1834 and ends, after an interruption of several years, with 21 July 1838. Neumann frequently made entries concurrently in both, and in content they often repeat each other. The French version of the *Journal* was published in English translation by William Nayden, C.Ss.R., over the period 1977-79 in *Spicilegium Historicum Congregationis SSmi Redemptoris*.

THE PRESENT COLLECTION OF ESSAYS

Our volume is divided into three sections of three essays each. There is a chronological and thematic progression from Neumann's early years to his priestly and episcopal ministry, and then to his theology and spirituality, which even found its way into one of the footnotes of the documents of the Second Vatican Council (1962-65).

Part I begins, appropriately, with Neumann's namesake. In his *Autobiography*, Neumann indicates that he was "named . . . John Nepomucene, in honor of the glorious Patron of Bohemia."[10] In his *Journal*, Neumann often invokes the intercession of St. John Nepomuk, as well as visits his grave in the cathedral of St. Vitus in Prague. Before leaving home to embark for America, Neumann records: "I made a pilgrimage to Nepomuc, the birthplace of my Patron Saint."[11] But who was John Nepomuk? This simple question has a complicated answer, as Paul Shore reveals. In "The Several Lives of St. John Nepomuk, A Patron Saint of Bohemia," Shore surveys the interpretation and re-interpretation of the John Nepomuk of history and legend over the course of three distinct periods of Czech history: the late fourteenth and early fifteenth centuries, the Baroque era, and the nineteenth century.

The next two essays focus on the critical period of Neumann's spiritual and theological formation as a seminary student in Prague. Augustinus Kurt Huber's "John N. Neumann's Student Years in Prague, 1833-1835" mines previously unused documents of the archives of the Prague seminary and theological faculty, together with more familiar sources, such as Neumann's *Journal* and *Autobiography*, Curley's and Berger's biographies, and the documents of Neumann's beatification process. This enables Huber to refine the picture of Neumann's seminary study in Prague. Neumann's disillusionment and negative assessment of this period is well documented. However, Huber argues that Neumann's sojourn in Prague "was not completely lacking in constructive experiences and impressions" (36),[12] including contact with important figures of the Catholic Restoration and visits to the city's churches, houses of religious orders, institute for the blind, National Museum and Imperial Library, and bookstores. Moreover, Neumann's *Journal* opens a window on his interior, spiritual development during these years. The *Journal's* testimony to Neumann's remorseless self-examination, clear consciousness of personal sinfulness, very tender, indeed scrupulous conscience, lamentations about temptations, interior aridity, and feelings of being deserted by God undercuts "all preconceived notion of an undeviating, upward movement towards sanctity" by casting into relief "the crises and problems in the evolution of Neumann the human being. Only human beings can become saints" (39). Huber's study is supplemented by two appendices, Neumann's *Autobiography* and his letter of 7 June 1834 to John Holba on papal infallibility. Neumann's student days in Prague are also the subject of Richard Boever's essay "Building a Foundation of Spirituality: St. John Neumann's European Years." Huber stressed that Neumann's *Journal* deserves more attention than it has received because it "spread[s] out before us his interior, spiritual development during his Prague sojourn," as well as "the religious psychology and piety of the Catholic Restoration" (37). Boever's close reading of the *Journal* yields the identification of six constitutive elements of the young Neumann's spirituality: (1) the desire to grow in virtue by God's grace; (2) the saints as guides and inspiration; (3) study of the Counter-Reformation spiritual masters; (4) Neumann's application of ascetical principles to his life; (5) the ascetical life expressed in ministry; and (6) a spiritual life that looked toward heaven.

Part II examines Neumann's pastoral practice and ministry as a missionary priest and then as bishop of Philadelphia in the service of an immigrant Church. In the title of her essay, Mary Charles Bryce, O.S.B., describes Neumann as "An Accomplished Catechist." Bryce, herself a noted contemporary catechist, studies Neumann's catechizing through both the spoken and written word—the former through the testimony provided in the biographies by Berger and Curley, and the latter through Neumann's *Bible History* and two catechisms. In the process, Bryce discovers the profound love that Neumann the priest and bishop had for people of all ages, especially children, and that was expressed in manifold ways by his ministry. "He was a people bishop. He enjoyed associating with people in the parishes, people in the diocese, people in the cities and rural areas where he lived. He learned the languages they spoke, the customs they cherished and the backgrounds from which they came to this 'melting pot' land. He loved them and they loved him. . . . [H]e was from beginning to end ever the model pastor" (98). Bryce also notes that while Neumann was regarded as an intellectual by many standards, yet there was never any distance between him and ordinary people: he adapted his language and approach to the people around him, never spoke to others in a condescending way, and possessed "that special quality of putting others at ease, of making them feel at home" (98) in his presence.

Complementing Bryce's study is "Blessed John Neumann, C.Ss.R., Pastoral Bishop," by Neumann's most authoritative English-language biographer, Michael J. Curley, C.Ss.R. This essay was first published following Neumann's beatification. According to Curley, Neumann's formation in the family, at the gymnasium, and in the seminary prepared him well for his future ministry, for it instilled in him industriousness, a disciplined and orderly method of approaching tasks, a compassionate understanding of student difficulties in learning, a readiness in formulating and expressing his ideas. These qualities were salient in Neumann's ministry. Although Neumann was criticized as inferior to his episcopal post by a Roman observer (Archbishop Gaetano Bedini) visiting this country, Curley counters that Neumann was an accomplished, if not a desk, administrator, a "human dynamo" who, with his great foresight, even anticipated some of the pastoral initiatives proposed at Vatican II. Among the many examples Curley cites to support his argument is "Neumann's *ad limina* report in 1854, one of the best, if not the best in the Propaganda [of the Faith] Archives for those years, . . . a living refutation of the charges leveled against him by his critics" (112-13). Moreover, Neumann's cause for remaining in Philadelphia was championed in Rome by no less than the archbishops of Baltimore, New Orleans, and San Francisco, who extolled him for his administrative talents, as well as his personal holiness and learning.

One of Neumann's most well-known achievements was his introduction of the Forty Hours devotion on a diocesan-wide level. This is the subject of Joseph C. Linck's essay "'The Brightest Jewel in their Crown': John Neumann and the Establishment of the Forty Hours Devotion in Philadelphia." After outlining the origins, historical development, theology, and spirituality of this devotion, Linck attends to the specific circumstances that prompted Neumann's resolve to introduce the Forty Hours to the city of brotherly love. For Neumann, the Forty Hours was "not mere uninformed piety" (129), but a chief component in the spiritual renewal of his diocese, "'a parish mission on a small scale'" (134). As Linck puts it, Neumann's "genius consisted in giving [this] traditional Catholic devotion an enhanced evangelical thrust" (134).

Part III turns to Neumann's spirituality and theology. An integral component of Neumann's spirituality and ministry was his fervent devotion to the Virgin Mary, as Thomas A. Thompson, S.M., documents in "'No More Powerful Friend Have We with God': The Marian Devotion of St. John Neumann." Thompson's comparative study of Neumann's *Journal*, a private diary not intended for publication, and his published catechetical works reveals "a great consistency between what Neumann taught and what he strived to attain in his personal life. That Neumann so sincerely practiced what he preached is no small sign of his holiness" (150). Thompson then analyzes Neumann's two pastoral letters on the Immaculate Conception—formal ecclesial documents lacking the personal style of the *Catechism* and *Journal*—the first issued immediately prior to his departure for Rome for the solemn declaration of this dogma (1854), and the second on his return to Philadelphia (1855).

Neumann scholars often note his veneration of St. Teresa of Ávila. However, an aspect of the reformer of Carmel's impact on the fourth bishop of Philadelphia that has been overlooked is how Neumann's reading of Teresa's testimony, in the *Book of Her Life*, chapter 6, to the power of St. Joseph's intercession sparked his devotion to the husband of Mary and earthly father of Jesus. This is the focus of Joseph F. Chorpenning's paper "St. Teresa Says She Never Failed to Receive Whatever She Asked of You!': St. Joseph in the Life and Ministry of John N. Neumann, C.Ss.R." Just as Teresa ascribed many roles to St. Joseph, so too does Neumann in his *Journal*: spiritual father, all-powerful intercessor, guide in all life's circumstances, protector at the hour of death, model of perfect resignation to the will of God, and teacher of the perfect love of the Infant Jesus. Neumann clearly merits a place alongside St. Thérèse of Lisieux and St. Bernadette Soubirous, other great nineteenth-century saints who also greatly loved St. Joseph.

It may come as a bit of a surprise that Neumann's name finds its way into one of the major documents of Vatican II, *Lumen Gentium*, the Dogmatic Constitution on the Church (1964). In the context of its emphasis on the universal call to holiness, the Council cites a document that both marked a turning point in Neumann's cause for beatification and canonization, and was truly a milestone in the history of defining sanctity: Pope Benedict XV's 1921 decree on the heroicity of Neumann's virtues. This fascinating story is masterfully recounted by Alfred C. Rush, C.Ss.R., in "The Second Vatican Council, 1962-1965, and Bishop Neumann."

In his sermon preached over Neumann's body at St. John's Pro-Cathedral, on Sunday, 8 January 1860, Fr. Edward Sourin, S.J., said of him: "He spared himself in nothing."[13] This phrase captures the essence of this saint who is a "[beacon] . . . [who] show[s] men and women the possibilities open to human beings."[14] We adopt this phrase of Fr. Sourin, one of the founding fathers of Saint Joseph's University, as the title for this book of essays that also seeks in its way to open a window on Neumann's particular type of holiness. At the same time, this book is not intended to be the final word on Neumann, but, hopefully, to foster a renewed interest in him and to serve as a stimulus for further scholarship on his life and legacy. Among the topics that future researchers might investigate are a comparison of Neumann's *Journal* with comparable spriritual diaries of the same period (1830s), his theology of preaching with his sermons, and his Christology with his theological and spiritual reading, such as Catherine Emmerich's *Dolorous Passion of Our Lord Jesus Christ*.

This project would not have been accomplished without the assistance and collaboration of many people. First of all, we thank the authors who contributed new essays to this volume. Thanks are likewise due to the scholars who served as readers for these new essays and offered suggestions for improvement to their authors. We are also grateful to the editors of the journals who graciously granted permission for the Neumann essays that originally appeared in their publications to be reprinted in this volume: The Catholic University of America Press for *American Ecclesiastical Review*; the Publishing and Promotion Services, United States Catholic Conference, and Our Sunday Visitor, for *The Living Light*; and Dr. Thomas R. Greene for *Records of the American Catholic Historical Society of Philadelphia*. Sincere appreciation is expressed as well to the institutions that allowed Neumann materials to be photographed and illustrated in this book: The Neumann Center, St. John Neumann Shrine, St. Peter the Apostle Church, Philadelphia; Office of Catholic Schools, Archdiocese of Philadelphia; Philadelphia Archdiocesan Historical Research Center; and the Redemptorist Provincial Archives, Baltimore Province, Brooklyn, New York.

NOTES

1. The original style and format of the reprinted essays have been retained; however, misprints have been corrected.

2. This overview of Neumann's life and writings is based on the primary and secondary sources here indicated, but not further noted unless quoted. Of primary importance are *The Autobiography of St. John Neumann, C.Ss.R.*, with introduction, translation, commentary, and epilogue by Alfred C. Rush, C.Ss.R. (Boston: St. Paul Books & Media, 1977) (hereafter *Autobiography*), and "John Nepomucene Neumann's *Spiritual Journal*," ed. and trans. William Nayden, C.Ss.R., *Spicilegium Historicum Congregationis SSmi Redemptoris* 25 (1977): 321-418 (Part 1: Oct. 1-Dec. 31, 1834); 26 (1978): 9-74 (Part 2: Jan. 1-Feb. 28, 1835), 291-352 (Part 3: Mar. 1-May 4, 1835); 27 (1979): 81-152 (Part 4: May 5, 1835-July 21, 1838). The most authoritative biographical studies of Neumann are by his nephew John A. Berger, C.Ss.R., *Life of Right Rev. John N. Neumann, D.D., of the Congregation of the Most Holy Redeemer, Fourth Bishop of Philadelphia*, trans. Eugene Grimm (New York: Benziger, 1884), and Michael J. Curley, C.Ss.R., *Venerable John Neumann, C.S.S.R., Fourth Bishop of Philadelphia* (Washington, D.C.: Catholic University of America Press, 1952). Also see the more recent important contributions to Neumann studies by Alfred C. Rush, C.Ss.R., and Thomas J. Donaghy, F.S.C., "The Saintly John Neumann and his Coadjutor Archbishop Wood," in *The History of the Archdiocese of Philadelphia*, ed. James F. Connelly (Philadelphia:

Archdiocese of Philadelphia, 1976), 209-70; Mary Charles Bryce, O.S.B., "An Accomplished Catechist: John Nepomucene Neumann," *Living Light* 14 (1977): 327-37; Francis Xavier Murphy, C.Ss.R., *John Nepomucene Neumann, Saint* (1977; Custom Editorial Services, 2000); Augustinus Kurt Huber, "John N. Neumann's Student Years in Prague, 1833-1835," trans. from German by Raymond H. Schmandt, *Records of the American Catholic Historical Society of Philadelphia* 89 (1978): 3-32; Richard A. Boever, C.Ss.R., *The Spirituality of St. John Neumann, C.Ss.R., Fourth Bishop of Philadelphia,* Ph.D. diss., Saint Louis University, 1983; and Joseph P. Chinnici, O.F.M., *Living Stones: The History and Structure of Catholic Spiritual Life in the United States,* 2nd ed. (Maryknoll: Orbis, 1996), 68-85.

3. See Paul F. Grendler, "The Piarists of the Pious Schools," in *Religious Orders of the Catholic Reformation: In Honor of John C. Olin on His Seventy-Fifth Birthday,* ed. Richard L. DeMolen (New York: Fordham University Press, 1994), 253-78.

4. On Baraga, see Bernard J. Lambert, *Shepherd of the Wilderness: A Biography of Bishop Frederic Baraga* (Chicago: Franciscan Herald Press, 1967), and Francis G. McManamin, S.J., "Missionary to the Indians: Bishop Frederic Baraga (1797-1868)," in *Portraits in American Sanctity,* ed. Joseph N. Tylenda, S.J. (Chicago: Franciscan Herald Press, 1982), 180-94.

5. Quoted in Alfred C. Rush, "The Second Vatican Council, 1962-1965, and Bishop Neumann," *Records of the American Catholic Historical Society of Philadelphia* 85 (1974): 123-28, at 126.

6. *Autobiography,* 17.

7. See *Autobiography,* 70, note 19.

8. Curley, 163.

9. Schmandt's translation of the *Autobiography* is appendix I to Huber's article on Neumann's student years in Prague.

10. *Autobiography,* 16.

11. Ibid., 24.

12. Page references in this section of the introduction are to the essays as they appear in this volume.

13. *Funeral Obsequies of Rt. Rev. John Nepomucene Neumann* (Philadelphia, 1860), 8-9.

14. José Saraiva Martins, C.M.F., "The lives of the saints show the world 'the divine in the human, the eternal in time,'" *L'Osservatore Romano,* Eng. ed. (16 Apr. 2003), 9-10, at 10.

PART I

THEOLOGICAL AND
SPIRITUAL FORMATION

THE SEVERAL LIVES OF
ST. JOHN NEPOMUK,
A PATRON SAINT OF BOHEMIA[1]

PAUL SHORE

The traveler to the modern-day Czech Republic will encounter at almost every turn an image unlike that of any other saint or hero found in Central Europe. The figure, portrayed in roadside statues or religious paintings, is of a man dressed in the garb of a seventeenth-century cleric, with beard, biretta, and cassock, cradling in his arms a large crucifix much as a mother might hold her child. His eyes are cast upwards to the beckoning heavens, which, when he is portrayed in painting, are sometimes filled with plump *putti* and angels, while a circle of stars is often shown floating at his feet (Plates 1–3). The figure is St. John (Jan) Nepomuk, a patron saint of Bohemia, special protector of the Jesuits, and an object of special veneration and enthusiasm among many nationalities in the region.

THE INITIAL PHASE OF NEPOMUK'S CULT

To understand the importance of St. John Nepomuk to Bohemia, one must reflect on three distinct periods of Czech history in which the saint, in one form or another, played a significant role. The first, the late fourteenth and early fifteenth centuries, was a period of political intrigue and upheaval that followed the "golden age" of the reign of Charles IV. The Bohemian king, Václav (Wenceslas) IV (1378-1419), the son of Charles, was engaged in a longstanding feud with Jan of Jenstejn, the archbishop of Prague.

This struggle centered not only on the boundaries between ecclesiastical and royal authority, but also contained echoes of the struggle for control of the Holy See going on in far-off Rome and Avignon, where a great schism divided the Church and produced rival claimants to the papal throne.[2] But popular legend disregarded the complexities of church-state relations and focused instead on the allegedly evil character of the king, who is remembered as a drunkard, bully, and weakling. According to pious legend, Jan Nepomuk was the confessor to Václav's wife, Queen Sophia, a lady of German birth.[3] The legend maintains that Nepomuk, pressed by the king to violate the seal of the sacrament of Penance and to reveal his queen's secrets, was tortured by the monarch's retainers and finally thrown off the Charles Bridge into the Vltava River in Prague. A circle of five stars is said to have appeared in the water where Nepomuk met a martyr's death, and, in the true style of a medieval legend, the Vltava ran dry the summer after his martyrdom. Interestingly, the earliest accounts of this tale, dating from about forty years after the incident, do not tell us what happened to Queen Sophia. The legend of Nepomuk is in no way a "macho" tale designed to appeal to those seeking an account of feats of military glory, and it is clearly one that appealed to women, but it is in essence the story of a man and a man's decisions.

Serious doubts have been cast on the connection of the legendary Nepomuk, about whom we are told many fascinating but doubtful facts, to an actual member of the king's retinue who ran afoul of the monarch's anger and was tortured to death in 1393.[4] No less a figure than Josef Dobrovsky, a former Jesuit and the father of Czech philology, in 1779 rejected the association of the legendary hero-martyr-saint, the confessor to the queen, with the priest Jan from the town of Pomuk who can be shown to have lived in Prague during the reign of Václav IV.[5] But the purpose of this essay is not to establish or demolish the veracity of the Nepomuk legend. Instead, let us briefly examine the impact of the legend of Nepomuk on Bohemian cultural and religious life in the centuries following his death. The historical Jan Pomuk was born about 1340 in the village of Pomuk; his father Welflin (or Wölflin) (also known as "z Pomuk" or "from Pomuk"; individuals in fourteenth-century Bohemia did not customarily have what we would consider today "last names") served as the village justice of the peace from 1355 until 1367. Jan never signed his name "Nepomuk," but always as "Joannes son of Welflin of Pomuk." The suffix "Ne" may be a variant spelling of "na," a Czech word meaning "on" or sometimes "at," thus giving us the possible meaning of "On the [tract of land of] Pomuk."[6] Ironically, Jan's family was apparently of German origin, and Jan himself mastered German at an early age.[7] By 1380 we find Jan working as a priest in the Cathedral of St. Vitus in Prague, and in 1389 he was made Vicar-General in Prague, in the service of Archbishop Jan (or John) of Jenstejn. The historical record shows that in a conflict between king and prelate that developed in 1393, several church officials were interrogated, tortured, and probably killed on the king's command. One of them may have been the historical priest Jan z Pomuk, but we do not know this for certain.

Another historical element must be considered before we turn to the implications of the Nepomuk legend itself. A century before the appearance of Martin Luther, Bohemia was convulsed by rebellion against the authority of the Church. The Hussite Wars, as they came to be known, had their roots in the reaction of the common people to clerical abuses and in a popular movement that sought to return the Church to what were held to be its primitive and pure origins. These wars spawned innovations in art and in literature that profoundly affected the development of Bohemian culture.[8] The spark that ignited the conflict, however, was the execution of the preacher and language reformer Jan Hus, who traveled to the Council of Constance in 1415 under a safe conduct to respond to charges against him, only to be seized, accused, and convicted of heresy and burned at the stake. Hus alive was a prolific writer and respected academic, a disseminator of the ideas of the English priest and reformer John Wyclif, and a rector of Charles University in Prague. After his death, Hus immediately became a symbol of Czech religious and cultural identity, and a rallying point of resistance to the authority of distant Rome. His death was likewise viewed as a martyrdom for his faith, and, because he was a champion, and to some degree codifier of the Czech language, for Czech culture as well. Hus was, in a sense, Bohemia's first "St. John," whose memory lived on among the people, who to the present day count him among the greatest of Czech heroes.

Bohemia first passed through the Hussite wars, and then in the next century experienced the penetration of the ideas of the Protestant Reformation. From 1526 onward the lands of the crown of St. Wenceslas (Bohemia, Moravia, and Silesia) were in the hands of the Habsburgs, who increasingly cast themselves in the role of defenders of Catholicism and who brought the Jesuits to Prague in 1556. By the early seventeenth century, the majority of the population of Bohemia was Protestant, and in 1619 war broke out between the Bohemian Estates, who had chosen the Protestant Frederick, Elector of the Palatinate, as their king, and the Catholic Habsburg dynasty, a family that came to equate religious heterodoxy with political unreliability. In the Battle of the White Mountain west of Prague in 1620, Frederick's V's forces were completely routed by the troops of the Habsburg Ferdinand II, and the forcible recatholicization of Bohemia, spearheaded by the Jesuits, began.[9]

A COUNTER-REFORMATION SAINT

Meanwhile the tomb of Jan of Nepomuk had been attracting pilgrims and miracle seekers.[10] While Jan of Nepomuk enjoyed local popularity among those who recounted his martyrdom and marveled at the miraculous way his tomb had escaped desecration by Protestants, the Bohemian Church itself had paid relatively little attention to the legendary royal confessor, perhaps because adequate documentation of his life and death was lacking. Towards the end of the seventeenth century, however, this began to change. A movement began seeking the canonization of the martyr, whose place of martyrdom on the beautiful bridge in view of the Prague Castle was also becoming a pilgrimage site.

The romantic qualities of the Nepomuk legend undoubtedly contributed to its popularity. A woodcut from 1602 illustrates this tendency, as well as hints at other sources of the legend's appeal

(Plate 4).[11] Nepomuk is shown hearing the queen's confession: in this pre-Tridentine setting, there is no confessional booth but instead a face-to-face encounter. The queen leans forward, almost resting on Nepomuk's breast to offer her confession, while the saint bends near to catch each word. It is a setting that, were Nepomuk's head not encased in a halo, might almost seem to be illustrating some popular romance of the period. Other details catch our attention: through the open window beyond the confessional scene flows the Vltava, and a tiny figure may be discerned falling from a bridge. Closer to the two figures an elaborate table with two candles serves as a representation of the elaborate metal furnishings of the saint's tomb in St. Vitus cathedral. The illustration thus summarizes simultaneously, in a fashion often employed in the late Middle Ages, the key elements of the Nepomuk legend: the faithfulness of the confessor (with perhaps a whiff—not officially sanctioned, of course—of the entire relationship between queen and confessor), his impending martyrdom, and the dignity and even glory that awaited the martyr.

A set of engravings, published in a book devoted to the saint more than a century later, provide further evidence of the evolution of Nepomuk's cult. We again see the saint hearing the confession of Queen Sophia, again in plain sight, in an open and geometrically structured interior space that emphasizes the vulnerability of the queen and the composure of the priest (Plate 5).[12] Elsewhere in the volume we see Nepomuk preaching from a Baroque pulpit to a congregation clad in vaguely seventeenth-century costume (Plate 6), placing his finger to his lips in the presence of the evil King Václav (Plate 7), and triumphing over a fallen figure whose tongue is protruding and who probably represents Discord or Fama (Plate 8).[13] In these illustrations, and in many others from the same period, Nepomuk personifies a devotion that is refined and courtly, full of humility yet with an aesthetic sense. Nepomuk, the patron of the Bohemian peasant, would retain these characteristics.

Why did the cult of an obscure court functionary steadily gain momentum during the Counter-Reformation? Some scholars have pointed to the efforts of the Jesuits to supplant the popular hero Hus with another homegrown hero who personified Catholic virtue.

Certainly the legendary Nepomuk's devotion *usque ad mortem* to the sacrament of confession, a sacrament given renewed emphasis in the post-Tridentine Church, gave ammunition to missionaries working in a land where so many of the symbols and sacraments—even the cross—had been discarded by the reformers.[14] Then, too the Nepomuk legend casts the Luxemburg king Václav IV in a very negative light, reducing him almost to the status of a "wicked king" in a fairy tale. In this instance the wicked king was of partially Czech ancestry, and his family was ultimately supplanted by the Habsburgs in 1526. The virtues and Catholic piety of the Habsburgs were advertised everywhere in public monuments in Prague and every other city that they came to dominate. The virtues of Nepomuk, a martyr endorsed by the Habsburgs, could therefore be contrasted with the evil behavior of a representative of a deposed dynasty, and his faithful service to the Church equated with the devotion of its champions, the Habsburg dynasty.[15] The saint-to-be thereby came to serve a royal house with which he had had no real contact during his life. But more amazing adventures lay ahead for the medieval cleric.

Other factors brought the popular enthusiasm for Nepomuk to a boiling point. The Baroque era, especially in Catholic lands, was a period obsessed with the body and its potentialities.[16] The body could be a source of danger and disease (the seventeenth century was a time of both virulent plague and epidemic venereal disease carried by the soldiers of the Thirty Years War), but it could also be the medium through which miraculous cures occurred. Bohemian Baroque literature abounds with accounts of weeping Madonnas answering petitioners' prayers, of bodies that resisted corruption, and of murder victims whose wounds continued to bleed after death.[17] The tale of the martyrdom of Nepomuk focused on his physical resistance (derived of course from his spiritual strength) to the unjust demands of his king, and, in particular, on his silence. Small wonder, that when in 1729 his tomb was opened in the presence of a distinguished gathering of religious and academic figures and a small embalmed object fell from his skull as it was raised, Prague rejoiced in the rediscovery of the miraculously uncorrupted tongue of the silent confessor. (In fact, modern forensic science has identified the object as probably a fragment of the saint's brain.)[18]

Moreover, the secrets that Nepomuk had refused to divulge themselves added to the intrigue surrounding the martyred confessor. Nepomuk's faithfulness to his sacramental duty coincided with his faithfulness to his queen, while the queen's fidelity is veiled by the sacrament itself. Fidelity was a commodity highly valued by the Habsburg dynasty, whose entire domestic policy during the seventeenth and early eighteenth centuries might be summed up in the term *Kaisertreu* (faithful to the Emperor). This mixture of officially sanctioned virtue and discreetly implied sexual innuendo together offered an appeal that was hard to resist. But beyond the draw of sexual innuendo was also the chivalrous notion of protecting the honor of women, an idea that has survived in the narratives of more recent Catholic martyrs of Central Europe.[19] The Church was often portrayed as a woman in Baroque allegories, as were the cities of Bohemia.[20] Defense of a woman's honor, therefore, could be read as a concretized expression of devotion to Church or community, and with the personality of Queen Sophia (whose name means "wisdom" in Greek, a virtue often personified as a woman) in the background, the transfer of this devotion to another object was all the easier. The more worldly might find the Nepomuk legend attractive because of the suggestion of courtly discretion, but others, steeped in the multilayered emblematics of the Baroque era, would easily extract a message where the female character personified an abstract idea, just as Nepomuk himself personified fidelity.[21]

Nepomuk now had a distinctive symbol that could be associated with his martyrdom, his silent tongue, which like St. Paul's sword and St. Lucy's eyes, could be used in art works to identify him to the illiterate. At the same time St. John Nepomuk evolved in other ways as well. Earlier iconography has merely portrayed him as a pious priest, either hearing Queen Sophia's confession or engaged in prayer. The image of Nepomuk, however, that came to dominate eighteenth-century art invariably portrayed him in the vestments of a contemporary priest, and gave him the physical appearance and dynamic body language of a man of the High Baroque. Even in the throes of torture Nepomuk remains handsome and even elegant.[22] The historical St. John Nepomuk, born in the late Middle Ages and killed—perhaps—in the midst of a sordid quarrel between king and archbishop, had now been recast according to the aesthetics and needs of the eighteenth century, a time when opera was arguably the most developed art form and Jesuit didactic theaters shaped the educational experiences of the elite of Bohemia.[23] Yet while this recasting was underway, elements of the visual telling of his story took on other features. The king's soldiers chosen to send Nepomuk to his death are sometimes portrayed in costumes recalling the uniforms of Roman soldiers present at Christ's crucifixion, a reference that would not have been lost on the faithful.

The recasting of a saint to suit the needs and taste of a later age is hardly unusual. Yet Nepomuk, the silent confessor, was put to some uses that tell us much about life in eighteenth-century Bohemia and about the attitudes common in Catholic Europe before the French Revolution.[24] His tomb, located in the Cathedral of St. Vitus, the coronation church of the lands of St. Wenceslas, was completed during the reign of the devout Maria Theresia, and exhibits a theatricality extravagant even by the standards of the day.[25] A metal canopy intended to resemble cloth and supported by *putti* hangs suspended above the huge tomb itself. The censers hanging around the tomb create a slightly Eastern flavor, reminding us of the Orthodox influences found in many parts of the Habsburg domains, while the location of the tomb in the most sacred precincts in Bohemia attests to the central role given to the saint in the retelling of Bohemian history. The Baroque re-creation of Nepomuk completely transformed the medieval man at the most basic level. Even the bones of the martyr were supplanted with those of pigs or other animals before they were wrapped in jewels and satin and reburied.

Nepomuk, offered to the Bohemians as a model of self-control, discretion, and fidelity to the sacraments, was meant to epitomize the ideals promoted by the Counter-Reformation. But the Catholicism of Bohemia was of uncertain depth and security. Investigations and interrogations conducted in the countryside throughout the century

10

reveal how widespread heresy was. Jesuits roamed the land burning tens of thousands of heretical books while crypto-Protestant beliefs simmered below the surface, only to burst into view when Maria Theresia's son, Joseph II, allowed limited religious toleration in the 1780s.[26] The promotion of Nepomuk occurred in a culture whose relationship to the Catholic clergy was not always characterized by reciprocal trust and respect, and while conversion was the choice of many, tensions between varying religious positions never completely disappeared.[27] The enthusiasm that Bohemians genuinely expressed for Nepomuk cannot therefore be attributed exclusively to their positive view of the clergy, or to a strong sense of connection between Czech national identity of the eighteenth century and Catholic orthodoxy.[28] Nor can Nepomuk be identified as a favorite of Germans as opposed to Czechs, for the saint had enthusiastic supporters from both ethnic groups in the general population, as well as among the Jesuits who promoted him. Much of the appeal of Nepomuk derived from his own personal characteristics as relayed in the legends surrounding him, as he evolved from a shadowy and scarcely remembered medieval ecclesiastic into a guardian and protector of the kingdom.

NEPOMUK'S ENDURING APPEAL

This appeal, which lasted well into the third stage of Bohemia's encounter with Nepomuk, i.e., the nineteenth century, derived from three sources. First, Nepomuk was presented to Bohemians as the suffering martyr. Bohemia in the seventeenth and eighteenth centuries had experienced more than its share of suffering and martyrdom: it was ravaged by armies in the Thirty Years War; its native aristocracy was either banished or reduced to poverty; its intellectuals were forced either to conform or to emigrate; its peasantry was perpetually on the brink of starvation. Thus, Bohemia understood well the experience of injustice and the frequent necessity of forbearance and silence. While it was true that much of the suffering inflicted on Bohemia had some of its origins in the same forces that were promoting Nepomuk, the linking of suffering with virtue struck a chord with many Christians already schooled in the details of Christ's Passion. In Bohemia, as elsewhere in Catholic Europe, the constant proximity of death, danger, and illness fostered a culture that sought deliverance through the intervention of saints whose sympathies were heightened through their own experience of suffering. Women who prayed to St. Anne or sprinkled themselves with "Ignatius water" during a difficult childbirth, and men who commissioned *ex voto* art when a child or crop was spared, responded to the kindly, loyal, and brave saint who understood what mistreatment and suffering were.[29] In this regard Nepomuk was similar to many other saints popular during the Baroque era whose relics provided a focal point for pious demonstrations. But Nepomuk was neither a remote figure clad in a stiff costume like the Infant of Prague, a figure of the Christ Child that attracted pilgrims to the Church of S. Maria de Victoria in Prague where it was displayed, nor a beardless youth like St. Stanislaus Kostka, who died nursing plague victims, nor a daring missionary like St. Francis Xavier who met death in some remote corner of the world. He was a Bohemian man whose experiences and geographical setting were immediately familiar. Nepomuk was an accessible saint, too: his "tongue" was placed within a jeweled container that was kissed by thousands during feast days. Because his piety could be localized in the organ that the common people believed had been preserved (even if the "tongue" consisted of brain tissue), Nepomuk was able to exercise a particularly potent appeal to those who sought a physical connection with the holy. As with so many Baroque saints, Nepomuk's spirituality not only became geographically localized, but physically localized as well. The genius of the Baroque aesthetic was its capacity to concretize the abstract, to lend a physical reality to the symbolic that could transcend the tawdry and sensational. Nepomuk retained (or regained) his physicality and even expanded its impact, as he was sometimes shown swinging from ropes while under torture, or sailing gracefully into the waters of the Vltava, all the time never losing his composure (Plate 9).[30]

Nepomuk the Baroque saint also had the advantage of being promoted by the Jesuits, the most visible and active of Catholic religious orders in the seventeenth and eighteenth centuries. The Jesuits had not enjoyed widespread popularity when they arrived in the train of the Habsburgs following White Mountain, but in the century that followed the order had gained control of virtually all the important educational institutions in Bohemia, as well as became major landowners and leaders in all aspects of intellectual life. The sodalities and congregations they had founded had taken root in communities, where they fulfilled important social needs.[31] Jesuit churches dotted the landscape, and the Klementinum, the Prague headquarters for the Jesuit Province of Bohemia, directed operations that reached as far away as Dresden and Transylvania.[32] The considerable power of this order was eagerly directed to the cult of Nepomuk, for the Bohemian saint possessed many of the characteristics admired by the order, not the least of which was a willingness to undergo martyrdom.[33] The Nepomuk revealed in the legends was virginal, prepared to make a sacrifice even when opposed by secular authorities (a common theme in Jesuit martyrologies), and received a distinctive martyrdom that afforded many compelling artistic renderings. While the historic Nepomuk may not have been a notable preacher, the Baroque saint was skilled in oratory, thereby resembling the Jesuits who promoted him. Like the original Bohemian saint, the tenth-century St. Václav (the Good King Wenceslas of the English carol), Nepomuk died because of a struggle within a royal household, and because he held to his convictions in the face of life-threatening circumstances.[34] His spiritual purity manifested itself in the incorruptibility of his tongue, his potency as a saint in the miracles attributed to his intercession. And last but not least, he appeared in paintings and sculpture in the form of a contemporary Jesuit![35] The model of restraint linked with strength that Nepomuk presented fit well with the moral curriculum taught in Jesuit schools, which placed considerable emphasis on rhetoric and self-discipline.[36] The Jesuit support of the Habsburgs and of that dynasty's understanding of royal legitimacy posed no problem for the Nepomuk cult, for, as we have seen, the king in the legend was a base fellow who did not merit rehabilitation.[37]

Finally, Nepomuk's identification with Bohemia, and, in

particular, with its Czech population, cannot be discounted. Yet while we can talk about the geographical location of a Baroque saint, it is difficult to talk about ethnic identity in the modern sense when discussing Central Europe in the seventeenth and eighteenth centuries.[38] Undoubtedly Nepomuk was understood to be of local origin, and his story was linked with the history of the Bohemian crown. Yet Nepomuk had devotees in many other parts of the Habsburg lands and elsewhere in Central Europe, and, in fact, might be called a Habsburg as much as a Bohemian saint. He was also popular among some of the rural aristocracy of Bohemia, who as of yet had no sense of their distinctly Czech identity.[39] It was in Bohemia, however, where the saint's cult reached its greatest extent. If it had been the conscious intention of the Jesuits and others to replace the first "St. John" Hus with John Nepomuk, they succeeded to the degree that Nepomuk came to represent Czech cultural (if not yet national) identity, although this identification of the saint with the land did not displace the status of the man schoolchildren are still taught to call "Master Jan Hus." The popular appeal of the Bohemian saint was unmistakable; the celebrations held in Prague to commemorate the fiftieth anniversary of his canonization were replete with living tableaux of scenes from his life, and processions that went beyond events staged by the clergy.[40] Nepomuk's life and sacrifice, the pathos of his death coupled with the Baroque portrayals of his ascension into glory, spoke to the temperament of eighteenth-century Bohemia, a land where—despite (or perhaps because of) material privations, repeated wars, and uprisings—thousands went on pilgrimages each year to rural shrines in places such as the "Holy Mountain" near Příbam.[41]

Nepomuk was embedded in folk culture in other ways. Soldiers and peasants reported that he appeared to them in dreams, and countless boys throughout Central Europe were given the names Jan (or in German, Johann) Nepomuk. While the cult was probably strongest in Bohemia, statues and monuments to Nepomuk, almost all of them created in the eighteenth century, are found in Poland, Austria, and throughout the eastern half of the Holy Roman Empire and into the Danube basin. Often these monuments appear in regions where, while there might be a large and devout Catholic population, there was also a sizable Protestant minority. Nepomuk, the epitome of commitment to the sacraments, served as an advertisement of the Catholic community's devotion in a time when religious identity was still being expressed in public ways. And if the statue bore an inscription, as many do, extolling the piety and virtue of either a local noble who had had it erected, or the Habsburgs, it might also serve as evidence of the Catholic community's political dependability. Nepomuk, among his many other incarnations, was also an expression of the *pietas Austriaca*, that special brand of Catholic piety associated with the Habsburg dynasty and with their own connections to the sacraments and public rituals of the Catholic faith.[42] The saint flourished in an environment that not only linked dynastic loyalty with religious conformity, but also reached his zenith of popularity at a time when all education in Bohemia was in the hands of the Catholic clergy, who were themselves tied to the Habsburg vision of an empire united in religion.[43] Nepomuk's heyday thus occurred before people—educated and uneducated— had given up the idea of transcendence and accepted a relativistic view of "reality" that did not allow for the miraculous or the romantic.[44] This moment passed. As the aristocracy fell away from the religious cults it had helped establish a century earlier, the common people remained loyal to Nepomuk, as they believed he had been loyal to them. The Jesuits supported him as long as they could, for they had other uses for him in the world of miracles that still occupied the Baroque imagination.[45] In the eighteenth century Nepomuk, in his artistically recreated form, could be an expression of an otherwise unstated Jesuit aesthetic, one that combined the otherworldly, the sensuous, and the emotional.[46]

Nepomuk in the Nineteenth Century

The third epoch to which the legend of Nepomuk belongs is the nineteenth century, which saw the rise of Czech national conscious- ness and the growing conflict between Czech and German speakers in the cultural and political spheres. The political and social developments of this period cannot be summarized here, but a few trends relating to the cult of Nepomuk can be identified. The most salient of these was the conservatism in popular and small-town visual and applied arts. The Baroque aesthetic sensibility that had faded west of the Rhine by 1750 survived well into the 1800s in Bohemia, as it did in many of the other Habsburg lands.[47] This conservatism meant that some of the venues in which Nepomuk had traditionally appeared, such as bridges and crossroads, did not cease to be created, and those representations that had been completed in the eighteenth century were in many cases preserved. Thus the visual rendering of the "heroic virtue" of the saints defined by Pope Benedict XIV in his decree *De Servatorum Dei* remained visible throughout the region, often manifesting itself in votive pictures of the saint created to commemorate a deliverance from danger.[48] And although Bohemia underwent a steady industrialization that climaxed in the decades before the First World War, the land remained and remains deeply conscious of its rural and small-town roots, as nineteenth- and early twentieth-century Czech scholars, writers, and educators searched for the unspoiled "essence" of Czech culture surviving in the byways of Bohemia, where they inevitably encountered Nepomuk.

While a segment of the country retained traditional forms of cultural expression, others, often academics or other products of the universities, sought self-consciously to resurrect the glories of the High Middle Ages. The gilded theatricality of Baroque displays of the sort that had glorified Nepomuk was replaced by the romantic neo-Gothic aesthetic influenced by forces as diverse as Violet-le-Duc and the Grimm brothers, an aesthetic that added unhistorical "improved" pointed towers to the city's medieval gates and erected idealized statues of Charles IV. Yet even these developments, and the increased interest in Bohemia's history, worked in favor of the saint's cult. Nepomuk's association with the Jesuits and with the Habsburgs by themselves would have been a liability in a society that increasingly ignored the Society and resisted the authority of the dynasty.[49] But as a character from the Bohemian Middle Ages and as an object of reverence on the part of the people, Nepomuk could be retained by some Czech nationalist enthusiasts who otherwise would have little reason to support a symbol of Counter-Reformation and Habsburg hegemony.[50]

Nepomuk also gained a more far-flung following. St. John N. Neumann, a namesake of the Baroque saint and the fourth bishop of Philadelphia, was one of Nepomuk's most articulate nineteenth-century devotees. In his diary for the years 1834 through 1838, there are numerous references to the Bohemian saint whom Neumann referred to as his "patron" and "counselor."[51] Nepomuk's special relationship to the administration of the sacraments thus persisted into a time and place far removed from the Counter-Reformation context in which this link was first forged. Even in the age of utilitarianism and revolution, the appeal of the Baroque saint was still powerful, with his virtues of fortitude and eloquence shaping the sensibility of another saint whose destiny would lie in a New World with no connection to the medieval world from which Nepomuk had emerged.

Nepomuk in his third phase became one of the symbols of the myth of "golden Prague," the medieval and to a lesser extent Baroque city that Czech patriots and romantics discovered and reshaped in the nineteenth century.[52] Part of the Austrian, and after 1867, the Austro-Hungarian monarchy, but filled with the sense of being denied a national identity, Czechs turned to the late medieval period, when Prague had been the center of a brilliant Central European culture, for inspiration.[53] The legend of Nepomuk provided both a glimpse of this earlier culture and created a connection with the folk culture of Bohemia, which was beginning to receive great attention from Czech writers and academicians. The statue of Nepomuk on the Charles Bridge in Prague that marked the traditional site of his martyrdom was gradually transformed from a shrine for the pious into a cultural landmark that tourists today still seek out. Nepomuk continued to have a following of the sincerely pious, but added to the passion of these devotees was a new awareness of his cultural significance driven by the desire of the Czechs to reconstruct a narrative of their own past.

CONCLUSION

While Nepomuk remains a symbol of Czech cultural identity, he is more than that. The saint reminds us of the risks inherent in dividing history into neat compartments labeled "Baroque," "Romantic," or "modern," and also how our understanding of the distance between elite and popular culture must be flexible enough to accommodate symbols that bridge these concepts. For St. John Nepomuk has a place in multiple historical and cultural contexts, and has played overlapping roles through much of his history. The highpoint of his visibility came at a moment when the pre-rational, pre-Enlightenment understanding of the body and the soul were flourishing in Central Europe, while the philosophes of France and England were mounting their own cases against the entire notion of a miraculous martyred saint.[54] Yet Nepomuk is much more than merely a relic from the early modern era. The adaptability of this saint serves as a useful metaphor for the Czech people themselves, who in the past three centuries have been compelled to adapt to drastic changes in fortune while still retaining a portion of their own identity uncorrupted, much as Nepomuk's reputed tongue was said to have done. Understanding the meaning of Nepomuk, and, in particular, grasping the way his seventeenth- and eighteenth-century devotees perceived him is not easy in our postmodern world. He simultaneously embodies the general and the particular, calling to mind as he does the universal human experiences of suffering, longing, and hope simultaneously with the recollection of the specifics of his legendary life and death that haunt the memories of his devotees. W. H. Auden, writing about the W. B. Yeats at the time of the great Irish poet's death, wrote, "he became his admirers."[55] So it has been for St. John Nepomuk. Not only has his historical personality been obliterated by successive levels of pious embellishment, but he himself has become a tool for understanding Czech culture at various stages of its evolution. We may view him as a suffering victim of injustice, as a conduit of Divine mercy, as a reminder of the imminent possibility that God will intervene in history, as a testimonial to fidelity and honor, as an object of affection and at times sentimental representative of a glorious Baroque aesthetic that survives into our own day. And if Czech society and culture undergo another metamorphosis in the post-Communist, free market era, do not be surprised if St. John Nepomuk will be recast in some way to embody the hopes and concerns of the future.

NOTES

1. This essay was supported in part by a Faculty Development Grant from Saint Louis University. The author also thanks the Institute of Jesuit Sources for its support, as well as Rich Sanker, Matthew Herrell, and the anonymous reader who reviewed the manuscript for Saint Joseph's University Press for their helpful suggestions.

2. Jaroslav V Polc, *Svatý Jan Nepomucký* (Praha: Zvon, 1993), and R. N. Swanson, *Universities, Academies and the Great Schism* (Cambridge: Cambridge University Press, 1979), 29-30.

3. Because Queen Sophia was a Wittelsbach, of the ducal (and later royal) Bavarian family, Nepomuk was also honored in Bavaria. See Thomas DeCosta Kaufmann, *Court, Cloister, and City: The Art and Culture of Central Europe 1450-1800* (Chicago: University of Chicago Press, 1995), 378.

4. One theory posits a Jan z Pomuka who was put to death 1383 for refusing to violate a confession, and a Johánnek (Jan) z Pomuka, who died in 1393 as a consequence of the struggle between king and bishop. Emanuel Vlček, *Jan z Pomuku / Sv. Jan Nepomucký: jeho zivot, umučení a slavné působení ve světle současné historie a antropologie* (Praha: Vesmír, 1993), 27.

5. Josef Dobrovsky, *Böhmische Literatur auf das Jahr 1779* (Prag, 1780), and Emil Valasek, "Der heilige Johannes von Nepomuk," *Archiv für Kirchengeschichte von Böhmen-Mähren-Schlesien 4* (1976): 192.

6. Another theory derives the word "Nepomuk" from the the verb "pomukávat" meaning "to communicate with sounds that do not constitute speech." Since a Cisterician monastery, where speech was forbidden, was nearby, "ne+pomuk" might be translated as "the place where people do not 'pomukávat,' i.e., where they speak normally." Robert B. Pynsent, *Questions of Identity: Czech and Slovak Ideas of Nationality and Personality* (Budapest: Central European University Press, 1994), 202.

7. We must be careful, however, not to make too much of the linguistic orientation of late medievel Bohemians, as nationalism as we now understand it was not fully developed. German-speaking Bohemians would still be listed in university records as belonging to the "Bohemian Nation." The term

"Czech" did not even gain common usage until centuries later.

8. The art of the Hussite period, as represented in illuminated manuscripts, is beautifully detailed in Karel Stejskal and Petr Voit, *Iluminované Rukopise Doby Husitské* (Praha: Grafit, 1991).

9. The Catholic perspective on the decades following White Mountain is found in Ernst Tomek, *Kirchengeschichte Österreichs*, 2 vols. (Innsbruck/Wien/München: Tyrolia Verlag, 1935-).

10. The most accessible recent work on the relation between religious practices such as pilgrimages and factors influencing social control is R. Po-Chi Hisa, *Social Discipline during the Reformation: Central Europe 1550-1750* (New York/London: Routledge: 1989).

11. Georgius Bartoldus Pontanus de Breitenberg, *Hymnorum Sacrorum de Beatissima Virgine Maria et S. Patronis S. R. Bohemiae libri tres* (1602).

12. *Der Neu=eröffnet=Joannäishcen Ehr=und Gnaden=Pforte...des Heiligen Joannis von Nepomuk* (1721), 143.

13. Ibid., 7, 10, 33.

14. In Prague, arguably the epicenter of the Nepomuk cult, the idea of martyrdom and fidelity was commemorated in an impressive illustrated volume by the Jesuit Mathias Tanner, *Societatis Iesu usque ad Sanguinis et Vitae Profusionem Militans...* (Pragae: Typis Universiatatis Carolo-Ferdinandeae, 1675).

15. Nepomuk, holding the palm of martyrdom, gestures approvingly from the heavens towards the armor-clad Habsburg emperor Charles VI in the frontispiece of J. T. Berghauer's *Protomartyr Poenitentiae*, published in 1736.

16. Some of the characteristics of the Bohemian Baroque are delineated in Antonín Kratchovil, *Das böhmische Barock: Ausgewählte Kapitel aus der tschechischen Kulturgeschichte* (München: Erasmus-Grasser-Verlag, 1989).

17. Shimon Abeles, a Jewish youth supposed to have been murdered by his father to prevent his conversion, is one example of an innocent victim whose body remained uncorrupted. See Antonín Novotný, "Prazská sensace A. D. 1694," *Adventinský magazin* 4 (1930): 10-17, and Gábor Klaniczay, *The Uses of Supernatural Power: The Transformation of Popular Religion in Medieval and Early-Modern Europe*, trans. Susan Singerman, ed. Karen Margolis (Oxford: Polity/Blackwell, 1990), 176ff.

18. The 1721 volume, cited in notes 12–13, includes an illustration of the saint's tongue rising on a cloud, supported by *putti*, and surrounded by a quotation from Proverbs 31:26: *Lex clementiae in lingua ejus*, "The law of clemency resides on his tongue," which might suggest that Nepomuk's taciturnity was motivated not merely by reverence for the

sacraments, but also by the necessity of protecting the queen from the king's wrath. *Gnaden=Pforte*, 375.

19. An exceptional example of the coupling of religious piety and chivalrous protection of women in the continuing hagiography of Central Europe is found in the story of Vilmos Apor, Bishop of Győr, Hungary, who was shot by Soviet soldiers in the spring of 1945 while trying to protect women who had gathered in his residence. The shirt of the martyred bishop, stained with his blood, is on display in the Treasury of the Diocese of Győr.

20. For example, the city of Jičín is shown as a woman wearing a crown made of the defensive towers of the city wall in a copperplate engraving commemorating the one hundredth anniversary of the Jesuit church there. See Jan Royt, *Obraz a Kult v Čechách 17. a 18. století* (Praha: Nakladatelství Karolinum, 1999), 125.

21. The literature on Baroque emblematics is considerable. A useful starting point is Karel Porteman, "The use of the visual in classical Jesuit teaching and education," in Marc Depaepe and Bregt Henkens, eds., *The Challenge of the Visual in the History of Education: International Journal for the History of Education* 36, no. 1 (2001): 179-96. Also see Eberhard Hempel, *Baroque Art and Architecture in Central Europe*, trans. E. Hempel and M. Kay (Baltimore: Penguin, 1965), 139ff.

22. See the fresco by Václav Vavřenec Reiner in the church of St. John Nepomuk in Prague, reproduced in Vít Vlnas, *Jan Nepomucký: česká legenda* (Praha: Mladá Fronta, 1993), unnumbered plate.

23. The literature on the artistic trends of the eighteenth century is extensive. Two useful starting points are Rémy Saisselin, *The Enlightenment against the Baroque: Economics and Aesthetics in the Eighteenth Century* (Berkeley: University of California Press, 1992), and Ernst Wangermann, *The Austrian Achievement 1700-1800* (London: Thames and Hudson, 1973).

24. Louis Châtellier, *The Europe of the Devout: The Catholic Reformation and the Formation of a New Society*, trans. Jean Birell (New York/Cambridge: Cambridge University Press, 1989).

25. The tomb was designed by the Austrian master Josef Emauel Fischer von Erlach and by Antonio Corrodini Johann and executed by Josef Würth.

26. Charles H. O'Brien, "Ideas of religious toleration at the time of Joseph II," *Transactions of the American Philosophical Society* 59, no. 7(1969): 25.

27. Marie-Elizabeth Ducreux, "La reconquête de l'espace Bohemien," *Revue des Etudes Slaves* 40, no. 3 (1988): 685-99.

28. The term "Bohemian" is geographical, and can be applied to any resident of the historic kingdom of Bohemia, as well as to inhabitants of

neighboring Moravia. There is no word in the Czech language equivalent with Bohemia. The English word "Czech," a term seldom employed in the eighteenth century, refers specifically to speakers of the Czech language, whose national awareness was only beginning to evolve at the end of the eighteenth century.

29. The mix of superstition and Catholic orthodoxy found among the Bohemian peasantry is described in Paul Shore, *The Eagle and the Cross: Jesuits in Late Baroque Prague* (St. Louis: Institute of Jesuit Sources, 2002).

30. The most complete recent survey of the iconography of Nepomuk is Joanna Baumstark et al., *Johannes von Nepomuk 1393-1993* (München: Bayerisches Nationalmuseum, 1993).

31. Châtellier, 192.

32. Petr Voit, *Pražské Klementinum* (Praha: Orbis, 1990).

33. Peter Burke, "How to be a Counter-Reformation Saint," in *Religion and Society in Early Modern Europe, 1500-1800,* ed. Kaspar von Greyerz (London: George Allen and Unwin, 1984), 45-55.

34. For the story of St. Václav, as retold in the nineteenth century, see Josef Virgil Grohmann, *Sagen aus Böhmen* (Prag: Verlag der J. G. Calvesschen k. k. Universitäts=Buchhandlung, 1863), 24ff.

35. The portrayal of Nepomuk as an identifiable type has a parallel with the Baroque devotional literature of Bohemia, which, as Arne Novák points out, "did not always limit itself to liturgical aims, and fostered the expression of feeling and sensuality..." (*Czech Literature,* trans. Peter Kussi, ed. W. Harkins [Ann Arbor: Michigan Slavic Publications, 1976], 81).

36. *Ratio Studiorum Superiorum Societatis Jesu* (Romae: Apud Curiam Preapositi Generalis, 1954).

37. Peter Sugar, "The rise of nationalism in the Habsburg Empire," *Austrian History Yearbook* 3 (1967): 91-100.

38. The devotion to the Virgin and other expressions of piety from this period in fact have a distinctly non-national quality. See Mary Lee Nolan and Sydney Nolan, *Christian Pilgrimage in Modern Western Europe* (Chapel Hill/London: University of North Carolina Press, 1989).

39. Emil Franzel, *Der Donauraum im Zeilalter der Nationalitätprinzips (1789-1918)* (Bern: Delp-Taschenbucher, 1958).

40. Nepomuk was beatified by Pope Innocent XIII on 31 May 1721, and canonized a saint by Pope Benedict XIII on 19 March 1729. *Paměti Františka Vaváka souseda rychtáře Milcického,* ed. Jindřich Skopec, 5 vols. (V Praze: Cyrillo-Methoděská Knihtiskárna V. Kotruba-Nákladem "Dědictví Sv. Jana

Nepomukého," 1907-), vol. 1, part 1, p. 125.

41. Johanna von Herzogenberg, "Heiligtümer, Heiltümer und Schätze," in *Bohemia Sacra. Das Christentum in Böhmen 973-1973,* ed. F. Seibt (Düsseldorf: Schwann, 1974), 465-74. No complete study of Bohemian pilgrimages of the Baroque period has been done; for German-speaking lands, in particular, Bavaria, see Rebekka Habermas, *Wallfahrt und Aufruhr: Zur Geschichte des Wunderglaubens in der frühen Neuzeit* (Frankfurt/New York: Campus, 1991).

42. Anna Coreth, *Pietas Austriaca: Ursprung und Entwicklung barocker frömmigkeit in Österreich* (München: R. Oldenbourg, 1959). A characteristic example of this connection between the dynasty and public, ritualistic expressions of Catholicism is found in the Corpus Christi procession undertaken by the ruling Habsburg each spring. See Paul Hofmann, *The Viennese: Splendor, Twilight and Exile* (New York: Anchor/Doubleday, 1988), 23-24. For the relation of these rituals to Italian culture, see Josef Polišenský, "Società e Cultura nella Boemia del Barocco," in *L'arte del Barocco in Boemia* (Milan: Bramante, 1966), 10ff.

43. Jaroslav Werstadt, "Politické dějepisectví XIX. století a jeho čeští představetelé," *Český časopis historický* 26 (1920): 3.

44. Mircea Eliade, *The Sacred and the Profane: The Nature of Religion,* trans. Willard R. Trask (New York: Harcourt, Brace and World, 1959), 202-203.

45. R. J. W. Evans, *The Making of the Habsburg Monarchy.* 1550-1700 (Oxford: Clarendon Press, 1979), 388, and Philip M. Soergel, *Wondrous in His Saints: Counter-Reformation Propaganda in Bavaria* (Berkeley: University of California Press, 1993), 224-25. Among the many tributes offered to Nepomuk in the late Baroque era, the following is representative: *Fortissimus dei miles et martyr invictus sanctus Joannes Nepomucensis S. Metropolitanae Ecclesiae Pragensis Canonicus sub annuis solemnis in templo honori ejusdem athletae...* (Vetero-Pragae: Per Jacobum Schweiger Archi-Episcopalem Typographum, 1763).

46. A noteworthy feature of the eighteenth-century debate on aesthetics is that the Jesuits, long known for their forays into theoretical and polemical regions, did not participate, but instead expressed their values through a series of visual archetypes, of which Nepomuk is arguably the most outstanding. For the issues raised in the debate, see Allen Megill, "Aesthetic Theory and Historical Consciousness in the Eighteenth Century," *History and Theory* 17(1978): 29-62.

47. Oldřich J. Blažíček, *Iskustvo Čěsskogo Barokko* (Leninigrad: Ministersvo Kulturi SSSR, 1974).

48. Marcus B. Burke, *Jesuit Art and Iconography 1550-1800: Introductory Essay and Exhibition Catalogue* (Jersey City: St. Peter's College Art Gallery, 1993), 4, and Lenz Kriss-Rettenbeck, *Das Votivbild* (München: Herman Rinn, 1958).

49. The Jesuits, suppressed by Pope Clement XIV in 1773, returned to Bohemia in the early nineteenth century but maintained a low profile, never again regaining their prominence in higher education. See Paul Shore, "The suppression of the Society of Jesus in Bohemia," *Archivum Historicum Societatis Iesu* 65 (1996): 139-56.

50. Many anti-German, anti-Habsburg Czech nationalists, however, ignored Nepomuk.

51. "John Nepomucene Neumann's *Spiritual Journal*," ed. and trans. William Nayden, First Part: Oct. 1- Dec, 31 1834," *Spicilegium Historicum Congregationis SSmi Redemptoris* 25 (1977): 357, 378.

52. Robert Auty, "Language and Society in the Czech National Revival," *The Slavonic and East European Review* 35 (1956-57): 240-48, and Robert Redfield, *Peasant Society and Culture: An Anthropological Approach to Civilization* (Chicago: University of Chicago Press, 1956), 67-104.

53. As late as the reign of Rudolph II (1576-1612), Prague was the capital of the Holy Roman Empire, and a major center of European culture. See R. J. W. Evans, *Rudolf II and His World* (Oxford: Clarendon Press, 1973). For Prague in the eighteenth century, see Marie Pavlíková, "Josefinská Praha," in *Pražský sborník historický* (Praha: Orbis, 1968), 85-112. When the historical and artistic significance—including the many monuments to Nepomuk—of the city were rediscovered in the nineteenth century, Prague had ceased to be a European capital of the first rank. However, by being largely spared the construction of boulevards and squares that typified the urban landscape of Paris, Rome, and Vienna, Prague preserved more of its older character.

54. G. W. Wentzlaff-Eggebert, *Deutsche Mystik zwischen Mittelalter und Neuzeit* (Berlin: Walter de Gruyter, 1969).

55. W. H. Auden, "In Memory of W. B. Yeats," in *The New Oxford Book of English Verse 1250-1950*, ed. Helen Gardner (New York: Oxford University Press, 1972), 919.

JOHN N. NEUMANN'S STUDENT YEARS IN PRAGUE, 1833-1835*

AUGUSTINUS KURT HUBER

TRANSLATED BY RAYMOND H. SCHMANDT

John Nepomucene Neumann, beatified by the Church in 1963, was born in 1811 in Prachatitz in southwestern Bohemia. After attending the gymnasium and, after 1831, the diocesan seminary in Budweis, he took the second half of his theological studies (1833-1835) in the archdiocesan seminary and the Theological Faculty in Prague. Then, having completed his studies, he departed for the United States where he was ordained in New York. In 1840 Neumann entered the Redemptorist Congregation. Tireless in serving the spiritual needs of German immigrants, he became Provincial in 1848 and then in 1852 Bishop of Philadelphia. Successful in every respect in the development of the diocese and of the parochial school system, Neumann is numbered among the pioneers of American Catholicism. Prematurely worn out, he died in 1860. His beatification process was introduced in Rome in 1886.[1]

Under the influence of the Cathedral Vicar Hermann Dichtl during his years in the Budweis seminary, Neumann discovered his missionary vocation and formed the plan of working among the German immigrants in the United States. He hoped that he would find the opportunity to acquire a thorough knowledge of French and English while completing his theological studies in Prague. For this reason he applied for one of the five scholarships at the Prague seminary that were at the disposal of the Budweis diocese.

In Prague Neumann completed his third and fourth years of Theology. The following pages attempt to enhance what was previously known of the Prague seminary and its Theological Faculty from the materials on this subject in the sources for Neumann's life. The effect of his Prague contacts on Neumann is generally known, although the picture can still be refined in a few areas.

The extant hagiographical literature on Neumann,[2] especially the modern American biography by Michael J. Curley, has not drawn on the archival sources of the Prague seminary and the Theological Faculty. Our information about these institutions is drawn chiefly from the two contributions of Josef Schindler in Heinrich Zschokke's collective work, *Die theologischen Studien und Anstalten der katholischen Kirche in Oesterreich* (Vienna-Leipzig, 1894).[3] The works of Eduard Winter on Bernard Bolzano and the Catholic Enlightenment[4] cast some light on the diocesan seminary under Dean Anton Rost, as do the writings about Karel Havlíček.[5] This very important Czech publicist entered the seminary in 1840, five years after Neumann, but he left after one year. The contrast between these two, who were unknown to each other, could not be more pronounced, yet both found much to criticize in the Prague seminary. Whereas Neumann judges his experiences in the seminary as a representative of the renewed Catholic pietistic spirit and of Roman orthodoxy, Havlíček's viewpoint is that of Bolzano's Catholic Enlightenment and of early liberalism. Furthermore, Havlíček had no well-defined vocational goal, for his outlook encompassed strong secular elements pointing toward his career as a popular educator and publicist. His rejection of the seminary is unsparing, absolute. Neumann's criticism, on the contrary, takes into consideration his recognition of his own limitations and tries to be more understanding. This will become clear in what follows.

The chief source for this essay is Neumann's diary. It begins with October, 1834.[6] Primarily spiritual in content, it is above all the record of his daily efforts at self examination and of his prayer life. Nevertheless, now and then it touches on the exterior experiences of life in the seminary and his studies. Along with this diary there are some pertinent passages in Neumann's short autobiography,[7] and a few letters from his days at the Prague seminary.[8] Curley's and Berger's biographies also include information handed down by word of mouth. The documents of the beatification process contain mostly statements by Neumann's contemporaries. This essay represents the first use of the documents of the Prague seminary archive and also of the archive of the Theological faculty.[9]

1. THE SEMINARY

From the time of the establishment of the Josephist General Seminary, the archdiocesan seminary was located in the imposing complex of the former Jesuit college, the Clementinum, in the old section of Prague near the Charles Bridge. Housed under the same roof were the Theological Faculty and other departments of the University, particularly the Royal and Imperial Library.

The seminary administration consisted of the Rector, Spiritual Director, Dean (called Vice-Rector before 1806), and after 1827 an Assistant Dean.[10] In Neumann's time Johann Büttner held the office of Rector. The Dean was at first Vincenz Prasky until he became a canon in Königgrätz in 1823; on July 10 of that year Anton Rost assumed the office.[10a] The names of the Spiritual Director and of the Assistant Dean could not be ascertained. Rector Büttner does not appear in Neumann's diaries, nor do the Spiritual Director or the Assistant Dean. Apparently Büttner had no real influence at that time.[11] In the life of the seminarians, the most significant office was that of Dean Rost's, as evidenced in the writings of both Neumann and Havlíček. To put it simply: both seminarians were disillusioned and even repelled by Rost.

Anton Franz Rost (1798-1879)[12] was selected by Archbishop Count Alois Ankwicz, who had been elevated to the See of Prague in 1833, with the intention of educating the new generation of clergy in the spirit of the Roman Catholic Restoration. This measure was intended to offer energetic opposition to the tide of the late Enlightenment which was still running strong in Bohemian theology, with its foremost representatives being Bernard Bolzano and his students. Originally himself one of Bolzano's students in

Prague, Rost had shifted into the new ecclesiastical movement, the Restoration, while in Vienna and Innsbruck, and he had become its eager champion. In 1847 he was dismissed from his post as Dean of the seminary by Archbishop Alois Josef von Schrenk (1838-1849), a man more favorably inclined toward the Bolzanist circle. Nevertheless Rost remained active even after his removal. In any case, he was one of the relatively few protagonists of the Catholic Restoration in Bohemia. Rost also enjoyed a reputation as a writer, chiefly for his attack on Bolzano's philosophy of religion whose dangerous elements he demonstrated to his readers.

Assessments of Rost up to the present, except for those in the Neumann biographies, derive entirely from Bolzanist circles and they paint a very unfavorable picture.[13] Accusations against him extend from fanaticism to dishonesty and hypocrisy. According to Havlíček he was a narrow bigot and hypocrite who rewarded tale-bearing and, on top of that, was said to have been an opponent of the national striving of the Czech people.[14] To a considerable degree Rost was the opposite of the ideal priest as exemplified in Balzano or in Franz Schneider, a religion teacher whom Bolzano influenced and who was the favorite spiritual guide of many of the seminarians.[15]

What was Neumann's experience with Dean Anton Rost? One would be inclined to think that the two of them, both conscious representatives of the new ecclesiastical currents in the midst of an environment that still bore strong traces of late Josephism, would see each other as allies—in so far as that was possible in view of their superior-inferior relationship. Yet this was not at all the case.

Neumann's first impressions are favorable. The Dean appears to him as pious and learned, a praiseworthy man.[16] His lecture on the chief tenets of religion pleased Neumann greatly.[17] When Neumann was late getting to class one day, the Dean did not rebuke him as the student expected.[18] Rost's spiritual inclinations are evident from the readings at table which he seems to have selected; for example, Friedrich Graf Stolberg's *History of the Religion of Jesus Christ.*[19] Rost himself reads to the seminarians from the writings of St. Charles Borromeo.[20] He considers papal infallibility a dogma.[21] He opposes Biblical criticism.[22] He rejects the established Church-State system.[23]

He entertains a favorable opinion of the Jesuits.[24] There is, however, no mention in Neumann's diaries of the battle over Balzano. The first indication of a critical attitude is the diary entry of December 11, 1834: "My feelings toward the Dean are too severe."[25] A week later follows a prayer to God: "Lead our Dean to his holy goals, for he has good intentions."[26] Later occur frequent signs of disillusionment and a complaint about the Dean's behavior. Neumann feels that Rost misunderstands him and is keeping an eye on him.[27] Unequivocal statements seldom are to be found in the diary. "When I try occasionally to get close to him he shuns me or seems to scorn me."[28] Neumann often has to struggle against feelings of aversion.[29] The diaries show no lack of introspection, of questioning whether the cause of their misunderstanding might be Neumann himself.[30] He wants to keep himself under control and merit confidence so that this zealous man Rost might become his spiritual guide.[31] Thus the months passed to the end of the academic year with thoughts and emotions alternating constantly, but with failure looming ever clearer. Only towards the end did Neumann decide to reveal to the Dean his missionary vocation; the Dean advised against it and urged him to join the Jesuits.[32]

The entries in the diaries unfortunately do not go into enough detail to admit of a precise, unambiguous portrayal of Rost's character. Neumann is clearest on April 13, 1835.[33] "Perhaps there is more against me than meets the eye. Were it not for our misunderstanding, I would not be so annoyed at him and he could help me very much. But his pronouncements, his extremely clever behavior towards us all, his secretiveness about his intentions, his lack of courtesy towards those who are failing because of mere ignorance, his seemingly cold heart that can only feign sympathy, all this constantly prevents my opening my heart and my thoughts to him. God forgive me that I sin against this zealous man. It could well be that my own terribly evil heart is the only reason for this wicked judgment, but up to now I simply cannot see things in a better light, and surely I cannot act against my conscience. To talk it over with someone else could damage the respect that he has to have while doing little for me. Other criticisms even more outrageous than mine are being voiced...." What are these pronouncements of Rost's that strike Neumann as peculiar? Once he jotted this down: "His moral principles contradict those that Prof. Teplotz taught us last year."[34] Unfortunately Neumann did not say anything more specific about Teplotz either, as we will see later; from the perspective of later years he seemed to Neumann too philosophical and therefore barely understandable. With some reservations one might formulate this generalization about Rost's character and pronouncements: he must have been a man with a rather unfortunate personality, with frustrations and complexes. Yet he too seems to have suffered from his unsatisfactory relationship with Neumann. Thus he once bade Neumann's friend Anton Laad to intervene: "He told Laad that he likes me, even though he does not show it."[35] Was it that he just found it difficult to switch from his tried and tested methods to newer tactics? Or did the Dean believe in the old rule that long served Jesuit pedagogy: "See everything, overlook much, say little about it"? Essentially that attitude aims to make this easy for all parties concerned but some consider it dishonest. As Neumann himself relates, Rost met with much resistance among the seminarians but he also had some adherents[36]—but what their motives were we cannot discern.

The situation becomes even more complicated by the fact that young Neumann does not entirely agree with Rost about the Catholic Restoration movement which they both desired to promote. Neumann was concerned at Rost's assertion of papal infallibility as a dogma.[37] One day Rost notices Neumann busy with a critical treatment of the Evangelists, and to the Dean's question whether hypotheses are permitted in Biblical interpretation, Neumann responded in the affirmative.[38] And finally, on the subject of Church-State relations: Rost denies that a person is bound in conscience to turn over to the state sums of money collected for the Church; Neumann disagrees, alleging that such a case does not impinge on anything essential to the Church, and that, furthermore, the Church demands obedience [to the State]. The Dean, however, expressed an opinion derived from pre-Josephist Moral Theology, namely, that this case concerned only penal laws [not moral laws].[39]

In these matters Neumann represents Josephist views, while simultaneously manifesting his integrity and tender conscience. Berger and Curley, Neumann's biographers, have suppressed these uncomfortable facts, despite their awareness of them. Nevertheless, Neumann did see Rost as a representative of the Catholic Restoration, or at least he realized his good intention. Whether Rost for his part was aware of his real community of spirit with Neumann is uncertain. A final question is this: does Neumann's assessment of Rost confirm that of Havlíček and the other followers of Bolzano? In part, yes. Rost was incapable of awakening confidence. Over and above the defense of Orthodoxy and Ecclesiology, this new religious integralism seems to have neglected the cultivation of the natural virtues so dear to the Enlightenment. Yet the judgments of the Bolzanist opponents are too one-sided and make no effort to understand the man and his motivation, whereas Neumann balanced his verdict carefully. The former object that Rost willingly used disciplinary means to protect the seminarians from the influence of Bolzanist ideas, but then they rejoice when Archbishop Schrenk dismisses their opponent from his position![40]

During Neumann's time the seminary limited its enrollment. From the mid-1820s, the number of clergy in the archdiocese had increased to the point where the newly ordained priests had to wait six to eight months for an initial appointment.[41] This superfluity, in Budweis too, was the reason why the bishop there postponed ordinations during the summer of 1835, which affected Neumann and disappointed him greatly.[42] For the academic year 1833-34 only twenty-five candidates were accepted at Prague. In 1835 there were 216 students in the Theological Faculty.[43]

Of life in the seminary we learn little from Neumann. The arrival of the new archbishop, Count Ankwicz, led to a strict regimen which caused Neumann the seminarian to feel his freedom seriously restricted.[44] Visits outside the seminary were limited to the two-hour community walks on Tuesday and Thursday afternoons along the route that led across the Charles Bridge into the so-called seminary garden, which included a large part of the slope of Mount Laurence. Neumann did not always observe the regulations to the letter. It even happened that on one occasion the Dean had to come and get him out of bed.[45] Sometimes he studied or conversed with his intimate friend Laad until past midnight.[46] In the seminary he particularly missed having a spiritual director and confessor in whom he could put his complete confidence.[47] For this reason he could not receive the sacraments as often as he wished and, apparently, as Dean Rost expected.[48]

II. THE COURSE OF STUDY

Concerning the Theological Faculty at Prague and its professional accomplishments during the nineteenth century there still exists no study that meets our modern needs. All that we have is information about the curriculum and the personal status of the teachers.[1] Occasionally we find in the literature information about the career of individual professors such as Maximilian Millauer. During the academic year 1833-34 Neumann had two classes daily in both Dogmatic and Moral Theology; in 1834-35 he took Pastoral Theology along with Homiletics and Catechetics. All other subjects (Sacred Scripture, Church History, Canon Law) he had already completed at Budweis.

The professor of Dogmatics was Hieronymus Zeidler.[2] The prescribed textbook was *Institutiones theologiae dogmaticae* (Vienna, 1789 and later editions) by Professor Engelbert Klüpfel of Freiburg. The author was an opponent of rationalism even though he denied papal infallibility.[3] Neither did Zeidler support infallibility, as Neumann reports. Once he himself did so in a very objective letter dated June 7, 1834, to a fellow student at Budweis.[4] Later, in the autobiographical sketch prepared in 1852 from the perspective of the ultramontanism that had developed with the passing of time, he draws a completely negative picture of Zeidler; he says that he was more against the pope than for him. He "offered such ridiculous objections that he lost our respect and could do no harm."[5] The official faculty history contradicts this view in describing the high esteem that Zeidler enjoyed; he frequently held important academic offices and also was well beloved.[6] To be sure, Zeidler was more of a

Josephist than a representative of the Catholic Restoration. His votes as government censor for religious literature (1842-43) reveal his critical attitude towards devotional books in the baroque tradition and with emphasis on sentiment.[7]

The moral theologian Stephan Teplotz[8] is judged more positively in Neumann's student diary. Neumann sharply contrasts Teplotz's moral principles with those of Rost, but without being specific on the subject.[9] The contrast seems to lie in the fact that Teplotz attributes to conscience, veracity and the natural virtues the decisive role in the life of a Christian. Unmistakably clear on this point was the deposition in 1822 by Adolf Koppmann, O. Praem., the New Testament scholar at Prague, concerning Teplotz when the latter applied for the Prague chair of Moral Theology. In that document Koppmann, spokesman for the Catholic Restoration, finds fault with the fact that Teplotz emphasized rational proofs and gave evidence of a thorough familiarity with Kant's philosophy; this "perverse method of demonstration is the reason for the wide-spread idea that there is no revealed truth that cannot be shown without Revelation to be good and useful."[10] Yet he could not have been a rationalist, at least in his later years, for the Necrology of his monastery describes him as pious, and he also composed a manuscript on the Veneration of the Most Pure Heart of Mary and an exposition of the invocations of the Loretto Litany.[10a] The faculty chronicle calls him a man whose knowledge far surpassed his teaching ability, who more effectively represented Christian morality through his lifestyle than through his teaching. To his students he was seen as "Moral Theology personified."[11] Neumann's later judgment that Teplotz was much too philosophical and therefore incomprehensible[12] thus corresponds in general to the facts. Neumann liked the textbook in Moral Theology that was then in use: *Theologia moralis in compendium redacta* (1827-31) and the *Epitome moralis* (2 vols. 1832) by Professor Ambrose Stapf of Brixen.[13]

It is strange that, from his later perspective, Neumann calls neither Zeidler nor Teplotz a Josephist, but rather the pastoral theologian Maximilian Millauer.[14] Neumann's diary entries[15] confirm the judgment of the faculty chronicle that as a teacher

Millauer handled his position "with the greatest conscientiousness and with accuracy down to the most minute detail."[16] Research shows not the slightest reason to call him a Josephist.[17] Why Neumann did so cannot be determined. It could be that he was adversely affected by the grades Millauer gave him, but that is scarcely conceivable in view of the tender conscience revealed in his diaries.[18]

Neumann is silent about the professor of Pedagogy and Catechetics, Franz Czeschik, who replaced Nicholas Tomek in 1835 and administered the examination to Neumann.[19]

The following grades that Neumann received can be found in the archives of the Theological Faculty:[20] In Dogma: Conduct—very good, Diligence—very good, Progress—first class; In Pastoral Theology: Conduct—good, Diligence—industrious, Progress—first class (Pastoral Theology and homiletic training); in Pedagogy and Catechetics: Conduct—good, Diligence—very industrious, Progress—first class. In regard to these grades, it might be noticed that Neumann received from Millauer in Conduct the second-best mark, "good." Of the fifty-nine students in the class, thirty-four received "very good" and twenty-five "good." In Diligence Neumann shared the second rank, "industrious," with half of the class. From Czeschik he also received the second rank, "industrious" in Diligence along with half the class. The reason for this evaluation cannot be determined. In the diary Neumann writes: "The 'first class' that Millauer gave me in Conduct soured all my pleasure at the termination of my long, arduous years of study."[21]

III. Conclusions

Neumann did not consider his Prague period profitable, neither in 1835[1] nor, even less so, later. While his diaries assess the seminary particularly as unsatisfactory, his later autobiography devotes only a few sentences to an adverse judgment of his professors and his studies. We know his assessment of the professors. He concludes his criticism in these words: "It took a lot of effort and self-control to bury myself in the study of subjects and ideas whose foolishness I had already come to realize. It is a pity that at such institutions so much more is done to preserve the splendor of scholarship than to propagate sound Catholic and certain truth. Hence I was heartily glad to return to Budweis in August, 1835, after the successful completion of my examination."[2]

In the diary he makes the comparison with Budweis where there lived a number of others who shared his views, "fine examples" and "pious and wise directors."[3] He eagerly awaited information of his friends there. More than anything else Neumann missed the Vicar Dichtl, his "spiritual father," "master and director of souls" as he often remarks.[4] This zealous representative of the new ecclesiology and its attitude towards the missions stands out in Neumann's diaries more than any other as the key priestly figure; he ranks next to Alois Klar and the somewhat less fortunate Rost among the precursors of the Catholic Restoration in Bohemia. We know of Neumann's complaint about not being able to find a suitable confessor. He felt isolated in Prague, not understood by his superiors or by his classmates. Anton Laad, who came with him from Budweis, was his only close friend in Prague. He was jeered at and derided for his "hyperorthodoxy."[5] Such evidence shows that a certain Enlightenment spirit still dominated the intellectual climate.

Neumann judged his Prague sojourn a failure primarily because he could not fulfill there his hope of systematically studying French and English. As a theology student he already understood eight languages, including Czech,[6] but he pursued language study to be better prepared for missionary work. He attended a few classes in French in the Philosophy Faculty but the new archbishop's general prohibition brought such elective courses to an end.[7] Thereafter Neumann studies languages privately.[8] He reports that English was not even taught at the university,[8a] but he finally found a substitute of sorts by associating with one of the English laborers who were employed in a textile factory in the city.[9] There is a report that the Prague civil Administration in 1835 wanted to hire a student with a mastery of languages, specifically Neumann, but he declined the offer.[9a]

The entries in Neumann's diary have elucidated somewhat more clearly the outlines of the personality and character of Anton Rost, but numerous points remain obscure. Concerning the opposite side, the Bolzanist faction, we learn nothing in the diaries. There is only a single letter that even incidentally mentions the Bolzano-Fesl affair as an aspect of the Catholic Restoration; this is Neumann's letter of December 31, 1833,[10] to a friend in Budweis in which Neumann describes the burial of retired Bishop Hurdalek of Leitmeritz who had died in Prague on December 27.[11]

Yet the Prague sojourn was not completely lacking in constructive experiences and impressions. First of all, there was Neumann's contact with the household of Alois Klar.[12] To be sure, this attractive representative of the Catholic Restoration, one of the few in Prague, had died on March 25, 1833, before Neumann's arrival. Yet his son Paul Alois continued his father's labors, chiefly those concerning the institute for the blind which he had founded. With Dichtl's cooperation he was also able to realize his father's last wish: the introduction of the Sisters of Mercy into Bohemia. Neumann of course had no direct contact with Klar—as he had none with Dichtl. His likeminded student friend Anton Laad did. Laad visited Professor Klar and from him learned a great deal about Dichtl and his plans.[13] In the seminary, Neumann copied one of Dichtl's letters to Klar and even gave it to Rost to read. Neumann's notations record only visits to Rosina Klar, Alois's widow, at the institute for the blind. He describes her manner as maternal, pious and charitable. Among other subjects she talked about the Tiecks in Dresden and also about Dichtl and the Carmelite nuns, one of whom, Theresa de Corde Jesu, was Dichtl's sister. Neumann's impression of the people who comprised the Klar group drew from him the remark: souls pure as angels, unconsciously using the expression of the contemporary Nazarene school for their artistic ideal.

From Neumann's diary entries we also learn that Rost and Dichtl came into contact with each other at this time. Dichtl seems to have had a high regard for Rost.[14]

What else did Neumann learn about Prague? In the diary he writes of visiting many buildings, chiefly ecclesiastical ones, but he fails to mention his impressions of works of art. He frequently assisted at church services.[15] He served as acolyte for the funeral Mass in the cathedral of St. Vitus for the deceased Emperor Francis I.[16] On the occasion of a procession to Sts. Philip and James at the Malá Strana Cemetery, he notices the still fresh graves of Bishop Hurdalek and Abbot Pfeifer of Strahov.[17] On Good Friday, 1835, he visited the "holy graves" at the Ursuline convent, at Emaus, at St. Stephen's church, St. Henry's, and at Our Lady of Týn. He was edified but he speaks critically of the profanation of the holy water in these services.[18] He seems to have frequently visited the grave of his patron St. John Nepomuk in the cathedral of St. Vitus.[19] Of the houses of the religious orders the Carmelite convent on the Hradchin seems to have attracted him more than the others. He had a very high regard for the Carmelite nuns and their contemplative, ascetic life.[20] At the house of the Brothers of Mercy where he visited the sick, he was deeply touched by the "care and sympathy with which the patients were treated."[21] Among the others he thinks that the only ones that were worth while were the Sisters of Mercy of St. Charles Borromeo, the Jesuits and the Redemptorists—even though the last two still had no houses in Bohemia at all.[22] Of the old Orders, most of whom were represented in Prague, he observes that their postulants are motivated by unworthy considerations—poverty, comfort, ambition.[23] Mention has already been made of the Klars' institute for the blind. Neumann makes a passing reference to a visit to the National Museum and the Imperial Library, that is, the university library in the Clementinum.[24] He was frequently to be found in the bookstores buying spiritual literature for himself and for the deacon in his home town.[25]

Neumann's diaries spread out before us his interior, spiritual development during his Prague sojourn. They deserve special study with regard to the religious psychology and piety of the Catholic Restoration.[26] The essential point is that Neumann's piety stands in the renewed classical-baroque tradition of Ignatius of Loyola, Francis Xavier, Peter Canisius, Louis of Granada, Theresa of Avila, Vincent de Paul, Francis de Sales, Joseph of Calasanza, Scupoli, Fénelon, Alphonse of Ligouri, Jean Crasset (1618-1692), Jean Crosset (1656-1738), Bourdaloue and the Roman Catechism.[27] Neumann was able to read the authors from the Latin countries in their original language. The great significance of French mysticism and theology had in fact induced him to learn French.[28] It is strange that his notes make no reference to the modern French authors of the Restoration such as Chateaubriand, De Maistre, Lammenais, etc., yet he seems to have been familiar with the Mainz *Katholik* in which the thoughts of these men were made available to the Germans.

An echo of Jansenism, part of the inheritance of the eighteenth century even in the Austrian lands, must be seen in his use of the expression "fear-provoking sacrament" once in reference to the Eucharist.[28a]

The contrast between the more utilitarian religiosity of Josephism, which was still to be found in the seminary, and Neumann's spirituality is complete. He knew, too, a kind of mysticism which he does not share in.[29] Another striking characteristic is his remorseless self-examination which frequently leads him to agonizing self-accusations; there are numerous lamentations in the diaries about temptations, interior aridity and being deserted by God, particularly in the final half year of his studies.[30] Everything bespeaks a clear consciousness of sin and a very tender, indeed a scrupulous conscience. For a considerable time he entertained the idea of approaching his vocation through the Jesuits or a missionary seminary.[31] Although he apparently never lost his interest in the natural sciences,[32] his scrupulous conscience would not permit him to read secular poetry because it threatened his chastity and, in a general way, because of its worldliness. Here we see a consistent bias in the piety of the Restoration, indeed a kind of anti-humanism.[33]

We must return again to a consideration of Neumann's attitude on the question of papal infallibility. We recall how Rost's assertion of the dogmatic character of this doctrine seriously disturbed him. The pertinent entry in the diary for February 10, 1835, reads: "He did not demonstrate for us the truth of this opinion; I feel sure that this is blasphemy an assertion [of a dogma] without regard for the consensus of the Roman Catholic Church. If it is a dogma, I am a material heretic. My God!" Eight months previously, in a detailed letter to his Budweis friend John Holba, Neumann had defended infallibility as a teaching, not as a Dogma—as it was not before

1870.[34] Here Neumann publicly took a stand on a rather crucial issue. Did this have anything to do with his interior crisis, whose symptoms we hinted at previously? Neumann did not live long enough to experience the dogmatic proclamation of the First Vatican Council. Even though there is no available documentation for his later views on this subject, he nevertheless was in agreement with the general tendency that led up to the famous dogma in 1870.[35]

Neumann's disillusionment with his student years in Prague has been transmitted through the biographical and hagiographical literature about him. The accepted view is that the Prague Theological Faculty—if not Prague itself—was a nursery of rationalism and Febronianism. Hopefully, the present investigation shows that more precise analyses of the sources can modify that picture somewhat. Neither was uniformity a characteristic of the Catholic Restoration. Furthermore, the hagiographical literature dealing with Neumann's early career should discard all preconceived notion of an undeviating, upward movement towards sanctity on his part, and it should not fail to note the crises and problems in the evolution of Neumann the human being. Only human beings can become saints.

APPENDIX I

Short [Auto]biography of Father John Nepomucene Neumann, Priest of the Congregation of the Holy Redeemer and Bishop-elect of Philadelphia in North America

My parents, Philipp Neumann from Obernburg in Lower Franconia in Bavaria and Agnes, born Lebisch,[1] had six children. The two oldest, Catherine and Veronica, each married a widower. I was the third child, born on Good Friday of the Year of the Lord 1811 and baptized on the same day in the local church of the Holy Apostle St. James the Great. My godfather Johann Marek was then mayor of the city. He gave me the name John of Nepomuck in honor of this glorious patron of Bohemia. The fourth child is my sister Johanna who, after my departure for America, entered the Sisters of St. Charles in Prague.[2] She was the first novice to enter this Order which had just been transplanted there from Nancy in Lorraine. With the name Sister Caroline she is presently superior at the hospital in Budweis. The next younger sister, Aloisia, is still at home and takes care of our elderly father who, following the death of our mother three or four years ago, has been unable to supervise the large household alone. However, she has already been accepted by the same Sisters of St. Charles and undoubtedly will follow her holy vocation as soon as her filial duty permits. The youngest of us, Brother Wenzel, learned our father's trade, stocking-weaving, and followed me to America. Since my coming to America my mother, my sister Veronica and my sister Catherine's husband have died back home. Because Catherine and her son have a sufficient income, we other sisters and brothers have agreed to renounce our share of the family inheritance in favor of our father during his lifetime; after his death it is to be used for the support of a hospital for the city of Prachatitz. The family home will serve very well for this purpose because of its size and because of the land attached to it. There will be no difficulty in transferring it to the Sisters of St. Charles.

Our education was traditional. Our parents were both very religious. From morning to night my father supervised the journeymen and employees, of whom at times there were five or six in the household. My mother never missed daily Mass, and she always took along one or the other of us, whoever was not in school. She often received Holy Communion and fasted both on the regular church fast-days and also at certain other times; my father was not happy about that. As for me, it took only the occasional promise of a coin or something of the sort to bring me to Holy Mass, to rosary services or to the stations of the cross. This caused one of my comrades, whose mother had called his attention to my zeal in going to church, to remark: "Give me a coin every day too and I'll be just like him."

On All Saints Day of 1818 I began to attend our local school. Since the Lord God had given me a good memory, I was always one of the best pupils during my six years there. The fact that my father always held one or another municipal office may have had an influence on my teacher. Meanwhile I had gotten from my father, who genuinely loved books, a real craze for reading. The time that others spent playing and snaring birds I spent poring over all kinds of volumes—anything that I could get my hands on. My mother often scolded me for being a book worm. In my seventh year I made my first confession, and in the summer of 1819 I was confirmed by the Reverend Bishop of Budweis. For as far back as anyone could recall, no bishop had visited our remote mountain village; as a result the huge crowd and the solemnity were indescribable and remained so vivid in my memory that ever since I can recall the most trivial detail of the occasion. Of the day of my First Holy Communion I have no recollection, for in Bohemia it is not the custom to observe the First Holy Communion as solemnly as in other countries. If I recall correctly, I was not yet ten years old when I mastered the larger catechism and thus was admitted to First Holy Communion with the other, older communicants at the school. Thereafter we received every three months.

I cannot say that I was aware of any definite inclination for the priesthood during my childhood. I did own a little altar made of lead, and I served Mass almost every day, yet my ideal of the priest was too high for it to seem attainable by me. One day when in our homey fashion I recited the prayer before meals and without thinking blessed myself in the Latin style instead of making three crosses on my forehead, mouth and breast, an old woman servant whom we had at home and who enjoyed a reputation for strict fasting, remarked: "Look at that, our little Johnny is going to become a priest."[3] My mother mentioned this incident on different occasions because she wanted me to become a priest some day. The idea, however, probably occurred to me more frequently later, especially when our other schoolmates decided on further education and, as was our custom, first spent a year or two taking Latin lessons from the priest who taught us catechism. I was asked if I wanted to do the same thing, and my parents consented at once. Consequently, during my last two school years, 1822-1823, I went every afternoon with eight or ten others to the home of our priest catechist to acquire the rudiments of the Latin language.

On All Saints Day of 1823 I and some twenty others left our town for Budweis to continue our studies at the gymnasium there

under the Piarist Fathers. I did not want to cause my parents any
unnecessary expense and so I shared room and board with three
others. Room and board were very cheap and cost no more than
sixteen florins for the ten months. I had very little studying to do.
The catechist at home, during our few lessons each week, had made
us learn so much that with little preparation we could have been
immediately promoted into the third class. That, however, was not
permitted. I used the many idle hours and days in more and more
reading—all kinds of books, whatever I could indiscriminately get
my hands on. Sometimes, of course, I played or went walking with
my colleagues, but not too often. The two old people whom I lived
with were very good, religious people, but they had no authority over
us. For that purpose, then, we were assigned to a teacher who,
because of his advanced age and his sociability, was addicted to drink,
and so we made little progress with our studies. In fact, I even forgot
much that I had already learned. During our third year this unfortunate priest came drunk to an examination being held in the presence
of the Reverend Supervisor of the school and was dismissed. Shortly
afterwards he shot himself. His successor was both learned and strict.
He aimed to repeat in a half year the curriculum of two and a half
years. After the neglect that we had enjoyed under his predecessor,
this was too much for most of the students and many simply stayed
away. I was even less satisfied with the religion teacher who was
dryness and dullness personified. He was obsessed with every word,
and I had a poor memory for words, so that my two religion classes
were the most boring ones. Every three months we went to confession. As far as I can recall, I was always very serious about receiving
the holy sacraments properly. The first instruction that I had had in
my own home town and the memory of the piety of my parents'
house saved me from the snares into which most of my fellow
students fell. At the end of 1827 I was very weary of my studies.
Once during vacation I thought of giving them up. Nevertheless, I
easily let my mother and my late sister talk me into continuing.
Actually I enjoyed the Liberal Arts subjects better, for we had a
teacher who showed a bit of affability towards us, even though he was
stricter than our second professor.

During the two years of Philosophy (November 1, 1829 to September 7, 1831), many changes occurred in my life. First of all, eight or ten of the students discovered that they had a strong inclination towards various sciences. We spent all of our free hours and every recreation day telling each other whatever we had each learned in his special field of interest. Then too, there was the good, blameless conduct of our professors, the Cistercian Fathers who were in charge of the Philosophical Institute.[4] They treated everyone with courtesy and to his complete satisfaction, even though they were inexorably strict when they discerned deceit or bad will. During these two years I industriously pursued my interest in the natural sciences, natural history, geography, physics, geology and astronomy. I applied myself most assiduously to algebra, geometry and trigonometry which had formerly been very distasteful to me. When the time came at the conclusion of the Philosophy course to decide on Theology, Law or even Medicine, I had more inclination for Medicine, particularly since only twenty out of eighty or ninety applicants for Theology were to be accepted. For Theology not only were the final certificates of study required but also letters of recommendations, which I did not want to bother with.

In this uncertainty about a choice of professions I came home during the Fall vacation of 1831 and found that my father had no objection to my studying Medicine in Prague, even though the expenses involved were considerable. My mother, however, was not very happy at this idea. Although I told her that I knew no one who would support my petition for admission to the Theology Institute (for which no tuition was required), she nevertheless thought that I should make the attempt. Then I wrote a request and sent it by special messenger to the episcopal consistory in Budweis. In a few days I received notice of my acceptance in the Theological Seminary there. From that moment on I never gave a thought to Medicine. Without any special effort I also gave up almost completely my study of physics and astronomy with which I had been keeping pleasantly busy. The studies that I had formerly pursued had at least the good result that I had not wasted my time and that my mind was better prepared for the more serious study of Theology. During Philosophy

I went to church even on weekdays; most of my comrades at that time did the same.

On All Saints Day of 1831 I began the study of Theology. Because of the limited space in the episcopal seminary only the two highest classes were permitted to live there. I therefore boarded outside. I studied *con amore* Old Testament, Hebrew, Church History, and so on, to my own satisfaction and to that of my professors who were diocesan priests. With the exception of the professor of Church History and Canon Law, who was by and large a Josephist,[5] a good spirit prevailed among them, and with great ease they taught us much useful material in a short time. At the end of the first year of Theology I was one of the few who were allowed to receive the tonsure and the four lower orders. This occurred on December 21, 1832.

In second year Theology we had to study the New Testament in Latin and Greek, with Hermeneutics and Canon Law. I found most interesting the Epistles of St. Paul, which the professor interpreted expertly.[6] About this time I also began to read the publications of the Leopoldine Foundation, especially the letters of the Reverend F. Baraga[7] and other missionaries among the Germans in North America. In this way there developed in one of my fellow students, Adalbert Schmid, and myself, on the occasion of a stroll along the Moldau, a sudden resolve to betake ourselves to North America as soon as we had attained our desired goal of ordination and acquired some experience. Two or three of our fellow students whom we invited to join us expressed admiration for our resolution but would make no promises. It was simply not their vocation. My decision was so firm and strong that from that moment on I could think of nothing else. We discussed how our proposal could be accomplished. We thought that the best thing to do was for me to apply to the Reverend Bishop of Budweis[8] for the recently vacated scholarship for a theologian of that diocese at the University of Prague, in the hope that I could learn French and English there. Knowledge of these languages seemed to us much more necessary than is really the case. The Reverend Bishop granted my request, but I found myself badly disappointed. I had barely attended a few classes in French at the

Clementinum when there appeared a decree of the Reverend Archbishop of Prague[9] that no seminarian should attend these lectures. I had even more difficulty learning English since this language was not taught at the university at that time. Similarly, I was very displeased in Prague with the professors of Dogmatics, Moral Theology and Pastoral Theology. The first was more against the pope than for him; however, he offered such ridiculous objections that he lost our respect and could do no harm. The second man was too philosophical for any of us to understand him. The third was an out-and-out Josephist.[10] It took a lot of effort and self-control to bury myself in the study of subjects and ideas whose foolishness I had already come to realize. It is a pity that at such institutions so much more is done to preserve the splendor of scholarship than to propagate sound Catholic and certain truth. Hence I was heartily glad to return to Budweis in August, 1835, after the successful completion of my examination.

Meanwhile, the Reverend Bishop of Philadelphia, Francis P. Kenrick, now Archbishop of Baltimore, had authorized Reverend Dr. Räss, Director of the Seminary at Strassbourg and now Bishop there,[11] to recruit young priests or, preferably, theologians for his diocese. Räss wrote about this to a very pious priest who held the office of Vicar of the Chapter at Budweis, in hopes of securing such individuals from Bohemia. Through a special disposition of Divine Providence, the Vicar, Father Hermann Dichtl, the man who had brought the Order of the Sisters of St. Charles from Nancy to Bohemia, happened to be the father confessor of my friend Adalbert Schmid, and he knew of our scheme of going to America. No one but he and three or four of our fellow students knew about it. He was overjoyed to see in the two of us his first recruits for America. In addition, on the occasion of his journey to France to bring three postulants to the sisters at Nancy he had become acquainted with the Catholic Institute of Foreign Missions in Paris. Full of zeal and courage in conceiving and executing great plans, Dichtl was thinking of launching a similar Institute in Austria. The request from Dr. Räss and our resolution seemed to him indications that his project would be attainable.

Because our Reverend Bishop, already over eighty years of age, was ill and there was no prospect of ordination for five or six months, Dichtl favored our departing as soon as possible. Nevertheless, he could not get the approval of either the Bishop or of the Chapter. The Leopoldine Foundation from whom we requested travel expenses refused; in their opinion not we but the Bishop of Philadelphia was supposed to have presented the request on our behalf. Despite such poor prospects, the Rev. Vicar succeeded in having the Bishop inform several of his clergy of our project and he allowed them to take up a collection among the priests of the diocese. But because nothing in the way of a recommendation or even a personal endorsement was forthcoming from him, scarcely enough money was realized to cover one man's expenses. So it was decided that I should depart alone. Dr. Räss having promised 400 to 500 francs to every missionary journeying to America to supplement his own travel funds, all difficulties seemed to have been overcome. After many requests and much correspondence, my passport, valid for three years, finally arrived. Very grudgingly my father consented; my mother, on the other hand, seemed delighted. Also, I received every possible encouragement from the clergy of our village, especially from the Reverend Deacon. And so, after I had made a pilgrimage to Nepomuck, the birthplace of my holy patron, I left my native city on February 8, 1836, without having really taken farewell. The necessary preparations for the journey kept me in Budweis for a few more days. On the 13th, however, after receiving the Bishop's blessing, I began the trip to Linz. My friend Adalbert Schmid accompanied me as far as his home which was situated along my route. The snow lay fourteen to fifteen feet deep along our road through the Bohemian Forest. In Linz I stopped at the episcopal seminary and was honored by the Reverend Bishop Ziegler with a Latin address and a splendid banquet. At that time a missionary, even a potential one, was considered something of a marvel, for it was (*illegible*).

Well supplied with letters of introduction, I left Linz on the evening of February 18 and headed for Munich. On the way we passed through Alt-Ötting, but it was dark and so I could hardly make out the famous pilgrimage church. In Munich I lodged with my cousin Philip Janson, a halbardier in the royal bodyguard. When I reached Doctor Phillipps,[12] the professor, I met there the Reverend J. Henni, Vicar-General of Cincinnati, now Bishop of Milwaukee, who gave me the strange news that the bishop of Philadelphia had just revoked the authorization he had given to Fr. Räss to recruit missionaries for his diocese, and that therefore there was no hope of my being accepted by him. Professor Philipps offered to write to the Reverend Bishop Bruté of Vincennes, who shortly before had passed through Munich on his way to Rome, to inquire whether he would receive me in his diocese. It was decided that I should wait in Strassbourg until I received word of a decision. In Augsburg, where I arrived on February 21, I received a very hospitable reception from the Reverend Canon Tischert and his Chaplain Dr. Schmidt, who later entered the Jesuits in Freiburg. When I reached Strassbourg on the last day of February, Dr. Räss also explained that I could not go to Philadelphia but that he would write to the Reverend Bishop Dubois of New York about his accepting me, since Bishop Bruté probably could not do so. An even more important bit of information was that he had already given to other missionaries from Lorraine and Alsace the travel funds that he had set aside for me. However, he promised to write on my behalf to a wealthy business man in Paris, a true friend of the missions, who would undoubtedly place a considerable subsidy at my disposal. Since the matter of my travel expenses caused him considerable concern, he advised me to depart for Paris immediately and to wait there for Bishop Bruté's reply. Therefore I left Strassbourg on March 3. In Nancy I visited the hospital of the Mother House of the Sisters of St. Charles where I also encountered two of the novices whom Fr. H. Dichtl had brought there. I had known both of them in Budweis. They were very happy to hear the latest bits of news from distant Bohemia. Here also I met a priest from Alsace who likewise wanted to go to America. He also had written to Bishop Bruté and planned to wait in Paris for an answer. I was very happy to have his company; he was a very pious and zealous priest and he spoke French fluently, while I, despite my certificate, had trouble with the French language in understanding a word now and then or in making myself understood. So we arrived together in Paris on the Saturday before Laetare Sunday. Despite all the testimonials and letters of introduction from Strassbourg, we could not find room with the Sulpicians. We were finally allowed in, after many refusals, at the Seminary for Foreign Missions, on the condition that we pay twenty francs for the month's rent for the room and took our meals at the hotel. The reason for our cool reception was the bad reputation of all German priests at that time on account of the petitions of the clergy of Baden and Würtemberg for the abrogation of the rule of clerical celibacy.

The wealthy Strassbourg business man could not be found, and my money had shrunk to about 200 francs. Although no answer had yet arrived from Bishop Bruté, I set out with my two leather suitcases and a large chest of books—a gift from Dr. Räss. When I got to the office of Lafitte and Company to depart for Le Havre, my coach had just left five minutes before. To overtake it and not lose my twenty-four francs, they advised me to take a cab and catch up with the coach. But it was too late. The cab driver let me out, after I paid him five francs, outside the city of Paris on the road to Le Havre. But I refused to turn back. Trusting in my sturdy feet, and even though the sun had already set, I marched confidently down the road towards the sea. It became darker and darker, and on top of that it began to rain softly. Thoroughly soaked but not at all tired, I passed on my nocturnal hike through Nanterre and reached St. Germain. Here I encountered a kindly old Frenchman who must have noticed my embarrassment. When I finally succeeded, after a hundred *quois?* and two hundred *s'il vous plais*, in making my adventures known to him, he went to the office of the Lafitte Company; within a short time he was helping me onto the loaded roof of the tall coach where I sat next to a Jewish man behind the driver's seat as we rolled through Rouen to Le Havre. I had to pay the driver only a trifling fare. Arrived in Le Havre on March 9, I quickly found on my first venture into the harbor the American three-master *Europa*, Captain Drummond. Through an interpreter I struck an agreement with him that he would give me a place between decks and take me to New York for eighty francs. Since, naturally, I had to supply my own food, I spent fifty-six more francs for potatoes, biscuits, salt, oil, butter and ham, and in addition an (*illegible*) and an (*illegible*). On the tenth there arrived the belongings that I had left behind in Paris. With them came the information that the Reverend H. Schaefer, my companion on the road from Nancy to Paris, had been accepted by the Bishop of Vincennes, but I had not. On the same day I had my things brought on board where I lived until we weighed anchor on April 20 at two o'clock in the afternoon and slipped out into the English Channel.

APPENDIX II

Prague
June 7, 1834

Rev. John Holba
Dear Friend:

In your last letter you informed me that the opinion generally prevails among your colleagues that the pope, in himself, *sensu stricto*, is infallible. You yourself apparently do not endorse the idea, since you say that it is not founded on Sacred Scripture nor on tradition or the *praxis ecclesiae*. Once I too opposed this idea. Perhaps you will recall the conversation we had about it. At the moment I have changed my mind, but of its full scope and truth I am still not as convinced as this alleged opponent of yours, who is something of a puzzle to me. Our Professor Zeidler dealt only cursorily with this question. He said that the Church has not yet made a decision on the matter, and that therefore it remains subject to debate, with limits set by other dogmas' boundaries, which should not be overstepped. As defenders of papal infallibility he cited a certain Kaestner, the Most Rev. Bishop Hille in Leitmeritz,[1] and Don Mauro Capellari, a Roman bishop.[2] He also numbered Ziegler[3] among the indirect defenders of this thesis. Personally, however, he bases his own interpretations on the opposite party: the *theologos saniores*. I have still read nothing on the subject, neither a book nor an article, and the grounds for my position are largely drawn from Canisius' Catechism. I know of no obvious proofs for the thesis of papal infallibility.

There are none, since it is not a dogma. You know as well as I the complete inadequacy of the human mind in trying to cope dogmatically even with truths of natural religion. Man in his present condition should accept without question the existence of a being the concept of which he comprehends only obliquely and indirectly. Where is the man whose upright, sensitive heart so precisely counterbalances his eye in its search for truth that neither faculty has an advantage over the other. Where, too, is the man who, unfortunately, does not often change his mind. Happy is he to whom, in this as in every other situation, there is allotted a pious *fides implicita* to sustain the superstructure of grace (Mk 9:23). Usually the old adage is confirmed: *homines quod volunt credunt*, which serves as compensation and justification for the lack of decisive motivation for a firm faith.

a. Now posit this situation. The Church has convened in a general council; a question is put to the assembled Fathers on which they disagreed among themselves even before the council, and they remain at odds. Only one of two or more factions can be the true one. With which should a Catholic take sides? To believe means to hold as true everything that the Roman Catholic Church says should be believed, etc. This is the mark only of those who agree with the Roman bishop. Their assent and consensus is my criterion of the truth, and who can deny that I am within the Roman Catholic Church when I adhere to it. When exercised in a council, therefore, I would maintain, his infallibility has the greatest possible probability.

b. [Another situation.] Disputes arise about the Faith in a time when no general council can be held. Whom should I turn to for instruction? Should I wait for a council? The matter is urgent. Irenaeus says: "*ad romanam ecclesiam propter potentiorem principalitatem necesse est omnem convenire ecclesiam, hoc est, eos, qui sunt undique fideles, in quo semper ab his, qui sunt undique, conservata est ea, quae est ab Apostolis traditio.*" Thus in the Roman Church (*illegible*). But how do I learn its pronouncement *in concreto*? Cyprian says: "*Etsi contumax ac superba obaudire nolentium multitudo discedat, ecclesia tamen a Christo non recedit, et illi sunt ecclesia, plebs sacerdoti adunata et pastori suo grex adhaerens. Unde scire debes, episcopum in ecclesia esse, et ecclesiam in episcopo; et si qui cum episcopo non sint, in ecclesia non esse.*" The dogmatic theologian simply says: The bishop is the representative of the Church. We must therefore assent to the pope's decisions. Moral theology demands this too in so far as it forbids the defense or even the holding of opinions condemned by the Roman popes. Does not Stapf[4] write so beautifully about Fénelon, who submitted immediately to the Roman See (*Epitome theol. moralis* Tom. I, 229, 4). So now, should not such an unconditional attitude underlie our own sense of duty? The concept of infallibility admits of no degrees. Just as in the first situation above the infallibility of the pope seems to exist in embryo from the point of view of dogma, so here it also seems that it should subsist when examined from the standpoint of moral theology.

c. I believe that my thesis is also confirmed in the concept of the Roman Catholic Church and of the pope. Canisius offers this definition: "*Ecclesia est omnium Christi fidem atque doctrinam profitentium universitas: quam princeps pastor Christus tum Petro Apostolo tum hujus successoribus pascendam tradidit atque gubernandam.* And then the negative: "*Nomen ecclesiae non merentur, sed falso arrogant sibi haeretici et schismatici omnes: qui etsi fidem atque doctrinam Christi profiteri videntur: tamen summi pastoris ac Pontificis, quem Christus ovili ecclesiae loco suo praefecit, et perpetua successione in romana ecclesia usque conservavit, oves esse detrectant.*" Thus truth and salvation exist only within the Church, where one is in communion with the Roman bishop. We conclude further: the pope represents the whole Church, for Cyprian says: "*Nec ignoramus, unum Deum esse, unum Christum esse Deum, quem confessi sumus, unum Spiritum Sanctum, unum episcopum in catholica ecclesia esse debere.*" And Jerome gives this interpretation: "*Propterea unus ex duodecim eligitur, ut capite constituto, schismatis tollatur occasio,*" and he goes on to say: "*si quis cathedrae Petri jungitur, meus est.*" St. Bernard says: "*Sunt quidem et alii gregum pastores sed tu tanto gloriosius quanto et differentius prae ceteris nomen hereditasti. Habent illi sibi assignatos greges, singuli singulos: tibi universi crediti, uni unus. Nec modo ovium, sed et pastorum tu unus omnium pastor. Unde id probem quaeris? ex verbo Dei* (Jn 21:17)." Does the conclusion not follow naturally that if the Church is infallible, its legitimate representative is also infallible?

Sacred Scripture seems to uphold it clearly enough in Luke, 22:32. Then Matthew, 16:17. Jerome comments on this last citation: "*Aedificabo super te ecclesiam mean etc. etc. et tibi dabo claves regni caelorum: omnia de futuro. Quae si statim dedisset ei, numquam in eo pravae confessionis error invenisset locum.*"

Among the holy Fathers the following speak in favor of my opinion: Augustine: "*Quoties fidei ratio ventilatur arbitror omnes fratres et coepiscopos nostros nonnisi ad Petrum, id est, sui nominis et honoris auctorem, referre debere, . . . quod per totum mundum possit omnibus ecclesiis in commune prodesse.*" Tertullian: "*Si Italiae adjaces, habes Romam, unde nobis auctoritas praesto est, felix ecclesia, cui totam doctrinam apostoli cum sanguine suo profuderunt . . . .*" Bernard to Innocent II: "*Oportet ad vestrum referri apostolatum pericula quaeque et scandala emergentia in regno Dei, ea praesertim, quae de fide contingunt. Dignum namque arbitror, ibi potissimum resarciri damna fidei, ubi non possit fides sentire defectum. Haec quippe hujus praerogativa sedis. . . . In eo plane Petri impletis vicem* (Lk 22:32), *cujus tenetis et sedem, si vestra admonitione corda in fide fluctantia confirmatis, si vestra auctoritate conterritis fidei corruptores.*"

Pope Leo I's legates to the fourth general Council of Chalcedon declare: "*Sanctissimus et beatissimus archiepiscopus magnae et senioris Romae Leo per nos et praesentem sanctam synodum uno cum ter beatissimo et omni laude digno beato Petro Apostolo, qui est petra et crepido catholicae ecclesiae, et ille qui est rectae fidei fundamentum, nudavit eum (Dioscorum) tum episcopatus dignitate, quam etiam ab omni sacerdotali alienavit ministerio.*"

The Council of Alexandria writes to Felix II: "*Tu profanarum haeresium et impetitorum atque omnium infestantium depositor, ut princeps et doctor, caputque omnium, orthodoxae doctrinae et immaculatae fidei existens. . . .*" At the sixth general Council Agatho's letter to Constantine [IV] was read aloud, in which it is stated: "*Luc. 22:31, qui fidem Petri non defecturam promisit, confirmare eum fratres suos admonuit: quod apostolicos Pontifices, meae exiguitatis praedecessores, confidenter fecisse semper cunctis est cognitum: quorum et pusillitas mea, licet impar et minima pro suscepto tu, divina dignatione, ministerio pedissequae cupis existere.*" And the Council sanctioned this letter.

But then there are many arguments against this opinion. It contradicts History, for Liberius and Honorius were heretics. Concerning Liberius, one should not be so quick to accuse him of heresy for we do not know which of the three Sirmium Formularies he signed. If it was the first, as Ruthenstock believes, he certainly cannot be numbered among the heretics (Cf. Ruthenstock, part 2, page 293 and the note on page 298). Honorius presents a more difficult problem. I find it hard to endorse Baronius's method of defending him. Every Council condemned him, but why? for heresy? or carelessness? That point is disputed, and Alexander Natalis defends him better than Baronius—(*apostolica sede illibatam fidem retinente*)—(cf. Ruthenstock, part 2, page 352, note 3, and page 472, note 2). Am I supposed to believe that the sun has been overwhelmed[5] just because storm clouds gather? No one has ever accused any pope of heresy before or after these two. Augustine writes beautifully: "*Petro successit Linus, Lino Clemens, Clementi Anacletus et caeteri; Damaso Siricius, Siricio Anastasius. In hoc ordine successionis nullus donatista episcopus invenitur. In illum autem ordinem episcoporum, qui ducitur ab ipso Petro, usque ad Anastasium, qui nunc eandem cathedram sedet, etiamsi quisque traditor per illa tempora subrepisset, nihil praejudicaret ecclesia et innocentibus christianis: quibus Dominus providens ait de praepositis malis: Quae dicunt facite, quae autem faciunt, facere nolite: dicunt enim et non faciunt, ut certa sit spes fidelis, quae non in homine, sed in Deo collocata, numquam tempestate sacrilegi schismatis dissipetur.*" As the exemplar of morality, moral theology holds up to us not the popes but only Jesus Himself!

My opinion seems rather probable to me, yet I do not believe it, thank God, with the same firmness with which I embrace the dogma of the infallibility of the Church, within or outside of a council. If the Church in my lifetime should make a declaration against this position, "*tunc qui leviter loquutus sum, Deo respondere quid possum? Manum meam ponam super os meum* (Job 39:34)." If she decides for it, then I would thank God for His grace in not leaving me insensitive to this truth, for having prepared my weak faith I would marvel at His wisdom and goodness which, to spare our blinded or enfeebled eyes, long withheld a light that would have injured them

STUDENT YEARS IN PRAGUE

in their weakness. Unhappily, though, there are many Christians so unfortunate that they comprehend only with difficulty a problematical article of belief even when the voice of God rings out for the salvation of believers through a venerable assembly of numerous Fathers who have grown gray in pious faith, in blessed hope, and in divine love.[6]

How difficult would it not be for a man to accept from an individual something that he now, richly supported by God's grace, accepts only with great effort from a large number of experts! If the situation remains unchanged, as I venture to hope, we thank God for His paternal goodness. May His Name be praised to eternity.

Now you have my opinion on the matter of papal infallibility. I have shared it with you because you insisted. In so doing I have intended nothing more than to satisfy your worthy request. Just discard it all if you do not care for it. I would not hesitate to do the same myself if I had more reason to do so. I have not shared my opinion with anyone else and would certainly not volunteer to do so. Premature opinions easily impede dutiful faith. To be sure, my fellow students asked me about it, but since I knew them only too well I answered: "I would be quite satisfied to know that the Church is infallible—whether or not the pope also is, I have no way of knowing. There are arguments pro and con for every opinion. In the final analysis, this is a transcendental matter whose existence or nonexistence can never be ascertained with certitude through rational processes, etc., etc."

I want to meet your opponent, and to learn his thinking on the subject. I will make a quick visit to Budweis about the 9th or 10th of August, for we all have to remain here until the 7th. I will personally thank Hani for his good wishes on my namesday.

Your friend John Neumann

*   This essay originally appeared under the title "Johann Nep. Neumanns Prager Studienzeit (1833-1835)," in *Archiv für Kirchengeschichte von Böhmen-Mähren-Schlesien*, II (1971), 36-61, published by the Königsteiner Institut für Kirchen- und Geistesgeschichte der Sudetenländer e.V.,

Königstein/Taunus, Germany. With permission of the author, who is also the editor of the *Archiv*, it has been translated by Raymond H. Schmandt of the Department of History, Saint Joseph's University of Philadelphia.

NOTES
SECTION I

1. *Philadelphien. seu Budvicen. Beatificationis et canonizationis ven. Servi Dei Joannis Nep. Neumann. . .Positio super virtutes* (Rome, 1907). The citations will be from the independently paginated section: *Summarium et sylloges super dubio: an constet de virtutibus theologalibus fide, spe et caritate....* (Abbreviated: *Positio...*).

2. Basic are: John N. Berger (Neumann's nephew): *Leben und Wirken des hochseligen Johannes Nep. Neumann* (Philadelphia, 1883), for its use of Neumann's diaries and letters, along with information from contemporaries; M. J. Curley: *Venerable John Neumann C.SS.R., Fourth Bishop of Philadelphia* (New York: Crusader Press, 1952), with sources and bibliography, but some errors in details; *Lexikon für Theologie und Kirche*, 2nd ed., VII, 914. Publications of edification and veneration: A. Reimann: *Böhmerwaldsohn und Bischof von Philadelphia—Joh. Nep. Neumann C.SS.R., 1811-1860* (Königstein/Taunus, 1960); N. Ferrante: *Il beato Giovanni Nep. Neumann, vescovo di Filadelfia* (Rome, 1963). See also *L'Osservatore Romano*, No. 135 (June 13, 1959), 3.

3. "Geschichte des prager fürsterzbischöflichen Clericalseminars," in H. Zschokke, *Die Theologischen Studien und Anstalten der kath. Kirche in Österreich* (Vienna, Leipzig, 1894), 838 ff. (abbreviated "Clericalseminar"); "Geschichte der theol. Fakultät an der k.k.Karl Ferdinands Universität in Prag.," *ibid.*, 157 ff (abbreviated "Theol. Fakultät").

4. *Bernard Bolzano und sein Kreis* (Leipzig, 1933), pp. 191 ff., 232, 235, 257; *Der Josefinismus und seine Geschichte* (Brünn, 1943), 395 ff., 400 ff., 455 ff. (abbreviated *Josefinismus*).

5. E. Chaloupný, *Karel Havlíček* (2nd ed.; Prague, 1921); E. Nittner, "Bernard Bolzanos geistiger Einfluss auf Karel Havlíček," unpubl. diss. (Prague, 1938) (abbreviated "Havlíček"); E. Nittner, "Havlíčeks Beziehungen zu B. Bolzano über F. Schneider," *Deutsch-slawische Wechselseitigekeit in sieben Jahrhunderten*, Veröffentlichungen des Instituts für Slawistik, 9 (East Berlin, 1956), 425-435.

6. To be precise, there are two diaries ("Mon Journal"), one in German (Gd) and one in French (Fd). Gd begins with March 22, 1835 and ends with Nov. 27, 1839, in 64 pages; Fd begins with October 1, 1834, and ends

with Nov. 4, 1835, pages 1-69c, with 69a and 69b missing. The Prague period in Fd ends with July 2, 1835, and in Gd with July 7. From March 22, 1835, he often made entries on the same day in both German and French, sometimes several hours apart; in content they often repeat each other. A few entries are composed in English. The entries are sometimes interrupted for days at a time. Preserved in Redemptorist Archives of the Baltimore Province, Brooklyn, New York.

7. "Kurze Lebensbeschreibung des P. Joh. Nep. Neumann, Priester der Versammlung des hl. Erlösers u. erwählten Bischof in Philadelphia in N. Am(erica)," 7 pp. Neumann composed this report on the eve of his episcopal consecration in Baltimore, on March 27, 1852. This autobiography, in so far as it treats of Neumann's life to the point of his leaving Europe, (pp. 1-4), is given in Appendix. 1. Preserved as above, n. 6.

8. There are nine letters: seven to his parents, one to John Holba (in Budweis?) on papal infallibility (published as Appendix II to this essay), and a fragment to a friend about the Bolzano-Fesl-Hurdalek Affair. Preserved as above, n. 6. The director of the archive kindly supplied photocopies of the items listed in notes 6 to 8. Miscellaneous notes and excerpts from Neumann's readings in the same archive were not available to me.

9. The archive of the archiepiscopal seminary today forms part of the Archiepiscopal Archive in the National Central Archive in Prague (Státní ústřední archiv, cited SUA). In the process of reorganization, some materials have been lost. Serious losses were sustained in the university archive which was added at the end of the war in 1945. The Archive of the Theological Faculty is a part of the University Archive (cited UA). To the administrators of both archives my thanks are due for their cooperation and assistance.

10. SUA Prague AP A II-IX-1349; Schindler, "Clericalseminar."

10a. SUA Prague AP A II-IX-6687, 6962. The designation "Praeses" has caused some authors to consider him the Rector. [The translation of Praeses as Dean is based on the similarity of function between that of Rost and the American official who would hold the title Dean in a seminary environment—Tr.].

11. According to the official chronicle on which J. Schindler based his work ("Clericalseminar"), Büttner is said to have ameliorated the discipline of the house and to have enjoyed a reputation among the seminarians of a concerned, kindly father; with increasing age he became somewhat eccentric. In Havlíček's day, a seminarian five years after Neumann, Büttner was an old, cultured, but ineffectual man. Cited from E. Nittner, "Havlíček," 108. In Havlíček's time the Spiritual Director was W. Siegmund and he remained indifferent to all the events of the time. *Ibid.*

12. Concerning Rost, in addition to the material by E. Winter cited in note 4, see *Allgemeine Deutsche Biographie*, 29, 272 f.; *Das katholische Deutschland*, 2, 4063 f., with a list of his works. According to the *Catalogus ven. cleri saecularis et regularis archidioecesis Pragenae 1869*, p. 18, Rost held a Ph.D. degree, had been a professor of religion at the University of Innsbruck before coming to Prague, later was Canon at Altbunzlau and Administrator of St. John Nepomuk in Skalka (Prague), but not Provost of Příbram as stated in E. Winter, *Josefinismus*, p. 429, who follows here a report of Bolzano. Rost, the Assistant Dean and the Spiritual Director are not mentioned in Schindler, "Clericalseminar."

13. See E. Winter, *Josefinismus*, E. Nittner "Havlíček," pp. 108 f.

14. E. Caloupný, *Karel Havlíček*, pp. 24 ff. (Havlíček wrote epigrams that made Rost seem foolish.)

15. *Ibid.*, p. 27; Nittner, pp. 42, 46 ff.

16. Fd Oct. 3 and 12, 1834; March 22, 1835.

17. Fd Oct. 30, 1834.

18. Fd Nov. 12, 1834.

19. Fd Oct. 27, 1834.

20. Fd Dec. 4, 1834.

21. Fd Feb. 10, 1835.

22. Fd April 18, 1835.

23. Fd Dec. 18, 1834.

24. Fd March 23 and June 24, 1835. Rost's brother was a Jesuit. E. Winter, *Josefinismus*, p. 395.

25. Fd

26. Fd Dec. 18, 1834.

27. Fd March 3, 22, 27, April 12, 17, 20, 21, 24, May 7, 8, June 12, 24, July 2, 1835; Gd April 8, 13, 16, 17, 18, May 9, 28, June 22, 1835.

28. Gd April 13, 1835. Neumann thought that Rost was urging him too insistently to enter the Jesuits. Gd April 20, 1835.

29. See note 27, Gd April 8, 16, 1835.

30. Fd June 12, 1835; March 22, 1834; April 16, 1835.

31. Fd April 17, 1835; Gd April 13, 16, 1835.

32. Fd April 23, 1835.

33. Gd

34. Gd April 18, 1835.

35. Gd April 15, 1835.

36. Gd April 16, May 17, 28, 1835; Fd April 17, 1835.

37. Gd Feb. 10 1835.

38. This is my interpretation of the entry in Fd April 18, 1835; "*je lisait*

l'Evangile inedité...."
39. Fd Dec. 18, 1834.
40. E. Winter, *Josefinismus*, p. 429. *Ibid* p. 396, quotes Přihonský mentioning that Rost was involved by Count Ledebur in an "annoying suit." Neumann's diary mentions the basic incident. He says that during Vespers before the exposed Blessed Sacrament in a church filled with pilgrims, the Count approached a girl sitting on a side bench—"the innocent soul looked resolutely towards Heaven as if begging for peace and protection from You, O God, the protector of innocence." Dean Rost, made aware of the situation by the seminarians, sent for two policemen standing outside at the bridge; after a brief but loud exchange of words with Ledebur they led him away. The next day, behind closed doors, the auxiliary bishop reconciled the church. Fd May 16 1835; Gd May 17, 1835.
41. Letter of Archbishop Chlumčanský, March 12, 1827, to the provincial administration of Bohemia: "The sad day is past when the shortage of theologians made it necessary even to abbreviate the theological curriculum." To provide employment for newly ordained priests, he suggests the founding of a house for priests in Prague. For the academic year 1833-34 only twenty-five candidates were accepted: SUA Prague AP A II-IX-1349.
42. Gd July 4, 7, 1835. In his autobiography (Appendix No. I) he gives as the only reason the bishop's illness.
43. F. Schindler, "Theol. Fakultät," p. 203.
44. Letters of March 14, June 22 and Nov. 20, 1834, to his parents. The new statutes were officially announced in a solemn ceremony on Oct. 16, 1834. See Fd.
45. Fd Feb. 18, 1835.
46. Fd Jan. 1, 28, 1835.
47. Fd Nov. 5, Dec. 10, 1834; May 8, 9, 1835; Gd April 3, 10, 1835. He occasionally mentions his confessor Fabian (Fd Oct. 4, 1834), spiritual director (Fd Jan. 31, 1835), Fr. Nitsch (Fd May 4, 1835). Fr. Franz Schneider is never mentioned in the diary. In Havlíček's time Schneider enjoyed the confidence of many of the seminarians, but because he belonged to the Bolzanist circle Rost rejected him. E. Winter *Josefinismus*, pp. 402 ff; E. Nittner, *op. cit.*, pp. 46 ff.
48. Gd May 9, 14, 16, 1835; Fd May 7, 8, 1835. There we find, however, complaint about the paucity of opportunities to go to confession: Gd May 2, 1835: "At last we finally can go to confession."

Section II

1. Schindler, "Theol. Fakultät." The faculty chronicle remains basic. In general see Zschokke, *op. cit.*, 66-78.
2. Born in Iglau, Nov. 5, 1790, died in Rome March 1, 1870. Premonstratensian of the monastery of Strahov, taught at the Theological Faculty from 1812 to 1835, elected Abbot of Strahov on Oct. 7, 1834 (not 1835), several times Dean of the Faculty, from 1839 to 1848 Director of philosophical studies, several times Rector magnificus of the university, ennobled in 1863, in 1869 became first Abbot General of the Praemonstratensians since the secularization of the Mother Monastery of Prémotré in France, and as such summoned to participate in the First Vatican Council, opposed among the inopportunists the doctrine of Infallibility. J. Schindler, "Theol. Fakultät," pp. 196 ff. C. v. Wurzbach, *Biogr. Lexikon des Kaisertums Österreich*, 59, 275-277; L. Goovaerts, *Ecrivains, artistes et savants de l'Ordre de Prémontré*, 11, 434 ff
3. Zschokke, *op. cit.*, p. 196; M. J. Curley, *John Neumann*, p. 26 f. In Neumann's day an excerpt by Dr. Geis was used; *Lexikon für Theologie und Kirche*, 2nd ed., VI, 355.
4. See Appendix II.
5. See Appendix I.
6. Schindler, "Theol. Fakultät," p. 196 f. (his elevation to abbot is erroneously recorded here for 1836). The political authorities attested to Zeidler's zeal, thoroughness and learning, and to his strict religious and moral life. SUA Prague C G Publ. 1826-35/97/3, 5976/360 a.
7. For example, Zeidler considered devotional books of the Confraternity of the Heart of Jesus and of the Scapular unnecessary since the corresponding associations were not recognized in Austrian law. He picked on many trivial passages and found many titles tasteless and meaningless; besides, there were too many devotional books anyway. Yet he often qualified his objections with the remark: "Otherwise in the spirit of the Catholic Church." On the popular *Allgemeine Religions- und Kirchenfreund* edited by the religious writer Fr. G. Benkert of Würzburg Zeidler writes: "One should not wish for things to be really so true all the time as the *Kirchenfreund* records." Apparently this was directed against Rost who wrote about Bohemia in the book. He did not care for the typography of the *Universalkirchenzeitung*, "otherwise a good paper." SUA Prague R D—Strahov Zeidler 1326 (8), No. 112, 147, 177, 189, 194, 245, 271.
8. Born in Varasdin, Croatia, December 12, 1795, died July 23, 1877. A Croatian, master of languages, Cistercian of the Monastery of Rein near

Graz, studied in Agram, Graz and Vienna. First lecturer in Old Testament in Graz, in 1823 Professor of Moral Theology in Prague, called to the University of Vienna in 1849, retired as emeritus in 1857 because of illness, returned to the monastery. The conventual library of Rein preserves the following unprinted works by him: Compendium theologiae moralis (MS 239); Die messianischen Erwartungen und Ansichten der Zeitgenossen Jesu (MS 280); Christologia in Litaniis Laurentanis (MS 288). Published was his *Ethica christiana* (Vol. I/1-2; Prague, 1831/34). *The Catalogue of Professed of the Monastery Rein* was made available through the kind cooperation of Fr. Gothard Ortner.

9.   Gd April 18, 1835.

10. A. K. Huber, "Das Stift Tepi im Aufklärungszeitalter,' *Annalecta Praemonstratensiana* 29 (1953), p. 101.

10a. *Professenkatalog des Stiftes Rein*, see note 8. I did not have the opportunity to examine his *Ethica christiana*.

11. J. Schindler, "Theol. Fakultät," p. 198; also the evaluation in the monastic necrology: "neminem laesit, omnes honor debito prosecutus est."

12. Autobiography, see Appendix I; Curley, *John Neumann*, p. 26, who makes use of material from the oral traditions of Neumann's circle of acquaintances (Berger and Landherr Papers), writes that Teplotz spent the time with labyrinthine, philosophical explanations of complicated, ridiculous difficulties, that he also bored his students with insipid ascetic digressions.

13. See the letter to Holba, Appendix II; Curley, *op. cit.*, p. 26; *Lexikon für Theologie und Kirche*, 1st ed., IX, 773.

14. Born Dec. 17, 1784, died June 14, 1840. Cistercian of the monastery of Hohenfurt in southern Bohemia, devoted himself to History (his teacher was Rev. Franz Kurz in St. Florian), from 1815 professor of Pastoral Theology in Prague, in 1822 Director of the Royal Bohemian Scientific Society, 1834 Rector magnificus. Millauer's chief area of activity was History; among other works he wrote an unpublished "Geschichte der Theol. Fakultät an der K. K. Karl Ferdinandeischen Prager Universität" (to 1821); MS in the National Museum, Prague, MS Division). He translated into German the official textbook on Pastoral Theology by Andreas Reichenberger (*Institutio pastoralis*, Vienna, 1819). Wurzbach, 18, 316-320; *Das Kath. Deutschland II*, 2999; still unprinted biographical study by J. Kadlec.

15. Fd May 11, 29, and June 3, 1935.

16. J. Schindler, "Theol. Fakultät," 200.

17. J. Kadlec, "Maximilian Millauer" (unprinted); E. Winter, *Tausend Jahre Geisteskampf* (Salzburg, 1938), p. 330.

18. Gd July 19, 1835.
19. *Catalog über die Hörer der Theologie im I., II., III. und IV. Jahrgänge an der k. k. Universität zu Prag im Schuljahr 1835*; according to Curley, *op. cit.*, p. 33, the textbook in Pedagogy was J. Peitl, *Methodenbuch oder Anleitung zur zweckmässigen Führung des Lehramtes* 1821).
20. *Classen-Cataloge über die theol. Zuhörer sämtl. vier Jahrgänge an der k.k. Universität zu Prag im Schuljahr 1834,* and *Cataloge....*(as in note 19), both in SUA Prague.
21. See note 18; "first class" meant "second best"; "Eminens" meant "best."

SECTION III

1. Fd May 31, 1835: "O Jesus, You know how much I have suffered since I have come to Prague."
2. See Appendix I. Actually Neumann left Prague in July.
3. Fd May 1, 2, 1835.
4. Fd Dec. 17, 18, 1834; on Dichtl see E. Winter, *Trausend Jahre Geisteskampf in Sudetenraum* (Salzburg, 1938), pp. 326, 330, 365, 373; Id., *Josefinismus,* pp. 455, 457, 459.
5. Fd Feb. 20, 1835, Dec. 10, 1834: "Böhm received a letter from Müller in Leitmeritz in which he made fun of my hyper-orthodoxy; he incited Nowak to bother me. The letter was read aloud in study hall." In the documents of Neumann's canonical investigation, his sister claims to have heard from Laad that Rost received an anonymous, slanderous letter which he caused to be read publicly so that Neumann had to endure being made fun of (*Positio,* 441). It is possible that the sister unknowingly brought together two separate facts. This man Nowak once took issue with Neumann and described canonization as ignorance and superstition: Fd March 27, 1835. One who seems to have shared Neumann's views, and who apparently was also inclined to join the Jesuits, was the seminarian Vavřík: Fd Jan. 27, 29, 1835.
6. Curley. *op. cit.,* pp 24, 28, 34; Berger, *Leben und Wirken,* p. 49.
7. Fd Oct. 12, 1834; Autobiography, see Appendix I. During the year 1835-36, however, two seminarians received permission to study French at the university: SUA Prague AP II—IX 1336, 7769/907.
8. According to Berger, Neumann is said to have taken the French examination after private study and to have been passed by the professor with the highest grade: *Leben und Wirken,* p. 47.
8a. Autobiography, Appendix I.
9. The diary mentions only two meetings with the Englishman: FD May 24, June 4, 1835.

9a. Berger, *Leben und Wirken*; Curley, *op. cit.*, p. 34.

10. See note 8, chapter 1.

11. The seminary rector named Fesl in Leitmeritz established a secret society; that was strictly forbidden by law. "They generally met at night, and he read to them different theological tracts of a kind that advocated the errors of Bolzano. Among other things, he taught the eternity of matter, that Christian slaves could do everything in their power to escape their masters etc., reviled the Church, the pope, the emperor etc., etc., until two students caused him to be arrested by night, to have his books taken away, especially his diary, and to be placed in the Servite monastery for several years where he responded to gentle treatment by renouncing his errors . . . ."

12. F. Weinolt, *Denkwürdigkeiten aus dem Leben Alois Klars* (Prague and Leitmeritz, 1835); Wurzbach, 12, 11-16; *Das kath. Deutschland*, II, 2143f; *Österr. Biograph. Lexikon*, III, 369; E. Winter, *Tausend Jahre Geisteskampf*, pp. 326 f.

13. Fd Jan. 27, Feb. 26, March 5, 19, May 5, 1835; Gd April 15, 1835.

14. Fd Feb. 17, 1835; Gd April 13, May 10, June 22, 1835. The entry for May 10, 1835, in Gd, is unclear: "Today I became better acquainted with Dean Rost from his analysis of the essay that H. P. Dichtl published in *Katholik*. Oh my Father, I call to Thee, he is your son also." The item in question most probably was the "Brief eines böhmischen Geistlichen an einen Geistlichen am Rhein" of Oct. 27, 1834, in *Der Katholik*, 15th year, volume 55, Appendix No. I, p. xvii-xx. It contains a general report about the religious condition of the country, historical perspectives, and the desirability of missionary vocations for America. It could have been addressed to Dr. Räss.

15. Fd Dec. 25, 1834 (Subdeacon at Vyšehrad), March 19, 1835.

16. Fd March 16, 17, 1835; he mentions that 230 three-pound candles burned at the catafalque.

17. Fd May 5 1835. This church was demolished in 1891.

18. Fd April 17, 1835.

19. Fd March 18, 1835; Nov. 19, 1834: "My patron saint, pray for me, that the Creator may grant me the grace of always telling the truth; that would be the most beautiful memory of Prague, that you have enlightened me through your immaculate teaching."

20. Fd March 19, April 25, May 26, 27, 1835.

21. Fd Oct. 29, 1834.

22. Gd May 15, 26, 1835.

23. Gd May 26, 1835; he considers political influences to be harmful.

24. Fd May 5, 6, 1835.

25. Fd Jan. 20, March 20, 1835.
26. Berger's biography reproduces many very long citations from the spiritual diary.
27. Fd April 2, Oct. 15, 26, 1834; Nov. 5, 7, 11, 12, 18, 1834; Dec. 25, 1834; January 7, 12, 28, 29, 30, March 18, 23, April 9, 1835; Gd June 11, 1835. He includes the Jesuit saints and St. Theresa of Avila among his protectors whom he often calls upon at the end of entries in the diary.
28. J. Berger, *Leben und Wirken*.
28a. Fd Nov. 22, 1834; March 22, 1835.
29. Gd Nov. 24, 1835. About his crisis of faith during his final year at the gymnasium, he writes in retrospect on April 8, 1835, Gd: "As regards religion I had the most dreadful prejudices, for Protestant poets and philanthropists were my reading . . . I considered humanity the peak of perfection; of nothing did I have as much horror as of the so-called mysticism . . . . At the end of Philosophy I felt some dislike for Theology; Medicine was more attractive to me."
30. Especially Gd March 22, 1835: "An overwhelming crisis looms in my spiritual life. I am forming it out of temptations in my Faith, in Hope, and in Love." Gd March 22, 1835 speaks of temptation of unbelief and of despair. Gd June 20, 1835: rejected by God. Towards the end of April, Gd April 24, 26, 30, 1835, he experiences disgust for his academic work and for the demands of his vocation.
31. Fd Oct. 13, 1834, Jan. 27, 1835; Gd April 27, May 25, 30, 1835.
32. Fd Jan. 29, 1835; Autobiography, Appendix I; *Positio . . .* 69, 79, 83, 99.
33. Fd March 17, 1835: scruples in reading Petrarch; Fd Oct. 13, 1835: the same for Shakespeare. Berger, *op. cit.*, pp. 81 f., mentions Neumann's giving up painting and chess.
34. See Appendix II.
35. See his remarks about his Dogmatics professor, Zeidler (Appendix I); also the deposition of Fr. Jordan, S.J., in the apostolic process in Philadelphia: "Devotissimus erat Sancto Patri utpote Dominum nostrum repraesentanti. Magnopere Primatum Romani Pontificis defendebat." *Positio . . .* 331.78.

Appendix I

1. This is the spelling used on Neumann's baptismal certificate issued on June 27, 1831, by the city official Philipp Enders, in the Redemptorist Archives of the Baltimore Province, Brooklyn. Neumann himself in this place used the form: Lebiš.
2. The Borromeo Sisters.

3. The text gives the quote in Czech.
4. These were members of the Cistercian community of Hohenfurt in southern Bohemia.
5. Franz Linhart.
6. Karl Körner.
7. Missionary in upper Michigan, first bishop of Sault Ste. Marie-Marquette.
8. Ernst Konstantin Růžička, Bishop of Budweis 1816-1845.
9. Andreas Alois Graf Ankwicz, Archbishop of Prague 1833-1838.
10. See the pertinent passages in Section II.
11. Andreas Räss (1794-1887), professor of Theology at Mainz, edited from there (since 1821) with the help of N. Weis the newspaper *Der Katholik*, 1829 dean of the seminary, 1840 Coadjutor and then in 1842 Bishop of Strassbourg.
12. Georg Phillips (1804-1872), legal historian and canonist, convert, 1834 professor in Munich, 1850 in Innsbruck, 1851 in Vienna, leading figure in the Catholic Movement.

APPENDIX II

1. Augustin Bartholomäus Hille (1786-1865), professor of Pastoral Theology, Rector of the seminary in Leitmeritz, bishop in 1832 worked on behalf of the Catholic Restoration.
2. Mauro Cappellari, Camaldolese monk, general of the Order, cardinal in 1826, elected Pope Gregory XVI in 1831. Consecrated bishop only after his election as pope. Author of the famous tract, *Il trionfo della Santa Sede* (1799 and many later editions).
3. Gregor Thomas Ziegler (1770-1852), former Benedictine of Wiblingen, after the secularization worked in Austria, professor of Dogmatics in Vienna from 1815, Bishop of Tyniec (Galicia) in 1822, Bishop of Linz in 1827, opponent of Josephism and Liberalism.
4. See above, Section II.
5. Accidentally Neumann wrote here "unbesiegt" when he clearly meant "besiegt."
6. [Neumann's syntax here is very confused, so that his meaning is obscure. Tr.]

BUILDING A FOUNDATION
OF SPIRITUALITY:
St. John Neumann's European Years

RICHARD A. BOEVER, C.Ss.R.

St. John Neumann is an American saint, the first male citizen of the United States to be canonized. His spirituality would come into full flower only in his ministry as a diocesan priest on the frontier of western New York State, as a Redemptorist in the eastern United States, and as the fourth Bishop of Philadelphia. However, like many of the great New World church figures of the first half of the nineteenth century, his roots are found in Europe, and it is there that the foundation of his spiritual life was set. The vision and conviction he had when he first set sail for North America would underpin his zeal throughout his ministry, and he would never lose these roots, as he would never lose his accent.[1]

NEUMANN'S HISTORICAL CONTEXT

The European roots of Neumann reach back to a time just twenty-two years after the French Revolution (1789-99), a pivotal point in the life of the European Church. The Church experienced a loss of both economic and cultural power. Years of economic prosperity and social standing affected the stance of even the most sincere churchmen toward the relationship of church and state.[2] While the Papal States, the center of Catholic Christianity, had inherited a recognized political status, an ongoing spirit of nationalism and emerging philosophies of government limited the freedom of the papacy to speak with the authority it once enjoyed. Far beyond politics, the Age of the Enlightenment,[3] with its emphasis on reason, distrusted theological speculation. For Neumann, this was particularly felt in his seminary education where Josephinism,[4] though largely ignored, remained on the books as a part of the legal system. While Neumann studied at the seminary in Prague (Praha), changes in the seminary curriculum and discipline still required only local approval, and students were not permitted to study in Rome. In his *Journal*,[5] Neumann was not slow to label a number of his professors as being tainted by Josephinism.

The Austrian Empire known to Neumann numbered 24 million Catholics, 80% of the total population. He was born in Catholic Bohemia, in the town of Prachatitz (Prachatice), located in the modern-day Czech Republic. The area had long boasted of a comfortable integration of Bavarian tradesmen since the time of the Thirty Years War, and John's father, Philip, immigrated from Bavaria to Bohemia at the beginning of the nineteenth century to remove himself from Napoleon's advances. In 1805, Philip Neumann married Agnes Lebis, a Czech, and together they had six children, John being the third, born 28 March 1811.[6] In his *Autobiography*,[7] which he was directed to write by his religious superior, Neumann described his home life: "We were brought up in the old-fashioned school. Our parents were both deeply Christian. While our father from morning to night supervised the apprentices and workers, . . . our mother never missed a day hearing Mass."[8]

Neumann's education followed the regular pattern of his day; he was a bright student. By the time he was in philosophy, he had an abiding interest in the natural sciences and studied these lessons with diligence. He received good grades for his effort. As he prepared himself for university study, his inclination was to pursue a career in medicine. He had given serious consideration to the seminary but, at the time, entrance into it was limited to twenty students each year. For every student accepted, four were rejected, and he feared he would not gain entrance. Despite his fear, however, at the urging of his mother, he did apply and, to his surprise, was accepted to the seminary at Budweis (Ceske Budejovice). In his *Autobiography*, he confided that "(f)rom that moment on I never gave another thought to medicine."[9]

In the country districts of Prachatitz, even while other parts of Europe were in a state of upheaval, the faithful continued to practice their faith in a traditional manner, and the seminary at Budweis, where he took his first two years of theology, was affected little by the turmoil. The years Neumann spent in Budweis were happy years for him; he was challenged by the studies, and he had good friends. He respected his superiors and teachers. He was especially moved by his scripture studies. Motivated by the enthusiasm of the faculty and inspired by the missionary journeys of St. Paul, Neumann and his friend Adalbert Schmid studied the accounts of missionary life in North America published in the Leopoldine Foundation publications and decided to dedicate themselves to missionary ministry.[10] Five seminarians of the Diocese of Budweis were sponsored each year for studies at the archepiscopal seminary in Prague, and Neumann won the bishop's approval for one of these positions for the fall term of 1833. There he hoped to study English and French, languages Neumann considered essential for ministry in North America.

Neumann finished his seminary studies in Prague, a place quite different from the pastoral setting of Prachatitz and Budweis, and it was difficult for the small-town boy to adjust to city life. The population of Prague numbered more than 100,000 people, three-fifths of whom where Czech and two-fifths German. The University of Prague had 3,000 students with four schools—theology, philosophy, medicine, and law. The seminary, the Clementinum, once a Jesuit school, numbered 140 seminarians. There he studied homiletics, pedagogy, and catechetics along with dogmatic, moral, and pastoral theology. These last three disciplines were taught by professors that Neumann labeled as Josephists. At Prague, Neumann came into contact with many of the currents of theology that were prominent in the Austrian Empire, including what has been referred to as the Roman Catholic Restoration,[11] which developed in response to the inadequacies that were becoming evident in the shortcomings of the Enlightenment.

On 8 October 1833, Neumann began his two years of theological study at Prague. His moral theology textbooks were *Theologia*

Moralis in compendium redacta (1827-31) and the *Epitome Moralis* (2 vols., 1832) by Ambrose Stapf of Brixen; Stephen Topoltz was the professor. Neumann found himself bored with the intricacies of the lectures given in class. Dogmatic theology was taught by Jerome Zeidler, who, Neumann claimed, was tainted by Josephinism, and, indeed, the textbook *Institutiones theologiae dogmaticae* (Vienna, 1789 and later editions) by Engelbert Klüpfel leaned that way. In his last year of theology, the subject matter included pastoral theology, homiletics, pedagogy, and catechetics. His professor of pastoral theology and of homiletics, Maximilian Millauer, who also was, in Neumann's opinion, guilty of Josephistic leanings, was not judged well by Neumann as a teacher. The textbook used for pastoral theology was that of Reichensberger. Pedagogy and catechetics was taught by Francis Czeschik, who used Peitel's *Methodenbuch*. These courses proved to be more inspirational to Neumann.

Neumann kept a copy of *The Catechism of the Council of Trent*, as well as St. Peter Canisius's *Summa Doctrinae Christianae*, on his desk in order to neutralize influences he considered negative. During the time of his theological studies, he must have been not only protective of his theological perspective, but also known for his opinions. His fellow seminarians would derisively categorize Neumann as "super orthodox." In his *Journal*, Neumann recorded that "Boehm received a letter from Mueller at Leitmerz in which the latter scoffs at my exaggerated orthodoxy and tries to get Nowak to take sides against me."[12]

Michael J. Curley, C.Ss.R., a biographer of Neumann, comments on Neumann's theological studies at Prague:

> His course of studies in theology at the University of Prague, judging from the skimpy textbooks employed and somewhat unorthodox professors whose lectures he attended, could hardly seem to qualify him for unusual proficiency in that science. The doubt fades, however, when one realizes the tremendous amount of private study he gave to the works of the greatest theologians of Christendom. From intense personal perusal of their works, he became thoroughly familiar with the teachings of Augustine,

Thomas Aquinas, Alphonsus de Liguori, Bellarmine, Canisius and a host of other standard authorities. The manuscript notes on theology, carefully written down on 2,000 closely written pages, are proof that for long years he collected an arsenal of theological lore for his own instruction and, in all probability, for future publication. . . . Likewise in the notes there is a heavy listing of ascetical authors like St. Francis de Sales, St. Vincent de Paul, St. Teresa of Avila, Louis of Granada and others.[13]

Though Neumann would never publish a book from these notes, they would prove helpful in developing the catechism he published ten years later in Pittsburgh, Pennsylvania, in the United States, and again when he was commissioned by the First Plenary Council of Baltimore in 1852 to publish a catechism for the German Catholic schools of the nation.[14] Another indication of the seriousness with which Neumann approached his studies during this period of his life is seen in his sketches of the Old and New Testaments. The "Exegesis Librorum Novi Testamenti, IIdi anni theologi, 1832" was written while he was a student at Budweis, and his "Exegesis Veteris Testamenti, Prachaticii" was sketched while he awaited word from North America of his acceptance into a diocese. Later in his ministry, in 1837 while working in western New York, he would compile a *Bible History* for his German students studying catechism.[15]

NEUMANN'S *SPIRITUAL JOURNAL*

Many of the comments about his professors and theological studies are found in Neumann's *Journal*, but even more significant is the revelation of his soul. His first entry is dated 1 October 1834. The *Journal* chronicles items as diverse as his daily schedule, his interactions with others, his discernment of lifestyle, his longing for friendship and spiritual direction, the books he bought for spiritual reading, his worries, his triumphs and defeats. This source reveals the evolution of his spirituality.

The transfer from Budweis to Prague awakened an uncomfortable feeling in Neumann, and his judgement on Prague was not favorable.

He was lonely, separated from family and friends, and he was disappointed that the study of French and English, a primary reason for his transfer to the archepiscopal seminary, had been forbidden by seminary officials.[16] Confronted with personal struggles and with few confidants, Neumann began writing his *Journal*, a practice he would continue through his years as a diocesan priest in the frontier of western New York State. The work served as a mirror for his soul. It was found among his personal effects at the time of his death. He had not made an entry in it for twenty years, and one can only guess why he stopped making entries. In his solitude, the *Journal* served Neumann both as a prayer and the conversation he lacked in friendships; it served him in his discernment, and through it he analyzed how God was acting in his life. The *Journal* reveals a man in process toward a goal set but often missed.

The *Journal* becomes the primary source for understanding the foundations of Neumann's spirituality, and it is important in reading it to be aware of the literary genre. Its purpose was not to list his successes, but to process his questions. As a result, the recordings tended to be concerned with problems. Neumann recorded the writers he consulted and the responses he made to their ascetical teachings. These sources of spirituality provided Neumann with the input he needed. The number of works he studied indicates the serious attention he gave to his spiritual growth. Since, however, he did not express a systematic spirituality, the best that can be hoped for in extrapolating a personal spirituality from writings not intended for publication remains only conjecture. The effort to identify a personal spirituality, therefore, makes it necessary to interpret the writings.

ELEMENTS OF NEUMANN'S SPIRITUALITY

From a number of possible paragraphs, the early entry of 25 October 1834 might be considered a basic outline of Neumann's approach to spirituality in the years he wrote in the *Journal* as a seminarian: "Let me grow in Your love, that the thought of Your Passion and Death may move my heart ever more deeply. Let my love for You prove itself in actions. May the virtue I attain by Your grace, enable me to await with joy the day of Your coming in judgement."[17] This statement presents an outline of topics that directed Neumann's spirituality—a desire for a closeness to God that would be expressed in ministry in the hope of eternal glory. These unfold in the individual circumstances of Neumann's life and are recorded in the *Journal*.

1. THE DESIRE TO GROW IN VIRTUE BY GOD'S GRACE

Neumann was painfully aware of his sinfulness. It was from this that his ascetical path began. He had a sensitive conscience and admitted it: "My conscience is already rather delicate. . . ."[18] At times, he was ruthless with himself and quite concerned with a need to confess his sins. He accused himself of a number of passions. Often enough, these seem to have been developmental issues that he spiritualized. He was driven by a self-image that suffered when he was not appreciated and became vain when he was praised. How others perceived Neumann was important to him, especially during his years of formation. This he openly recognized, and he brought this personal struggle into his ascetical life. "In my spiritual exercises, I seek the praise of my fellows, and it is rather hard for me to be fervent when I suspect someone may scoff at me."[19]

To avoid the derision of others, Neumann admitted that he would not always tell the truth. Once in homiletics class, he failed in his delivery and reflected on what had happened:

> I was doing fairly well as they say, when of a sudden my memory went blank. I paused and finally had to leave the pulpit. Without any great need, I tried to make excuses that really had nothing to do with my lapse of memory. Though no one pressed me, I lied in saying I knew the text in Latin but not in German—which was not true. My conscience was, by Your grace, telling me not to lie; nevertheless I repeated the lie several times, without any need to do so, because no one was asking me about it.[20]

Neumann faced his weakness. He lamented: "O horrid vanity of mine! You have already corrupted me so much. How many times have you deprived me of God's grace, the gift of my endlessly loving Father? Why do I still rely on you [vanity] when I know you are so thoroughly deceitful?"[21] His struggles with his self-image were often brought into a spiritual context but still they affected his behavior, even in matters as small as deciding to stay at home because he was embarrassed about a cassock that was shabby[22] and avoiding conversation in which he felt inept.[23]

His self-awareness made him long for a spiritual director to accompany him, or a close friend to help him discern his personal growth in the spiritual life. The importance of a good spiritual director was a common recommendation in most of the ascetical writers Neumann consulted, yet during his seminary years he never found one to whom he could entrust his soul. Normally, a spiritual director was appointed for this purpose at the seminary, but Neumann does not mention one nor is a name noted for that position in the seminary records.[24] He longed for the spiritual companionship he had at Budweis with Victor Dichtl, his "spiritual father, master and director of souls."[25] Without the help of a director, Neumann relied on his own musing in the *Journal*, and, at times his response was not productive.

2. The Saints as Guides and Inspiration

The lives of the saints and their example was a consolation. During his seminary years, Neumann records many of these. He claimed St. Teresa of Ávila (1515-82) as a patron and prayed that she would send him a spiritual guide: "St. Teresa, since God has deigned to bless you with so many graces and visits here on earth, you too be my patroness in the court of our mutual Father. I shall bend all my efforts to be like you. Ask God to give me a devout, wise and strict spiritual director who can lead me to Himself."[26]

Neumann began reading Teresa's *Autobiography* with intensity on Christmas Day 1834, and he continued during his holidays until he completed the work on 12 January 1835. The work tells the personal story of Teresa's spiritual journey through the disclosure of the failures and graces she experienced.[27] Teresa's personal revelations seemed to captivate Neumann; it is, however, questionable whether he took her mystical teaching as his own. Mysticism was a topic about which he once commented, "of nothing did I have as much horror as of the so-called mysticism. . . ."[28] He read Teresa in the context of his time and did not amplify her ideas; although his notes from Teresa filled many pages in his *Anthology*, they were quotes without any indication of their direct application to his life. After reading Teresa, Neumann continued his desire for moral conformity, as it was understood in the early nineteenth century.

Huber places Neumann's piety "in the renewed classical-baroque tradition of Ignatius of Loyola, Francis Xavier, Peter Canisius, Louis of Granada, Teresa of Avila, Vincent de Paul, Francis de Sales, Joseph of Calasanza, Scupoli, Fénelon, Alphonsus Liguori, Jean Crasset (1618-1692), Jean Crosset (1656-1738), Bourdaloue and the Roman Catechism."[29] These were, indeed, the authors Neumann consulted. The absence of other writers likewise helps us to identify Neumann's approach to the spiritual life. "It is strange that his notes make no reference to the modern French authors of the Restoration such as Chateaubriand, De Maistre, Lammenais, etc., yet he seems to have been familiar with the Mainz *Katholic* in which the thoughts of these men were made available to the Germans."[30]

In the same autobiographical genre as Teresa's *Autobiography*, Neumann read Augustine's *Confessions*. "Reading St. Augustine's *Confessions*, IX, 9, 10, 11 has given me considerable help in submitting to Your holy will, for I know how long St. Monica prayed for the conversion of her son and that You answered her prayers only after many years."[31] Augustine (354-430) touched Neumann. In the nineteenth century, Augustine "was prized, with his emphasis upon the manner in which God speaks to the soul through the conscience,"[32] and this would certainly tie into the introspective approach so many of Neumann's jottings exhibited during this period of his life. Neumann resolved: "from this moment on, O God, I promise You I shall lead a truly Christian life, mortified and humble just as Augustine did after his conversion."[33]

Beyond the autobiographical works of the saints, biographical accounts of holy men and women were of interest to Neumann. They served him as examples of the kind of life he wanted to live. He confessed an "inordinate desire to have a copy of the *Life of St. Francis Xavier*,"[34] and a loss of recollection in what he described as an adventure due to the arrival of the biography of St. Vincent de Paul,[35] as well as considerable edification in reading the life of St. Joseph Calasanctius.[36] In his *Anthology*, Neumann outlined sermons given by Bourdaloue[37] on the lives of SS. Andrew, Francis Xavier, Thomas, Stephen, John the Evangelist, Genevieve, Francis de Sales, Francis of Paola, and John the Baptist, again without personal comment.

The lives of the saints served Neumann as a source of information and inspiration, but he was painfully aware of his imperfections and greatly troubled by them, as is evident in the *Journal*. Huber comments: "An echo of Jansenism, part of the inheritance of the eighteenth century even in the Austrian lands, must be seen in his use of the expression 'fear-provoking sacrament' once in reference to the Eucharist."[38] Neumann was intense in his search for a deeper understanding of the ascetical life and was well read in the classical spiritual writers.

3. Study of the Counter-Reformation Spiritual Masters

In the first month of his *Journal*, Neumann reported that he had read Louis of Granada (1505-88) and thought it to be "quite good."[39] In April of the following year, he purchased another book by Granada, the *Memorial of the Christian Life*. The author of these works was born Luis de Surriá, but later changed the family name to honor the place where he grew up, namely, Granada. Though he lived in poverty after the early death of his father, Granada was well educated by the Dominicans whom he joined in 1524. His contemporary, St. Teresa of Ávila, said he was "a man given to the world by God for the great and universal good of souls,"[40] and St. Charles Borromeo, another contemporary, commented: "Of all those who up to our time have written on spiritual matters . . . it can be stated that no one has written books either in greater number or of greater selection and profit than Fray Louis of Granada . . . In fact I do not know if in matters of this type there is today a man more beneficial to the Church than he is."[41]

Granada's great work *The Sinner's Guide*, was published in 1556 and sought to demonstrate that living the Christian life was the only true way to happiness. It explored the value of virtue and considered the motives for its practice, followed by consideration of both the advantages of living this way and the folly of not doing so. Consciously practicing virtue and combating sin, the opposite of virtue, comprised the ascetical life. St. Francis de Sales recommended this work and this approach to his directees. It is not surprising to read that Neumann resolved "to overcome my sluggishness in performing my duties."[42]

Neumann also chose to read Lorenzo Scupoli (c.1530-1619), a Theatine, who was probably the most rigorous of the ascetical writers Neumann studied. Neumann recorded that he had Scupoli in his hands in November 1834: "Pardon me, help me, be kind to me! Let the book I bought today, namely Scupoli's *The Spiritual Combat*, lead me to perfection for that is the goal of my existence."[43] The title of the work expresses Scupoli's approach. Neumann's reading did not go without resolve. "Today I set about battling my enemy, apathy, in the way Father Scupoli suggests. I was successful on several occasions, because God's grace gave me greater strength."[44] Perfection, according to Scupoli, "results from the combined effort of the virtues which cause us to die to ourselves in order to be fully subjected to God through love."[45]

According to Scupoli, four arms are needed to lead a spiritual life: "Distrust of ourselves . . . ; trust in God . . . ; the good use of the faculties of soul and body; finally, the exercise of prayer."[46] Neumann responded: "I ask anew for the grace to distrust myself and place all my trust in You. . . .Your grace is the key that will open the door for me."[47] A virtuous life, Scupoli insisted, required combat. Throughout his *Journal*, Neumann confronted, one at a time, what he called his "predominant passions." These vary from day to day. He identified vainglory, laziness, indifference, apathy, pride, tepidity, and excessive distrust in the performance of seminary duties as his own. More importantly, as Scupoli taught, when he noted a shortcoming, he confronted it. "What an ugly thing lying is! My soul, together we have fallen so far that I lie even to myself. So, I shall have to observe my fast tomorrow."[48] Five days later, he wrote: "I was lackadaisical about my duties today, and so, tomorrow, I shall have to fast: no bread at all, and I shall leave half the soup and half the fish portion for the student in charge."[49] Four days later: "Almost all day today I was quite tepid both in my clerical duties and in my spiritual exercises. So tomorrow I shall be fasting, in the hope that God will pardon my indifference."[50]

By Neumann's time, the *Homo Apostolicus* of St. Alphonsus Liguori (1696-1787) was available to him. This particular writing was not one of Alphonsus's ascetical works but a part of his moral theology, specifically written for priests in their role as confessor. Alphonsus had found a middle ground between rigorism and laxism in the moral theology debate of his day which sought to state norms in making moral decisions. He would be declared a Doctor of the Church in 1871, less than a century after his death, and in 1950 Pope Pius XII named him patron of moralists and confessors. Alphonsus was concerned about the practical practice of confessors: "The Church grows sad when she sees so many Catholics on their way to Hell due to the ignorance and carelessness of bad confessors."[51] Neumann confided that he himself found consolation in Alphonsus's assurances: "Today I took up again the writings of St. Alphonsus Liguori and I read there that when one has made a general confession, he should be of good heart—and from that moment my own inner peace returned."[52]

Alphonsus was a great moral theologian, but he was also known for his ascetical works. He placed ascetical practice in the context of a response given by the individual to God's intense love. Neumann needed this balance in his strictness, and recorded that he went beyond Alphonsus's moral theology to his inspirational *Visits to the Most Blessed Sacrament*, a work filled with the enthusiasm of a heart overwhelmed with being so greatly loved by God. Neumann even rose early in the morning to translate the work.

St. Francis de Sales (1567-1622) also entered Neumann's repertoire of spiritual guides. "Today, I arose at 4:30 a.m. I have in mind to make a daily meditation from among those of St. Francis de Sales, in order to get a fresh start in this business of my future ministry."[53] Six weeks later, Neumann was still reading the work of de Sales:

"Today in *Philothea* I read that haste in the performance of works of devotion is reprehensible."[54]

Francis de Sales was a practical man. He wrote in response to the questions of individuals who sought his wisdom in spiritual matters, and many of their questions were Neumann's own questions. De Sales's *Introduction to the Devout Life* was first published in 1609, with many editions and translations thereafter. "St. Francis helps the reader see himself for what he is, for what he ought to be, and for what he can be if he cooperates with the grace that God will give to him."[55]

Concerning worship and devotional life at the time, it has been remarked "that devotional classics had a wide circulation, [an] indication that private prayer and meditation were widespread. Some of the classics were inherited from earlier days; others were fresh creations."[56] Neumann does not record a long list of his contemporaries as authors he consulted, but he does note Anne Catherine Emmerich (1774-1824). In October 1835, Neumann stated that he had "obtained a copy of Catherine Emmerich's *Passion of Our Lord Jesus Christ*."[57] She recorded her visions and inspirations, which were quite detailed, in this case of the passion and death of Jesus. They followed the Gospel accounts, with great attention to characters, settings, and conversations. Literary studies have attempted to filter out what she called her revelations from the additions of her secretary, who wished to give a fuller presentation of the life of Jesus as Catherine envisioned it and freely added his own material. Catherine herself was a pious and sincere woman, and her cause for beatification is being considered. Neumann does not comment much about the writing, but it is clear that he had a copy and read it with devotion; later, while serving as a pastor in New York State, he requested another of her books.

Neumann mentioned reading Jean Croiset's *Meditations* on the second day of his *Journal*.[58] Croiset (1656-1738) was a popular retreat director whose devotional writings on the Sacred Heart of Jesus interested Neumann. The devotion met a need as a "reaction against the austerity of Jansenism and the cold rationalism of the Enlightenment. . . .To some degree it was fostered by romanticism."[59] In this, Neumann was in the spirit of his times.

4. Neumann's Application of Ascetical Principles to His Life

Neumann would never be easy on himself, but, as the *Journal* continued, his own inner turmoil in the quest for perfection and the experience of failure forced him to expand his understanding of the spiritual life. "You are mankind's all-wise physician; be also my physician despite my unworthiness."[60] In one entry, Neumann compared himself to Bartimeus, the blind man in Mark's Gospel: "Son of David, have pity on me. My creator, I am even worse off than he —what should I do? . . . With all the confidence Your grace has instilled in me, I cry out, 'Help me!'"[61] This cry, from the depth of Neumann's soul, was not a formality; he felt himself sinking into a great darkness, possibly despair. He had no one to turn to in friendship, and his attempts to reach perfection by his own efforts failed; he had nowhere to go except to God. His inner struggles were further aggravated by the fact that, as his seminary days were drawing to an end, his hopes of ordination were slim. The number of ordinations allowed for the Diocese of Budweis was very limited because there were few positions available for priestly ministry; neither had he received the promise of ordination from a bishop in North America. In 1835, the civil administration was interested in hiring Neumann for a position because of his ability in languages, but he studied foreign tongues for ministry and rejected the offer.[62] His *Journal* reveals the depth of his depression as he came to the end of his seminary days, and for months he lost all enthusiasm for life. At one point, his reflection is startling, coming in the context of all his efforts: "My God, do not let this despair of mine continue. . . . it could lead me to suicide."[63] Two months later, he was still in the same state when he recognized and confided that he would no longer trust his own strength but only God's goodness: "As far as my spiritual life is concerned, at present I am so listless that all my devotions are dry and quite monotonous. I seem to perform them just out of rote. . . . Dear Jesus, I have not lost my trust and faith in You, my God, but I am indeed so miserable that I might well collapse 'neath the weight of these temptations to despair! Would that my misery might help me in my quest for perfection, but I no longer feel that I can muster the firm will to resist temptation with all my strength. O Jesus Christ! Strengthen me . . . do not forsake Your disciple in his struggles! I praise You, my Lord, with my whole heart and soul. I love You and I shall always do so. But do not abandon me in my despair! Have pity on me, sweet Jesus!"[64]

Neumann seemed to have come to a point where he not only theoretically but also experientially knew he could trust only in God; still, he did not excuse himself. There seems, however, to be a subtle difference in his writings. Earlier, he had recorded that after each fault, he would impose upon himself a penance as a means to conquer what he considered his human weakness. Toward the end of his seminary years and throughout the days he kept his *Journal* in North America, he continued to face his failings, still ruthlessly, but he seemed to have a bit more peace about them even in the midst of the despair he also experienced.

> I was worse than lax most of the day, for I often actually took delight in the impure thoughts that occurred to me. I was glad that I had them and maybe even coddled them! I also let myself be roused to anger once, though briefly. I was lazy and careless about my work. I no longer value humility or make an effort to acquire it because of my tepidity, lack of love, wavering faith and my despair of recovering God's grace. Indeed, the condition of my soul is simply astonishing. . . . Right now I would gladly quit this particular path of salvation I have trod for so long! Oh, Jesus, is it possible that You may still comfort and console me? Come to me! I am Yours. Do come to me, my Jesus![65]

The self-imposed penance is lacking, and its absence is probably not an accident, nor an oversight. Neumann's self-reliance is replaced by the cry for God's mercy.

5. The Ascetical Life Expressed in Ministry

Though the seminary life of Prague did not include apostolic endeavors as such, the ministry always occupied the attention of Neumann the seminarian. As his journaling continued later in North

America, this would be even more obvious, but it was evident in the seminary as well, especially as the days of formal study were coming to a close. "My longing grows every moment to direct others on the path of perfection."[66] All Neumann's studies and asceticism were ultimately aimed at the ministry. "This will be my thanksgiving: I shall make you known and loved, while for myself I ask of You and the whole court of heaven, the light I need to follow the way of Your law."[67] Ministry required the dedication of the entire self and all one's expertise and talent for the task. "I want to dedicate my every effort to Your glory, to spread Your Kingdom over the face of this earth which You have loved enough to become the God-Man."[68] A spirituality which identified ascetical practice with the service of ministry marked Neumann's life after this time of formation. He would be tireless in his apostolic endeavors all the way to the very last day of his life evidenced in his death while on an errand of kindness.

6. A Spiritual Life That Looked toward Heaven

In the end, the hope of heaven was the end of all Neumann's effort. "You are indeed most fortunate! One day you shall behold Him, you will not pass away like the world or the vast stars in the sky. Because of His goodness to you, you will behold him for all eternity. . . . Oh, permit me to speak to You and acclaim Your mercy and Your power! I would like to praise and bless You in my own person for that is why You made me and that is my greatest happiness."[69] Even in the midst of his reflections on his imperfection Neumann was aware of his ultimate end. "You have injured yourself by refusing to reflect on God our Creator, on your life's purpose which is to give glory to Him, on your final destiny which is the ultimate happiness, namely the blessed vision of God Himself."[70]

CONCLUSION

In Neumann's cause for canonization, there was doubt as to whether he lived a life of the kind of heroic virtue required for his process to advance. The comment was made: "The testimony shows the Venerable Servant of God to have been indeed a good and pious man and bishop, remarkably zealous for God's glory and the salvation of souls, but it does not show that he surpasses the bounds of ordinary virtue of the sort that any upright priest, missionary, religious, or especially bishop would have."[71] This critique of Neumann, while intended to be negative in his cause, actually identifies for us the very point that makes John Neumann accessible to us today. He worked no miracles. He was not an extraordinary preacher. Though admired, he was still criticized for not being the personality that people wanted him to be, especially in the sophisticated society of Philadelphia. He was "ordinary" in every sense of the word. It took the words of a pope to set the record straight.

> The merits of an active man are measured not so much in the number of deeds performed, as in their thoroughness and stability. For true activity does not consist in mere noise; it is not the creature of a day, but it unfolds itself in the present, it is the fruit of the past and should be the good seeds of the future. Are not these very characteristics the mark of the activity of Venerable Neumann? Bearing all this in mind, no one will any longer doubt that the simplicity of the work performed by our Venerable Servant of God did not hinder him from becoming a marvelous example of activity. The very simplicity has forced us . . . to impress on our children . . . the proclamation of the heroic virtues of Neumann, since all find in the new hero an example not difficult to imitate.[72]

In his decree affirming the heroicity of Neumann's virtues, Pope Benedict XV "unraveled the question and taught openly that the one norm for heroic virtue is the faithful, perpetual and constant carrying out of the duties and obligations of one's proper state in life."[73] This declaration aptly describes St. John Neumann, C.Ss.R., a man who did the ordinary extraordinarily well.

NOTES

1. Archbishop Francis P. Kenrick would comment on Neumann's accent in his letter to Rome concerning his preference for Neumann as his successor in Philadelphia: "He speaks both German and English fluently, but I cannot deny that one thing against him in so great a city is the fact that he is a Bohemian and, because of this, not so eloquent and less likely to please the ear" (*Acta S.C. de Propaganda Fide*, 1852, vol. CCXIV, fol. 53).

2. See Hubert Jedin, ed., *History of the Church*, vol. VIII (New York: Crossroad Publishing Company, 1981), 3.

3. The term "Enlightenment" came from the German *Aufklärung* and refers to the thought of eighteenth-century Europe. According to the basic assumptions of this current of thought, only that which can be attained by reason should be believed. Reason was applied to all human science, including the relationship of the human person to others in morals, economy, legal practice, and nature itself. In general, though not exclusively, the Enlightenment was hostile to the Church.

4. Josephinism (also called Josephism) refers to the principles of Joseph II, who, at the death of his mother, Maria Teresa (1780), instituted a series of laws that changed the status of the Church's relationship to the state in the Austrian Empire.

5. John Neumann's *Journal* can be found in the archives of the Redemptorists of the Baltimore Province, Brooklyn, New York. William Nayden, C.Ss.R., has translated into English the French entries, which were published in four installments in *Spicilegium Historicum Congregationis SSmi Redemptoris* 25 (1977): 321-418 (Part 1: Oct. 1-Dec. 31, 1834); 26 (1978): 9-74 (Part 2: Jan. 1-Feb. 28, 1835), 291-352 (Part 3: Mar. 1-May 4, 1835); 27 (1979): 81-152 (Part 4: May 5, 1835-July 21, 1838); hereafter *Journal*.

6. The Neumann children included Catherine, Veronica, John, Joan, Louise, and Wenceslas. Three of these, John, Joan, and Wenceslas, became religious, and the fourth, Louise, lived with a religious community after caring for her father in his old age. Veronica married John Kandla, and Catherine married Mattias Berger. After her husband's death, Catherine became a member of the Third Order of St. Francis and her son, Johann, became a Redemptorist and the first biographer of Neumann.

7. Neumann's *Kurze Lebensbeschreibung des P. J. Neumann, Priester der Versammlung des Hl. Erloser u. erwahlten Bischof v. Philadelphia in N. Am.* This autobiography was written in Gothic German script on the eve of Neumann's episcopal ordination in obedience to his religious superior. The original manuscript of approximately 6,000 words is in the archives of the

Redemptorists of the Baltimore Province. English translation: *The Autobiography of St. John Neumann, C.Ss.R.*, with introduction, translation, commentary, and epilogue by Alfred C. Rush, C.Ss.R. (Boston: St. Paul Books and Media, 1977); hereafter *Autobiography*. For another critical edition of Neumann's autobiography, as edited by Andreas Sampers, C.Ss.R., see *Spicilegium Historicum Congregationis SSmi Redemptoris* 11 (1963); for another English translation, see Appendix I of Augustinus Kurt Huber, "John N. Neumann's Student Years in Prague, 1833-1835," trans. from German by Raymond H. Schmandt, *Records of the American Catholic Historical Society of Philadelphia* 89 (1978): 3-32, at 14-22; hereafter Huber.

8. *Autobiography*, 22.

9. Ibid., 21.

10. Ibid., 22: "About that time I began to read the reports of the Leopoldine Society, especially the letters of Father Baraga and other missionaries among the Germans in North America. This is how there arose in one of my fellow students, Adalbert Schmidt, and in myself on a walk along the Moldau (Ultva) River, the determination to devote ourselves to North America as soon as we acquired some experience after ordination. . . . From that moment on, my resolution was so strong and lively that I could no longer think of anything else."

11. See Huber, 5.

12. *Journal*, 10 Dec. 1834. Boehm was a seminary companion to Neumann; Mueller at that time was studying in the seminary at Leitmeritz in Austria.

13. Michael J. Curley, *Bishop John Neumann, C.Ss.R.* (Philadelphia: Bishop Neumann Center, 1952), 163; hereafter Curley.

14. Neumann's smaller catechism (*Kleiner Katechismus*) was approved by the bishop of Pittsburgh in 1842. It had nineteen pages of questions and answers, as well as thirteen pages of prayers, the Commandments, and laws of the Church. By 1889, it had gone through thirty-eight editions. The larger catechism, commissioned by the First Plenary Council of Baltimore in 1852 (*Katholischer Katechismus*) was 147 pages, with thirty-one pages of prayers. It continued to be used for a period of time even after Neumann's death.

15. Neumann compiled his "Bible History" (*Biblische Geschichte*) in 1837. Curley says of the *Bible History*: "While awaiting his call to America, he had written out his exegetical notes on both the Old and New Testaments. In Williamsville in 1837 he began a German Bible history. This appears to have been the basis of the German *Biblische Geschichte* published by

Neumann in Pittsburgh in 1844. . . . Like the catechism, it enjoyed a wide circulation for many years. However, it was never translated into English and the later *Bible History* published by Bishop Richard Gilmour of Cleveland superseded it in American parochial schools" (162).

16. *Journal,* 12 Oct. 1834.
17. Ibid., 25 Oct. 1834.
18. Ibid., 10 Mar. 1835.
19. Ibid., 15 Nov. 1834.
20. Ibid., 23 Dec. 1834.
21. Ibid., 8 Oct. 1834.
22. Ibid., 28 Dec. 1834.
23. Ibid., 10 Mar. 1834.
24. Huber, 5.
25. *Journal,* 17 and 18 Dec. 1834.
26. Ibid., 5 Nov. 1834.
27. In the introduction to his and Otilio Rodriguez's translation of Teresa of Ávila, *The Interior Castle,* The Classics of Western Spirituality (New York: Paulist Press, 1979), Kieran Kavanaugh, O.C.D., describes St. Teresa's spirituality thusly: "The asceticism as well as the concept of prayer in her doctrine is based on friendship. All comes to center on the divine Friend . . . . The goal is viewed not in terms of the ordering and perfecting of human passions and instincts but rather in terms of loving communion with His Majesty and good works done in His service. . . . As with any friendship, prayer develops from the initial attempts at mutual knowledge to the final simplified and intense relationship of complete union" (13).
28. *Mon Journal,* (German), 8 Apr. 1835.
29. Huber, 13.
30. Ibid.
31. Kenneth Scott Latourette, *The Nineteenth Century in Europe* (New York: Harper & Brothers, Publishers, 1958), 367; hereafter Latourette.
32. *Journal,* 23 May 1835.
33. Ibid.
34. Ibid., 29 Mar. 1835.
35. Ibid., 9 Apr. 1835.
36. Ibid., 23 Mar. 1835.
37. "Bourdaloue, of the Society of Jesus (+1704), who . . . was more vigorous and solid, and must unquestionably be ranked as one of the greatest pulpit instructors and orators" (John Alzog, *Manual of Church History* [Cincinnati: Robert Clarke & Co., 1878], 522).

38. Huber, 13.
39. *Journal,* 26 Oct. 1834.
40. Quoted by Álvaro Huerga, O.P., in his introduction to the reprint edition of Louis of Granada, *The Sinner's Guide,* trans. A Dominican Father (1883; Rockford, Il.: Tan Book and Publishers, 1985), xx.
41. Ibid.
42. *Journal,* 27 Oct. 1834.
43. Ibid., 7 Nov. 1834.
44. Ibid., 28 Nov. 1834.
45. Pierre Pourrat, S.S., *Christian Spirituality, Part II: From Jansenism to Modern Times* (Westminster, Md.: The Newman Press, 1955), 240.
46. Ibid., 240.
47. *Journal,* 15 Nov. 1835.
48. Ibid., 11 Oct. 1834.
49. Ibid., 16 Oct. 1834.
50. Ibid., 20 Oct. 1834.
51. Alphonsus Liguori, *Praxis Confessarii* (Oconomowoc, Wi.: C.Ss.R., 1978), 5.
52. *Journal,* 15 Feb. 1835.
53. Ibid., 29 Jan. 1835.
54. Ibid., 10 Mar. 1835.
55. John K. Ryan, "Introduction," to his translation and edition of St. Francis de Sales, *Introduction to the Devout Life* (New York: Image Books, 1989), 15.
56. Latourette, 355.
57. *Journal,* 23 Oct. 1835.
58. Ibid., 2 Oct. 1834.
59. Latourette, 359.
60. *Journal,* 15 Feb. 1835.
61. Ibid., 1 Dec. 1834.
62. Curley, 34. Curley lists German, Bohemian, French, English, Spanish, and Italian as languages Neumann could speak. He would, of course, also be able to read and translate Latin and Greek. Later, in his ministry, Neumann would continue to learn more languages as the needs of the apostolic life required, including Gaelic.
63. *Journal,* 4 Mar. 1835.
64. Ibid., 13 May 1835.
65. Ibid., 10 June 1835.
66. Ibid., 27 May 1835.
67. Ibid., 1 Oct. 1834.

68. Ibid., 11 May 1834.
69. Ibid., 29 Jan. 1835.
70. Ibid., 31 Jan. 1835.
71. Nicola Ferrante, C.Ss.R., "La Causa di Beatificazione e Canonizzazione di S Giovanni Nepomuceno Neumann (1886-1976)," *Biblioteca Historicum Congregationis SSmi Redemptoris: Studia Neumanniana*," vol. 4 (1977), trans. in *The Province Story*, 3, no. 2 (Oct. 1977): 41.
72. "Decretum approbationis virtutum in causa beatificationis et canonizationis Servi Dei Joannis Nepomuceni Neumann," *Acta Apostolicae Sedis* 14 (1922): 23.
73. Alfred C. Rush, C.Ss.R., "The Second Vatican Council, 1962-1965, and Bishop Neumann," *Records of the American Catholic Historical Society* 85 (1974): 125.

PART II
MINISTRY

AN ACCOMPLISHED CATECHIST:
JOHN NEPOMUCENE NEUMANN

MARY CHARLES BRYCE

Recently canonized John Nepomucene Neumann, Philadelphia's fourth bishop, lived a short forty-nine years (1811-1860). More than half of those years (twenty-four) were spent in the United States—from May 29, 1836, the day he arrived in New York City, to the day of his death, January 5, 1860. Neumann has been hailed as a pastoral bishop who personally knew the clergy, most of the families, the children, the religious sisters and brothers of his large diocese. His zeal, dedication and loving concern for others is detailed in the several biographies written about him. What is frequently treated with unjustified brevity is his catechetical ministry which was central to his total pastoral mission. That ministry illustrates a special aspect of his concern for others, that of providing the people he served with a better understanding of their faith. Neumann wrote four major works which are rightly called catechetical: a manual for the clergy, a Bible history and two catechisms. This brief study will introduce those works, which, in the context of his pastoral mission, caused a contemporary to describe him as an "accomplished catechist."[1]

LIFE AND EDUCATION

The third child of Philip and Agnes (Lebis) Neumann, John Nepomucene was born March 28, 1811 in Prachatitz, Bohemia,[2] a mountain village in the large Austrian-Hungarian Empire. He grew up in that German-speaking town, attended the elementary school there and then went to the gymnasium in nearby Budweis.[3]

Neumann began his theological studies for the priesthood in 1831 at the diocesan seminary in Budweis where he stayed for two years. Upon obtaining a scholarship to the School of Theology at the University of Prague he transferred there for the last two years of preparation for ordination. Toward the end of his final term of study he learned to his dismay that the bishop had decided not to ordain any more priests—the diocese already had far more than it needed. That forced young Neumann to turn to a long-cherished ambition of becoming a missionary in the United States.[4] After several abortive attempts at being accepted in an American diocese he set sail for the U.S. uncertain about his real destination. Arriving in New York on May 29, 1836 he learned that three weeks previous to his coming he had been accepted for the diocese of New York by that city's third bishop, John Dubois. One year later Dubois ordained Neumann and for the next four years the young Bohemian priest served the people in the regions of Buffalo and Rochester.

His earlier desires to become a religious surfaced again[5] as Neumann felt the need for a supportive community and at the same time witnessed the influence of the Redemptorist clergy in the area. On September 4, 1840 he wrote Father Joseph Prost, C.S.S.R., requesting admission into the Congregation of the Most Holy Redeemer. John Neumann began his novitiate in Baltimore in December 1841. On January 16, 1842, in old St. James Church, Baltimore, he made his profession, the first Redemptorist professed in America.[6] For the next ten years he ministered to the people in Baltimore, Pittsburgh and Baltimore in that order. In 1852 Pope Pius IX named him bishop of Philadelphia and Archbishop Francis Patrick Kenrick consecrated him on March 28, 1852. From a reluctant bishop he became in eight years an exemplary pastor. On June 19 of this year the Church acknowledged his extraordinary pastoral dedication by officially calling him a saint.

Neumann's Writings,
Bible History and Catechisms

Impelled by a talent for writing as well as a zeal for spreading the Word, Neumann wrote a lot. He developed a style that reflected his incisive intellect and clarity of understanding. If one judges by the 2000 hand-written pages of notes, his major interest was theology, for the largest amount of those many pages are theological in content. His biographer, Michael Curley, observed that:

> So complete were these notes that his brother priests designated them as Neumann's *Summa Theologica*, although he himself never used the term. Covering every field of dogmatic, moral and ascetical theology, they are divided into ninety-one treatises, carefully arranged under the general divisions employed by St. Thomas Aquinas in his celebrated work of the same name. . . . As the notes stand, they are unfinished. . . . He had not finished the material he found into a smooth, polished and unified whole for publication.[7]

Although he was considered an intellectual by many standards, Neumann nevertheless did not lose touch with the general populace and the less learned. In fact his published works were written for them. He is credited with a series of informative newspaper articles that appeared in the early 1840's in Baltimore. The articles are unsigned but Max Oertel, the editor of the German-Catholic weekly, *Katholische Kirchenzeitung*, attributed them to him.[8] It is safe to presume that Neumann perceived the catechesial significance of newspaper writing and thus cooperated with Oertel.

Neumann's best known works are two catechisms but he also wrote a Bible history and a manual for the clergy. The latter was actually composed before the others but remains in manuscript form in the Redemptorist archives in Brooklyn. The other three were published and used extensively in German-speaking communities of the U.S. during the mid- and late 1800's.

The proposed manual for pastors, *Synopsis Catechismi ad Parochus*, a sixty page Latin manuscript, was written some time before the two published catechisms, though the exact time of origin is uncertain. Curley describes the work as "a resume of the great catechism of Peter Canisius."[9] One must admit that a certain tone and unction similar to that of Canisius pervades the work but in one essential way they differ. Neumann followed the sequence of Trent's manual, namely creed, cult, code—faith in the context of the Apostles Creed, a study of the sacraments as Christ-events in human history, followed by a treatment of the commandments as Christian response. Canisius presented the doctrinal content of his manuals in the order of creed, code, cult.

Neumann's two catechisms, small and large, were among his earliest publications. His biographers maintain with ample evidence, that those two German manuals were published while he was stationed in Pittsburgh probably in 1842. Though unsigned and not dated the sixteen page *Kleiner Katechismus* carried the approval of Bishop Michael O'Connor, then the ordinary of Pittsburgh. The larger, *Katholischer Katechismus* was 147 pages long and dates from the same period. A second printing of the latter work is among the library holdings of Catholic University in Washington, D.C., and bears the date, 1846.[10] The Redemptorist Archives in Brooklyn has copies of both catechisms bound in one volume. In a letter to Archbishop Samuel Eccleston, Baltimore, Neumann told of issuing a third edition of the smaller catechism in 1848.[11] Neither edition carried a by-line.

Public credit for his two catechisms came to Neumann only after the first Plenary Council of Baltimore in 1852. The vexing matter[12] of catechisms which had persistently troubled the bishops of this country from the time of John Carroll, rose again at that first full gathering of bishops. The multiplicity of catechisms appeared to disrupt unity and the bishops desired a single manual to serve, in this case at least, the German-speaking Catholics in the entire country.[13] The Council commissioned the newly appointed prelate of Philadelphia either to write a catechism for the German-speaking faithful or to choose one already written and submit it for approval to the other ordinaries who spoke German. Neumann turned to his own previously written manual. Thus in August, 1853 Bishop

Neumann's large catechism appeared. It bore his by-line and the approbation of the first plenary Council of Baltimore.[14]

Unlike his earlier manuscript for the clergy the two popular catechisms more closely followed the sequential treatment of creed, code, cult. By the nineteenth century that order of presentation had become sort of traditional. It can be ascribed to Peter Canisius only in a skeletal way but it was popularized by Edmund Auger in France,[15] and, quite independently of either Canisius or Auger, it was adopted by Robert Bellarmine in Italy.[16] The basic structure of Canisius' catechetical works was twofold: 1) Concerning wisdom ("If you desire wisdom keep the commandments" [Sirach 1:23]) and 2) Concerning Justice. In the first part he introduced the three theological virtues and the sacraments. Under faith, he treated the Apostles Creed; under hope, the Our Father; under Charity, the ten commandments and the precepts of the Church; then the sacraments. The second part, concerning justice dealt with good works and the various kinds of sin. A careful examination will indicate that the creed-code-cult sequence extracted from Canisius' overall structure is skeletal. Such a bare-bones treatment is understandable, however, when one is faced with compiling a simple manual which can be easily handled and quickly memorized. It is particularly interesting to note that Neumann adhered faithfully to the last part of the sequence in his inclusion of good works and the various kinds of sin. However successful Peter Canisius was in projecting the corpus of the Christian reality, and it may be assumed that he was at least somewhat successful, when his work is so condensed as to be treated under three main headings one cannot be too optimistic about presenting comprehensively and clearly the correlated elements of Christian doctrine. The saving feature for John Neumann was his own winning personality and exemplary life which projected a living, inter-related unity of what he taught.

In 1844 Neumann published a 108-page volume he had been working on for about seven years. That was his Bible history, *Biblische Caschichte des Alten unde Neuen Testamentes zum Gebrauche der Katholischen Schulen.*[17] Writing that work was like returning to an early love. In his second year at Budweis Neumann had studied biblical hermeneutics, Greek, philology, introduction to and exegesis of the New Testament. Inspired by Professor Karl Koerner's enthusiasm and knowledge of the sacred text, he studied with increased interest and determination. Sacred Scripture became his dominant interest. Reading "the Scriptures were his daily bread,"[18] a fellow-student observed in correspondence with Berger. "What appealed to me most were the Letters of the apostle St. Paul," Neumann noted.[19] He made long and detailed notes on both the Old and New Testaments. Then during the interim before he sailed for the United States he re-wrote and edited those notes packing them into several hundred note-book pages.

It was from those notes that the future bishop wrote his Bible history in German. He began it in Williamsville in 1837, working on it in the late night hours after his daytime pastoral activities were finished. It was published in Pittsburgh seven years later. But Neumann did not stop with that. He prepared a much more detailed history as a long unpublished manuscript shows. That manuscript, among the archival holdings in Brooklyn, was probably written during his second stay in Baltimore (1847-1852). Although the published volume enjoyed a good circulation for a number of years, Neumann's Bible history was not translated into English. It seems to have been superseded by the 1869 *Bible History* of Cleveland's Ordinary, Richard Gilmour.[20]

THE CATECHIST

Neumann's catechisms were actually the fruit of long and serious concentration in the catechetical ministry. Consistent with his personality, his convictions and his vocation, he spent himself in proclaiming God's word. The description currently circulating in the *General Catechetical Directory* fit him well for as bishop he recognized himself as "head of the community and teacher of doctrine."[21] In describing his pastoral activities his biographers refer to his celebrating the liturgy, to his homilies and to his catechesis. Curley wrote that Neumann was not a great orator but, what was more important, he had the "unction and the power to move hearts, which is the ultimate purpose of sacred eloquence."[22] One illustration of such compelling persuasiveness came from Neumann's only visit to his hometown in 1854. After hearing one of the native son's sermons a self-proclaimed anti-cleric was heard to mutter, "If I listen often to that man, I shall be converted whether I want to or not."[23]

It is as catechist, however, that Neumann is better known. During his episcopacy administering the sacrament of confirmation[24] provided him the most frequent opportunities for catechizing. He established the practice of giving at least two instructions prior to confirming young Christians and newly baptized adults.[25] Inasmuch as he was, according to some, "a born catechist,"[26] those catecheses were simple, appealing and "intelligible to children"[27] and grown-ups alike.

Catechizing was not something that Neumann had to learn after he became Philadelphia's chief shepherd. It was, in fact, almost second nature to him by that time. According to his autobiography, he was "thoroughly familiar with the Large Catechism [sic]" before he was ten years of age.[28] Later he excelled in catechetics during his seminary days. At the end of one session he earned the comment "*eminentem*" in that "important, if underrated division of theological study."[29] Circumstances and individuals played no small part in leading him to become such an effective catechist.

The first major influence on young Neumann, outside of his family, was made by Peter Schmidt, catechist and director of the city school which John attended. Father Schmidt evidently attracted John by his personality, his willingness to converse and to answer questions on a wide range of subjects. "The youngster was often in the garden with the catechist and first learned from him the wonders of plants and flowers and the intriguing story of stars and planets"[30] as well as Christian doctrine. His association with Schmidt continued. A prerequisite for acceptance into the gymnasium was a basic knowledge of Latin which the elementary school did not offer. To provide this for interested and bright students Schmidt held evening classes in his home. "And so," Neumann wrote, "the last two years of school, 1822-1823, I went every night with eight or ten others and the catechist to learn the rudiments of Latin."[31]

Neumann's next encounter with a catechist and catechesis came about in a circuitous way. Soon after beginning his studies at the University of Prague he found himself surprised and "displeased with the professors of Dogmatic and Moral Theology as well as of Pastoral Theology [sic]."[32] The Austrian empire was at that time asserting itself in an autocratic way in its relationship with the Church. Under the Emperor Joseph II (1780-1790) referred to in some circles as "Joseph the sacristan"—state sovereignty had been established calling for subordination of the Church to the state. Under that policy the Church became a department of the state. The system had significant repercussions for the role of the Church in society. Many of Neumann's Prague professors were embued with the prevailing pro-state view. In addition, further aspects of Josephinism plus the related ideologies of Febronianism, and Gallicanism, held sway at Prague.

Neumann was not so gullible as to accept such positions unquestioningly. But the situation forced him to seek an alternative. He began to study on his own and for this he used the works of Peter Canisius, especially his *Summa Doctrinae Christianae*, the Catechism of the Council of Trent, Robert Bellarmine's catechisms and the works of the early Church fathers including Augustine and Gregory the Great. It was in those circumstances at Prague that Neumann's interest in catechesis developed further. Besides reading the works of the early fathers and the great sixteenth century catechists, he came under the influence and guidance of Dr. Francis Czeschik, professor in pedagogy and catechetics. Czeschik instilled in him "a thorough knowledge" of and solid grounding in the principles of catechizing.[33] Czeschik also introduced him to the concept of methodology which in application enhanced his natural ability of lucidly explaining things. Thus he acquired a professional approach to presenting concisely the truths of faith to inquirers in ways they could best comprehend. It was a skill which he continually refined and applied throughout his life.

Neumann's reputation as a catechist became established almost immediately after his ordination. On the day after arriving at his very first assignment in Rochester he was catechizing. He reached that city on July 4, 1836 where he found the German-speaking community in a sad and neglected state. The next day he rounded up the young German children and began teaching them the cate-chism.[34] The event served a double purpose. It informed the children and it let the community know that there was one who appreciated them, spoke their language and was concerned about them.

"No duty awakened livelier interest in Father Neumann," wrote John Berger, "than the instruction of youth."[35] Williamsville, a small town ten miles northeast of Buffalo, where Neumann was sent after Rochester, witnessed that fact. He assumed the responsibility of instructing the children in the school there. He spent two hours in the morning and two hours in the afternoon catechizing them. Sunday afternoons found him catechizing those unable to attend the week-day sessions. Endowed with a gift for teaching children, "he knew well how to suit his words and demeanor to the age and capacity of his scholars," Berger observed.[36]

The pattern was repeated in every missionary parish Neumann served. Circumstances and external characteristics differed but the parishioners and their children quickly discovered that the young Bohemian Redemptorist adapted himself to them and presented the life and message of Christianity in a winning way.

Mother Caroline, a School Sister of Notre Dame, summed up Neumann's catechizing in a letter to his nephew, John Berger.

> When Father Neumann was Superior of St. Alphonsus in Baltimore, I had charge of the girls' school; consequently I had ample opportunity to admire his virtues and eminent qualities. He was an accomplished catechist and a great lover of children. His gentleness and meekness, and perseverance in communicating religious instruction to the children often awoke my astonish-ment, and the salutary impression he made upon even the most faulty and troublesome of our little people was remarkable.[37]

From various accounts it is possible to discern certain method-ological characteristics. Not by question-and-answer only did he instruct those he faced. Because he had an abhorrence of rote memo-rizing, Neumann endeavored to present the truths in numerous ways that would assist people in comprehending their meanings. He shared his own insights and experiences. He interwove scripture narratives to acquaint people with the rich heritage and tradition that illustrated God's steadfast love and solicitude for them. In addition to his ability to adapt to the age and capacity of his listeners Neumann used stories to reinforce and emphasize points and doctrines. In short, he anticipated and personified the description the *General Catechetical Directory* provided for the model catechist:

> In the name of the church, he (catechist) acts as a witness of the Christian message, one who ministers to others, shares with them the fruits of his own mature faith, and wisely orders the joint study toward the accomplishment of its purpose (par. 76).

Conclusions

Neumann was a people bishop. He enjoyed associating with people in the parishes, people in the diocese, people in the cities and rural areas where he lived. He learned the languages they spoke,[38] the customs they cherished and the backgrounds from which they came to this "melting pot" land. He loved them and they loved him. All of which is a way of saying he was a Godly man whose delight was to be with the people of this world (See Prov. 8:31). That is also a way of illustrating that he was from beginning to end ever the model pastor.

He manifested his love for people in a variety of ways. He arbitrated their differences, he gave to the needy—often out of his own pocket, he was a compassionate and understanding confessor, he visited the sick, he was always eager to be helpful. According to Curley, he possessed that special quality of putting others at ease, of making them feel at home.[39] In a sense he did not seem to distinguish between his love for God and his love for humankind except to be a channel through which that love could be experienced and personified. That fact stands out in his catechetical apostolate. He catechized with the ease and confidence born of dedication and commitment. He adapted the images and language to the people around him without sacrificing any element of the message's richness and profundity.

Knowing that Christianity is a perduring reality he did not confine his catechizing to the spoken word only. In fact he seemed to recognize the quality of permanency which the written word has over the oral one. In print the word is captured for future referral, to be reread, pondered, critiqued. And so Neumann wrote. That he be credited with his first writings did not appear as important to him as that they be disseminated. Thus there was no by-line. After he was consecrated bishop the opportunity for further dissemination was made and his works were more widely circulated. Then they bore his name, were translated into English and enjoyed far more extensive use. But the man himself was unaffected by their proliferation. Neumann remained the clear-sighted, dedicated shepherd who fed and led his sheep. He was a good pastor who responded to the Lord's call and to the people's needs in an honest, unique and tireless way. He catechized and served them without any hint of belittling them, his office nor the catechetical ministry itself. Like the Lord, he emptied himself and in so doing brought honor to both his flock and himself (Philip. 2:07).

NOTES

1. From a letter written by Mother Caroline, S.S.N.D., to Neumann's nephew, John Berger; Milwaukee, April 21, 1874. The writer has a faithful copy of this letter, the original of which is in the Redemptorist Archives of the Baltimore Province in Brooklyn, N.Y.

2. Prachatitz is identified by a variety of spellings: "Praehatitz," "Srachatic" and the present spelling, "Prachatice" as it is found on a map of Czechoslovakia.

3. Budweis was about twenty miles from Prachatitz. The gymnasium there was staffed by the Piarist Fathers, a sixteenth century congregation founded by St. Joseph Calasantis.

4. *The Autobiography of John Neumann*, trans. Alfred C. Rush, C.SS.R. Boston: Daughters of St. Paul, 1976, p. 27.

5. See John A. Berger, *Life of Right Rev. John N. Neumann, DD*, trans. Eugene Grimm. New York: Benziger Brothers, 1884, p. 158, 217. Also Michael J.

Curley, *Venerable John Neumann C.SS.R.*, Washington: Catholic University of America Press, 1952, pp. 34, 63-4, 79. John Berger, Neumann's nephew, collected many letters from former classmates and friends of John Neumann. Those papers contributed to his biography cited here. They are held in the Redemptorist Archives in Brooklyn.

6. *Autobiography . . .* p. 44; Berger, 251; Curley, 92.
7. Curley, 163.
8. Curley, 163, 431, n45.
9. Curley, 162. Peter Canisius published his first catechism, *Summa Doctrinae Christianae* in 1555. It was published anonymously but was received enthusiastically. Because it did not meet the needs of the common people a second manual of fifty-nine questions and answers was published the following year. In 1568 a third catechism, *Catechismus Minor seu Parvus Catholicorum* appeared. This last became the most popular of the three. All three of these are available in the two volume set edited by Fridericus Streiher, *S. Petri Canisii catechismi latini et germanici.* Rome: Gregoriana, 1933-36.
10. This volume is 178 pages in length, was published in Pittsburgh and bears the approval of "Dr. Mich. O'Connor, Bishop of Pittsburgh" on the title page.
11. Baltimore Cathedral Archives, 27 A F 3. Neumann wrote that letter to Eccleston when he (Neumann) was at St. Alphonsus parish in Baltimore, March 27, 1848.
12. Peter Guilday, *A History of The Councils of Baltimore (1791-1884).* New York: Macmillan Company, 1932, p. 176.
13. See the minutes of the session, Fifth Private Congregation, of the First Plenary Council; Baltimore Cathedral Archives, 32- B-F-1, p. 14.
14. *Katholischer Katechismus*, verfasst von JoHann Nep. Neumann, Bischof von Philadelphia. Aehnte Auflage. Mit Genebmigung des National Conciliums von Baltimore. Baltimore: John Murphy, 1853. The writer possesses an 1855 copy of this catechism. Bernard Beck wrote that by 1889 the smaller catechism had gone through thirty-eight editions and the larger, twenty-one. See Beck, *Goldenes Jubiläum des Wirkens der Redemptoristeväter an der St. Philomena Kircke in Pittsburgh and Umgebung*, Illchester, Md.: Collegium zu Illchester, 1889, p. 154.
15. Edmund Auger, *Catéchisme et sommaire de la religion chretienne.* Lyon, 1563.
16. Robert Bellarmine, *Dottrina cristiana breve* (Rome, 1597); *Dichiarazione piu copiosa della dottrina cristiana* (Rome, 1598).

17. According to Curley this was first published in Pittsburgh. Maurice de Meulemeester cites this work in his *Bibliographie Génerale des Ecrivains Redemptoristes*. Louvain: Imprimerie Saint-Alphonse, 1935, p. 294. The *National Union Catalog*, Vol. 411, shows that the St. Vincent Archabbey library, Latrobe, PA., has a copy of this Bible history.

18. Cited in Berger, 41.

19. *Autobiography*, 27.

20. Richard Gilmour, *Bible History*. New York, Cincinnati: Benziger, 1881.

21. *General Catechetical Directory*, No. 126.

22. Curley, 340.

23. Berger, 403; Curley, 243.

24. Neumann kept a record of his visitations and confirmations in the parishes within his diocese. They cover 56 pages of single line entries recording the times he visited each parish and the number of persons confirmed on each occasion. See *Records of the American Catholic Historical Society* Vol. 41 (1930), 1-26, 162-192. It is significant that the diocese entrusted to him in 1852 covered 35,000 square miles which included the eastern half of Pennsylvania, the state of Delaware, and southern New Jersey. See Curley, 184.

25. Curley, 34-41.

26. Curley, 55, 162.

27. Berger, 264.

28. *Autobiography*, 23.

29. Curley, 33.

30. Berger, 18; Curley, 6, 9, 11.

31. *Autobiography*, 24.

32. *Autobiography*, 28, 88 n54.

33. Curley, 33.

34. Berger, 156; Curley, 62.

35. Berger, 166.

36. Berger, 166; Curley, 68.

37. Mother Caroline, Berger Papers, Redemptorist Archives in Brooklyn.

38. Neumann had learned Latin and Greek in order to study the scriptures from the text itself. He learned modern languages in order to communicate with the people he lived with, to be able to converse with them, read their literature and hear their confessions. Thus he came to master six modern languages: German (his native tongue), French, Italian, Spanish, Czech and the Gaelic tongue of the Irish. See Joseph Manton, *Bishop John Nepomucene Neumann CSSR., DD*. St. Paul: Catechetical Guild, 1960, p. 99. Also Curley, 21.

39. Curley, 375.

BLESSED JOHN NEUMANN, C.Ss.R., PASTORAL BISHOP

MICHAEL J. CURLEY, C.Ss.R.

On October 13, 1963, John Neumann, C.Ss.R., fourth Bishop of Philadelphia, became a world figure. The very humble prelate who had only two bishops at his consecration in Baltimore in 1852,[1] and only four at his obsequies in Philadelphia in 1860,[2] was proclaimed Blessed by Pope Paul VI in the basilica of St. Peter in Rome before an historic assemblage of over forty cardinals, hundreds of archbishops and bishops, and an over-capacity audience of the faithful. He is the first male citizen of the United States and the first bishop of the American hierarchy to win that high honor. The words of the sovereign pontiff on the occasion epitomized the saintly bishop's career: "This Blessed Bishop attracts us and charms us by his pastoral charity."[3] It was strange how all the elements of a successful pastor on the American scene were fused in the European formation and education of the new *Beatus*.

EARLY TRAINING

John Neumann was fortunate in having good parents. His father, Philip Neumann, the Bavarian-born stocking weaver, was a steady worker and dedicated family man, respected and admired by the townfolk at Prachatitz in Bohemia where John was born on March 28, 1811. Agnes Lebisch, the Czech mother of Philip's six children, was an exemplary Catholic who organized her family on solid Christian principles. Much of the piety that later characterized Blessed John was instilled into him by his hard working Catholic mother. She encouraged him likewise when he sought to enter the Gymnasium at Budweis after he completed his six-year course of learning in the local school in 1823.[4]

For the six more years he studied at the Gymnasium he had a very good record,[5] but his studies were almost terminated before he completed his full course. The trouble started in the third year when an old and easy-going teacher was succeeded by a more energetic professor bent on making up for lost time. His pace was so fast and his methods so exacting that many of John's classmates abandoned their studies. John was none too keen on the new teacher's system of having the pupils learn by rote, but he obtained passing grades, nevertheless. During his next year young Neumann lived in a boarding house with several room companions, noisier, less studious and more pleasure seeking than he. Their distracting influence hindered his studying so much that he failed to obtain the grades he might have. Philip Neumann called his son during that summer vacation and spoke to him sternly, "John, you do not seem to have your mind on your work. Perhaps it would be better if you stayed at home and took up a trade." John had passing grades but his father was disappointed, believing that his son was not applying himself as he should. Fortunately Philip Neumann called on a neighboring professor to examine his son privately and to see what was wrong. The professor saved the day when he said that the intelligence of John and his grasp of his subjects was greater than the grades he had received from the reforming professor.[6] It was a small incident but it could easily have turned the career of John Neumann and diverted him from the priesthood. It didn't. It gave him an outlook and an understanding of student difficulties he might never have had if he had sailed along serenely. Philip Neumann changed his son's boarding house and there was no further slacking of the pace in John's scholastic career. When he studied philosophy from 1829 until 1831, in the same Gymnasium building, he obtained fine grades; and what was more his study of the sciences taught him a disciplined, orderly method of approaching his tasks.[7]

As a seminarian of the Diocese of Budweis John Neumann spent his first two years from 1831 until 1833 studying theology at the Budweis Diocesan Seminary. In every way they were brilliant years both scholastically and spiritually. Because he sought to study modern languages for which he had an aptitude and because he wished to know English and French better for work on the American missions, he took his last two years of theology at the Theological Seminary of the Charles Ferdinand University in Prague. He did well here, too, but he was not so happy with his course as he was in Budweis, because of the Josephistic leanings of some of the professors.[8] In both seminaries the courses given him were in a special way adapted to form the pastoral side of the priestly vocation. There was a strong emphasis on pedagogy and cate-chetics. Out of that training in catechetics came an accomplished catechist, a man who could instruct in a simple and clear manner. It was an asset that served Neumann well throughout all his years.[9]

There was a good preaching course given in the Prague seminary. The young seminarians had to mount the pulpit for practice preaching regularly; and their efforts were graded. To foster their ideals in sacred eloquence, they were obliged to write out portions of sermons by eminent preachers, and they had to attend the sermons and instructions in the University Church every week.

One of John Neumann's first attempts at practice preaching at Prague ended in disaster; he forgot his lines and had to get down from the pulpit in confusion. He had tried to memorize the sermon, word for word and line for line. His old antipathy against verbal memorization upset him. The next time he mounted the pulpit, things were different; he was a glowing success.[10] In time he acquired a great facility in expressing himself because he employed many hours in writing his so-called diary. This was in reality an examina-tion of conscience which he wrote almost daily for several years to help his spiritual growth. An important side effect of this *nulla die sine linea* practice was the readiness he gained in formulating his ideas clearly throughout his life. This, together with his deep and wide habits of reading and his attachment to the cause of Christ, enabled him later to speak with such unction that he became a most effective preacher.[11]

One part of his training might have disqualified him from being a good pastor, his course in theology. The textbook in moral theology, the abridged edition of Ambrose Staf's *Institutiones Theologiae Moralis*, was skimpy, giving little space to the treatises on human acts, conscience and matrimony. Besides, the moral professor was too philosophical and obscure in his lectures. For dogmatic theology he used Engelbert Klüpfel's *Institutiones Dogmaticae* in epitomized form. The text lacked solidity of doctrine, and the professor teaching it seemed more against the pope than for him. Neumann sought to offset any deficiency by privately studying the *Homo Apostolicus* of Saint Alphonsus; the *Catechism of the Council of Trent*; the *Summa Doctrinae Christianae* of Saint Canisius, and the works of Saint Robert Bellarmine. The result was that he was well prepared to be a good confessor, especially since he possessed that most important ability of distinguishing the essential from the accidental in judging cases of conscience. As a bishop he was to become known as a distinguished theologian; and many sought him as their confessor.[12]

Most important in the formation of this future pastor was the central fact that early he acquired great energy, quiet energy, but energy nevertheless. His training at home by his father and mother had developed in him steady habits of industry. One of his boyhood companions, Dean Iglauer, later pointed out that Neumann's restless energy was evident in him even as a boy.[13]

Underlying all this was his love of God and his love of souls. Pious from his youth, John Neumann said that a book, Bode's *Betrachtungen über die Weltgebäude*, read in 1829, turned his mind more closely to God.[14] He fell in love with his Creator and no other love, be it comforts of life, honor or prestige, was going to displace it. How he pleaded with the Almighty in his daily examination of conscience for that love, day after day! In setbacks, in defeats, in frustrations, in anxieties, as well as in successes, always there sprang up from him a cry for God's love. Everything else could fail; he did not want to be defeated in his desire to love God.[15]

Allied to that love of God, there arose in him a keen, incisive desire to win souls for Christ. We can pinpoint the hour when the overwhelming urge came upon him to devote his life not only as a priest, but as a missionary priest, bringing the message of salvation to a mission land. Neumann had been reading the *Berichte*, the missionary reports of the Austrian Leopoldine Foundation, with their accounts of mission work in America. The letters of the missionaries were begging for helpers, for more workers in that vineyard of the Lord. Plea after plea came, urging others to come over the ocean and save abandoned souls. John Neumann was moved.[16] Now he was in the classroom during his second year of theology listening as Father Karl Koerner explained the eleventh chapter of the Second Epistle of Saint Paul to the Corinthians. The professor's burning words on the flaming zeal of Saint Paul, travelling over the world's highroads, on land and sea, in prisons, among friends and among enemies, everywhere seeking souls for Christ, galvanized in the mind of John Neumann and another seminarian resolved to be a missionary in America.[17]

ARRIVAL IN AMERICA

Characteristically putting his resolve into action, he applied for a post in the New World and was accepted by an intermediary for the Diocese of Philadelphia. Neumann hoped to be ordained before setting out, but when the ordination was delayed because of the illness of the Bishop of Budweis, he boldly began his journey to America. In spite of the tears of his family who had fondly hoped to see him robed as priest of God, and notwithstanding the defection of his fellow seminarians who once planned to accompany him, he steadfastly moved to his goal, the mission field in America.[18] Before he left Europe, he learned with dismay that the post promised him in the Diocese of Philadelphia had been given to another. Undeterred, he travelled on, hoping to be accepted as a missionary in a land where priests were badly needed.[19]

With only a dollar in his pocket, his clothes grown shabby and his shoes worn out John Neumann in 1836 arrived in New York with no place to go. The rain was pouring down on the sidewalks that Feast of Corpus Christi as he walked up the streets of New York, alone. Fortunately, a zealous missionary, Bishop John Dubois of New York, received him with open arms, for he was in need of men with apostolic zeal. He ordained him in a little over three weeks, June 25, 1836. After saying his First Mass the next day, John Neumann penned his thoughts in his diary. "Give to me holiness," he asked, and with it was a prayer that all the living and the dead might one day be with him eternally with his "dearest God." The pastoral formation was complete now; time would gauge its effectiveness.[20]

The young German-Czech missionary left New York in a new suit provided by Father John Raffeiner, a New York priest, and money for traveling expenses donated by the bishop. A Hudson River steamer took him to Albany, and a canal boat along the Erie Canal brought him to Rochester, N.Y. Here he preached, baptized and heard confessions for the first time. He was thrilled.[21] A week later he was moving along the canal again, and came to its western terminus, Buffalo, on July 12, 1836.[22]

At the time, Buffalo had one Catholic pastor, Father Alexander Pax, caring for St. Louis' Church, though another priest, Father John Mertz, was away temporarily, collecting funds in Europe for a church in Eden, New York. John Neumann began his pastoral caring for the faithful on the outskirts of Buffalo. There were three main centers in his parish, and each of them had an unfinished church, Williamsville to the northeast of Buffalo; North Bush (now Kenmore) to the north; and Lancaster to the east. There were more than half a dozen other settlements scattered around the perimeter of Buffalo, and Neumann's apostolate carried him to all of them from Niagara Falls to Batavia and beyond, wherever a call came for priestly help. Certainly a parish of over a thousand square miles afforded full scope for pastoral zeal. His wide-ranging districts were settled by recent immigrants struggling to clear the land and establish farms. His parishioners had the faith, but in every other sense of the word they were poor.

Because it was centrally located, Neumann first set up his headquarters at Williamsville, boarding with a Catholic family because no rectory was in the place. The head of the house was friendly enough, but his volatile disposition could mount to fiery explosiveness. Seven months after his arrival, the young missionary transferred his headquarters to North Bush, boarding again with a Catholic family. Only by November 1838 did he acquire a small two-room log cabin rectory. At last he had badly needed privacy, and the Blessed Sacrament, his "Dearest God" could be reserved close at hand.

For four years the pastoral zeal that burned in the heart of John Neumann took him up and down, over and across the wide-rolling hills with a Mass kit on his back, going from place to place, often on foot, sometimes on horseback, along dusty, swampy corduroy roads, bringing the words of salvation to the scattered Catholics.

It was a hard life, a lonely life, but the pastoral charity of the young priest shone luminously under difficulties. He completed the churches; he organized the schools, going into the classroom himself to teach for months at a time. Instructions in catechism and in choral singing were regularly given to the children who long remembered him for his kindness and clear explanations. To encourage them he rewarded them with holy pictures and rock candy. Ceaselessly he visited the people of his districts, and long before Cardinal Vaughan of England had said that a house-going priest makes a church-going people, he effectively illustrated it. He never imposed on the kindness of his parishioners, and for that reason he never visited the farmers at mealtimes lest his entrance at this hour be construed as a subtle request for a meal. Folks could tell he never cooked much for himself at the rectory in North Bush for the tell-tale smoke rarely issued from the rectory's chimney. He was generous to those in need; he lifted the courage of those in trouble; he defended the Catholic Faith against those who would impugn it, though he did not believe in upbraiding people, even those who were against him.

His journeys were so long and exhausting that several times his health threatened to break. Often he was near collapse on the road.[23] His health finally did break in 1840; for some months his younger brother Wenzel, whom he had summoned from Europe to act as his cook, stable boy and teacher in school, was left alone in the outskirts of Buffalo. Convalescing in the city of Rochester at St. Joseph's Redemptorist foundation, John Neumann resolved to become a Redemptorist that he might live in the company of priests and be a member of a community rather than a lone pastor.[24]

JOINS REDEMPTORIST FATHERS

Late in 1840 he journeyed to Pittsburgh to join the Sons of Saint Alphonsus as a novice. He wanted to live a life of seclusion during his novitiate year, and he got everything but that. Sent from Pittsburgh, to New York, to Rochester, to Buffalo, to Norwalk, Ohio, his novitiate was spent for the most part in travelling with raucous immigrants going west on canal boats, stage coaches and on primitive railroads, or in listening to the bickerings of church trustees with parishioners or of church trustees with other church trustees. The conditions were such that he became a general utility priest, shifted from one post to another without a chance to stay long or operate effectively in any of them.

One thing was evident from this wandering novitiate—John Neumann could eliminate quarrels. His gentle, peaceful manner helped many a soul and brought peace where discord raged before. By nature he had a meek manner, and grace made him even still more meek. Even in those days he could take a tongue lashing or an insult humbly, not allowing any rebuff to inflame his emotions into a spirit of anger or revenge, and thus cut himself off from those with whom he had to work. He could pass over the more disruptive qualities in his neighbor's character and make use of his more co-operative tendencies. He had that all important quality of getting along with people, the prime talent for a successful pastor. He used it effectively, and the Redemptorists were happy to see him, their first novice in America, professed on January 16, 1848 in Baltimore.[25]

For two years after his novitiate, Father Neumann was a curate in the twin parishes of Saint James and Saint Alphonsus in Baltimore, but mostly at Saint James. Together they formed a hurly-burly immigrant parish in those days with buildings going up and buildings going down, while the Fathers shifted from one home to another. But Neumann had a full day's work guaranteed for him every day both in Baltimore and in the outmissions. He travelled west to Wheeling and south to Richmond and all over Maryland, helping small Catholic groups to hold fast to their religious principles.[26]

From 1844 until 1847 his pastoral zeal was given a chance to operate in a big city parish back at Saint Philomena's, Pittsburgh.

Here he had the difficulties of many pastors in a fast-growing immigrant age, the problem of building a large church with little or no income. This particular handicap had been so great at Saint Philomena's that Neumann's predecessor had given it up as an impossible task. Neumann worked so hard to get that great church completed and a rectory started that again his health broke. His three years in Pittsburgh, however, established his reputation as a pastor of unusual talents, and Bishop Michael O'Connor was to remember him later when bringing up his name for a bishopric. Neumann and his two assistants were called by the Pittsburgh prelate, "The three saints of Saint Philomena's."[27] Nevertheless, because his health was threatened, Father Neumann was relieved of his post at Pittsburgh early in 1847.[28]

At the very time his superiors in America thought of giving him a rest, a higher superior in Europe appointed him to govern all Redemptorists in America, scattered in ten struggling foundations. The biggest problem facing him as vicegerent and later as vice provincial in America was to keep the finances in proper equilibrium without impeding the growth of the houses under him. Many irritating circumstances added to his burdens, but he did balance the budget. It was during his tenure of office, too, that the Redemptorist foundations in America began to reach the forefront in erecting and staffing parochial schools, thanks to his shrewd move in acquiring the services of The School Sisters of Notre Dame to teach in them.[29]

Succeeded in the vice provincial office by the famed mission organizer, Father Bernard Hafkenscheid, Neumann was retained by him as a consultor. He performed so well in that hidden office that Hafkenscheid called him "My right arm." Hafkenscheid left the command of the vice province once again in Neumann's hands while he journeyed to Europe to help establish the Redemptorist houses in America into a province. In January 1851, Hafkenscheid became provincial, and Neumann was made the first canonical rector of the great parish of Saint Alphonsus in Baltimore. Neumann really had three parishes under him now, for Saint James' and the new Saint Michael's, each of parochial size, were united under his command. Neumann's tasks were complicating and exhausting, but here again his orderly methods enabled him to function very successfully, and he himself aided in all the parochial activities, especially in the confessional.[30]

Kind and clear thinking, he was an excellent spiritual director. Among his penitents was the Archbishop of Baltimore, Francis Patrick Kenrick. The archbishop was seeking to send to Rome the names of suitable candidates for the office of Bishop of Philadelphia in the fall of 1851. Bishop Michael O'Connor had previously told him of Neumann's executive talents. When Kenrick himself had learned to know him as his confessor, the archbishop advanced the name of Neumann for the Philadelphia post. Many other bishops seconded the proposal of the Baltimore prelate.[31]

BISHOP OF PHILADELPHIA IN 1852

Only in obedience to the command of Pope Pius IX did Blessed John Neumann undertake the office of Shepherd of Philadelphia in March 1852. Because it was then considered the largest diocese in the country, Neumann seemed in the eyes of some a little inferior for the post. In fact, one Roman authority after visiting this country wrote that very thing,[32] but neither those in Philadelphia who so appraised him, nor the Roman authority knew Philadelphia's needs and the pastoral charity in the Fourth Bishop of Philadelphia. Neumann's *ad limina* report in 1854, one of the best, if not the best in the Propaganda Archives for those years, was a living refutation of the charges leveled against him by his critics.[33] These must have been stunned in heaven, if such things occur, when the full story of John Neumann's executive accomplishments and virtues became known to them.

Better than anyone else he learned the complete problems that Philadelphia faced at that time. Philadelphia, with 75,000 souls in the city and 75,000 more in the country sections, was a diocese that stretched over South Jersey, Delaware and the eastern two-thirds of Pennsylvania. Schools had to be erected, new churches built, orphans provided for, and future parishes planned. Immigrants were pouring into the diocese. Had Blessed John Neumann been a desk executive, he might have lived an easier life. But he well knew that if the Faith of the immigrants was to be preserved, a bishop had to move; and John Neumann was a Shepherd who moved. He went out to meet the immigrants. Year after year he moved up and down and across that diocese, spending four to six months tirelessly visiting villages, often conducting services in court houses, in private homes and town halls. Everywhere he encouraged the faithful to hold regular services whether a priest was present or not. During the recent session of the Second Vatican Council, one bishop recommended that liturgical or quasi-liturgical services be arranged for priestless mission places. More than a century ago, John Neumann had done exactly that.[34]

This Philadelphia bishop was a human dynamo. What made his activity noteworthy, however, is that while working at top speed he kept his mind on God—a living example of holiness in action. Father Edward Purcell, who preached at the consecration of Bishop Wood in Cincinnati in 1837, declared that Bishop Neumann's apostolic zeal was known to the whole American Church.[35] It should have been. Many remember Bishop Neumann as the prelate who introduced the diocesan-wide celebration of the Forty Hours in the United States. He did much more than that. In his ninety-three months as bishop he carried out an amazing church construction program. Seven churches begun before his time were completed; ten others were rebuilt; sixty-six more were entirely new; and eight more were started.[36] The number of Catholic school children was multiplied eighteen times and, what was more lasting, a Catholic diocesan school system was organized for the first time in America. The Sisters of Notre Dame du Namur, the Holy Cross Sisters, the Sisters of the Immaculate Heart of Mary, The Christian Brothers, and the Holy Cross Brothers were brought in to provide teaching staffs. He founded the Franciscan Sisters of Glen Riddle to do social work, and he brought in the Benedictines and the Franciscan Conventuals to aid his priests. With a foresight that few had in his day, he established the Philadelphia Preparatory Seminary to insure vocations for the priesthood.[37]

He had his critics, plenty of them but, while profiting from just criticism, he never allowed unjust censorious remarks to disturb the peace of his soul or to keep him from working steadily for God.

In an effort to promote the welfare of his diocese, and that was his only motive, he twice offered to leave Philadelphia and go to a smaller diocese.[38] He never went. Three times Archbishop Francis Patrick Kenrick wrote to Rome that he should be retained in Philadelphia, saying on each occasion, "He is loved by the priests and the people."[39] Solid testimony of their love came when they buried him in the candle-lighted basement of Saint Peter's Church in Philadelphia. Lay people sought to snip off pieces of his robes to preserve them as relics, and priests cried openly.[40] The Jesuit, Father Edward Sourin, preaching over Neumann's body, said of him, "He spared himself in nothing."[41] Tears welled up in the eyes of the people as Archbishop Kenrick, delivering the funeral sermon, spoke of Blessed John:

> Truly he has been an active and devoted pastor living only for his flock. To his clergy he has been full of tenderness . . . their affections were daily more and more won by him without any effort on his part beyond the constant exhibition of paternal kindness . . . To the laity he was a devoted pastor, always accessible and ready to discharge the duties of his office . . . the poor, the humble always found him kind, condescending, indulgent. His charities were abundant . . . It is as a pastor watching over his flock that he is specially worthy of our veneration.[42]

NOTES

1. Joseph Bernard Code, *Dictionary of the American Hierarchy* (New York, 1940), 254; Johann Berger, C.SS.R. (nephew of the bishop), *Leben und Wirken des hochseligen Johannes Nep. Neumann* (New York, 1883), 291; Michael J. Curley, C.SS.R., *Venerable John Neumann, C.SS.R.* (Washington, D.C., 1952), 436, n. 1.

2. *Funeral Obsequies of Rt. Rev. John Nepomucene Neumann* (Philadelphia, 1860), 14-17.

3. *L'Osservatore Romano*, 14-15 Ottobre, 1963, p. 1.

4. Redemptorist Archives, Baltimore Province, Brooklyn, N.Y. Neumanneana (cited hereafter as RABP, N), *Kurze Lebensbeschreibung des P. Joh. Nep. Neumann, Priester der Versammlung des Hl. Erlösers u[nd] erwählten Bischof*

114

v[on] Philadelphia in Nord America (cited hereafter as KL), a four-page (three of them double pages), MS autobiography written under obedience on the eve of his consecration, l; P. Emmanuel Kóvař, *Ctihodný sluha boží Jan. Nepom. Neumann* (Brünn, 1910), 12; Berger, *op. cit.*, 16-23.

5. RABP, N. Budweis Gymnasium, has the semi-annual reports of his progress.

6. KL, 1; RABP, N. Budweis Gymnasium, the semi-annual report dated Budweis, September 7, 1827; RABP, N, Mon Journal under date of April 9,1835, in German. This is a MS diary or, more correctly, an examination of conscience, written almost daily for several years, beginning October 31, 1834. There are two parts to Mon Journal, one in French and the other in German (cited hereafter as MJF and MJG). MJG places the incident in 1828, but Neumann's autobiography, the scholastic reports, as well as other internal evidence indicate it took place in 1827.

7. RABP, N, Budweis Gymnasium, "Austritt-Zeugniss aus den Philosophischen Studien," dated August 5, 1831, and signed by the Bishop of Budweis; Curley, *op. cit.*, 16.

8. KL, 2; Dr. Lad. Dvořák Biskupsky Kněžský seminář v. Č. Budějovicich (Budweis, 1905), 41-56; RABP, N. Seminary Years, 1831-1835, "Caesaro-Regius in Alma Caesarea Regiaque Carlo-Ferdinandea Universitate Pragensi Theologicae Facultatis Praeses et Director," dated Prague, August 3, 1835, gives his grades both for his courses in Budweis and in Prague.

9. *Ibid:* Dvořák, *op. cit.*, 52; Curley, *op. cit.*, 33. Mother Caroline Friess, SSND, called Neumann "a born catechist," RABP, N. Berger Papers, Mother Caroline, SSND, to Berger, Milwaukee, April 21,1874.

10. MJF, December 23, 1834; MJF, June 3, 1835.

11. Mon Journal, *ut supra* n 6. For an appraisal of his preaching see Curley, *op. cit.*, 339-40.

12. KL, 2; MJF, February 15, 1835; MJF, October 9, 15,1835; MJG, June 11, 1835; RABP, N, Neumann Data, 1835, "Aus dem Gebiethe der Theologie," Heft XXII, XXV; Curley, *op. cit.*, 162-63.

13. This native of Prachatitz said of Neumann, "Schon in seinen Knabenjahren was er stets rastlos thätig," Berger, *op. cit.*, 30. Later, Neumann's confrere, Father Francis Tschenhens, was reported as saying that the holy bishop, in imitation of Saint Alphonsus Liguori, made a vow never to lose a moment's time, RABP, III, John Berger, Berger to his aunt, Cumberland, Md., April 15-25, 1860.

14. MJG, April 9, 1835.

15. MJG, April 10, 1835; MJG, July 6, 1835; MJG, August 22, 1835; MJG,

February 13, 1836, and in many other places of his journal.

16. KL, 2; *Berichte der Leopoldinen—Stiftung im Kaiserthume Oesterreich* (cited hereafter as *Berichte*), Heft I (1831); Heft II (1831) and Heft III (1832).

17. KL, 2; RABP, N. Berger Papers, Laad to Berger, Kotoun, April 11, 1872.

18. KL, 2. MJG and MJF have many entries concerning the resolution and how it was carried out.

19. KL, 2; MJG, February 20, 1836; MJG, March 2, 4, 14, 1836.

20. KL, 2-3; MJG, June 9, 19, 20, 22, 26, 1836; *Berichte,* Heft X (1837), 52-55, Neumann to Dean [Endres], New York, June 27, 1836.

21. MJG, Feast of SS. Peter and Paul (June 29), 1836; MJG, July 5, 1836.

22. MJG, July 13, 1836.

23. KL, 3; Curley, *op cit.*, 64-78; Berger, *op. cit.*, 152-202; RABP, N, Berger Papers, Theodore Noethen's MS "Aus dem Leben des Hochwürdigsten Herrn Bischofs John N. Neumann"; *ibid,* George Pax to Berger, Williamsville, February 16, 1872. The various letters of Neumann at this time are cited in Curley, *op. cit.*, 414-16.

24. KL, 3; Joseph Prost, C.SS.R., "Die Geschichte der Gruendung unserer Congregation in den Vereinigten Staaten von Nordamerica vom Jahre 1832 bis zum Anfang des Jahres 1843," in Joseph Wuest, C.SS.R., *Annales Congregationis SS. Redemptoris Provinciae, Supplementum ad Volumnia I, II, III* (cited hereafter as Wuest, *Suppl.*), Part I (Ilchester, Md., 1901), 198.

25. KL, 4; Curley, *op. cit.*, 81-92, 374: "Kirchliche Nachrichten," Beilage zur *Sion* (Augsburg), 11 Jahr. num. 20 (February 16, 1842), 184.

26. The Redemptorists had two parishes in Baltimore at the time, Saint John's and Saint James'. St. John's was razed, and on it the Church of Saint Alphonsus was being built. The Fathers were shifted to St. James' rectory until the rectory of Saint Alphonsus' church could be completed. At the same time a new novitiate was being built at St. James'; Budweis Diocesan Archives, Rodler Papers, Neumann to his parents, Baltimore, October 12, 1842; *Berichte*, Heft XVII (1844), Neumann to the Archbishop of Vienna, Baltimore, December 6, 1843.

27. Berger, *op cit.*, 235-57; Bernard Beck, C.SS.R., *Goldenes Jubiläum des Wirkens der Redemptoristenväter an der St. Philomena Kirche in Pittsburg und Umgegend* (Pittsburgh, 1889), 150-64; Henry Borgmann, C.SS.R., *History of the Redemptorist at Annapolis, Md., from 1853 to 1903* (Ilchester, Md., 1904), 217.

28. RABP, N, Pittsburgh Years, Peter Chackert (Czackert), C.SS.R., to Joseph Müller, C.SS.R., Baltimore, January 19, 1847.

29. Curley, *op. cit.*, 121-53.

30. Bernard Hafkenscheid, C.SS.R., "Actes authentiques concernant le Vice-Provincialat de la Congrégation du très- Saint Rédempteur dans les États-Unis," in Wuest, *Suppl.* II, 26; Budweis Diocesan Archives, Rodler Papers, Neumann to his father and sisters, Baltimore, June 10, 1851; *ibid.*, Neumann to his father and relatives, Baltimore, September 10, 1851.

31. *Spicilegium Historicum Congregationis SSmi Redemptoris*, XI (1963) 322-48, has printed the pertinent Roman documents concerning the selection of Neumann as bishop.

32. Archives of Propaganda Fide, Rome (cited hereafter as APF), Scritture riferite nei congressi America Centrale dal Canada all' istmo di Panama (cited hereafter as SRC, America Centrale), XVII (1855), fols. 43r-113v, "Relazione completa remissa da Mons. Bedini all' Emo. Sig. Cardinale Prefetto dello stato di quella vaste regioni nell' anno 1855." See James F. Connelly, *The Visit of Archbishop Gaetano Bedini to the United States of America: June 1853-February 1854* (Rome, 1960), 234-55, where the phrase of Bedini, "meschinità di persona e neglegenza di modi," is, I believe, erroneously translated as "lack of personality and his neglect of proper manners." There is a variety of opinions concerning the translation of certain words, but I think the phrase would be rendered better in English by the words "unimpressive appearance and neglect of the fashion." Neumann's small size made him unimpressive to one meeting him for the first time. Moreover, his wide-ranging trips to the country districts did not always allow him to dress in the style of the desk executive, but he always had good manners. See Curley, *op. cit.*, 284-85, 363.

33. APF, SRC, America Centrale, XVI (1852-1854), fols. 852r-857v, "Relatio Status Ecclesiae Philadelphiensis in Foederatis Americae Septentrionalis Statibus A.D. MDCCCLIV." The report was dated December 16, 1854.

34. Philadelphia Archdiocesan Archives, Saint Charles' Theological Seminary, Philadelphia, has the MS Visitation Record of Blessed John Neumann. A printed copy of it is in *Records of the American Catholic Historical Society of Philadelphia*, XLI (1930), 1-26, 162-92. See Curley *op. cit.*, 218.

35. Philadelphia *Catholic Herald and Visitor*, May 2, 1857, p. 138.

36. Curley, *op. cit.*, 219-20, 517-18.

37. *Ibid*, 207-11; *ibid.*, 261, 264, 355-56.

38. APF, Udienze di Nostro Signore, 1855, Seconde Parte, CXXII (1856), fols. 1834-1835, Neumann to "Most Reverend and Illustrious Monsignor" [Barnabò], Philadelphia, June 4, 1855; APF, Acta Sacrae Congregationis (cited hereafter as Acta), CCXX (1856), fols. 440r-441r, Neumann to the Cardinal Prefect (James Franzoni), Philadelphia, May 28, 1855; APF, SRC,

America Centrale, XVIII (1858-1860), fols. 386rv, Neumann to Barnabò, n.p., n.d., See Curley *op. cit.*, 470, n. 79.

39. APF, Acta, CCXX (1856), fols. 441r-442r, F. P. Kenrick to the Cardinal Prefect, Baltimore, July 4, 1855; APF, SRC, America Centrale, XVIII (1858-1860), fol. 339, F. P. Kenrick to Barnabò, Baltimore, October 4, 1858; *ibid.*, fol. 971r, F. P. Kenrick to Propaganda, Baltimore, September 1, 1859.
Archbishop Anthony Blanc of New Orleans also wrote against changing Neumann from Philadelphia, pointing out his sanctity and apostolic work, APF, Scritture riferite nelle Congregazioni Generali, 983, fols. 668rv, Blanc to Barnabò, New Orleans, June 7, 1858. Similarly, the Archbishop of San Francisco wrote that Neumann should not be transferred from Philadelphia where he was shining by his learning and piety, *ibid.*, fols. 666r-667r, Joseph Alemany to Barnabò, Downieville, Upper California, July 15, 1858.

40. Berger, *op. cit.*, 381-98; Curley, *op. cit.*, 395-96.

41. *Funeral Obsequies of Rt. Rev. Nep. Neumann*, 9.

42. John N. Berger, C.SS.R., *Life of Right Reverend John N. Neumann* (trans. by Eugene Grimm, C.SS.R. [Philadelphia, 1884]), 432-33.

"THE BRIGHTEST JEWEL IN THEIR CROWN":[1]
JOHN NEUMANN AND THE ESTABLISHMENT OF THE FORTY HOURS DEVOTION IN PHILADELPHIA

JOSEPH C. LINCK

On 10 October 2000, the archbishop of Philadelphia, Cardinal Anthony Bevilacqua, came to the Church of St. Philip Neri to preside at the closing of an archdiocesan-wide celebration of the Eucharistic devotion known as the "Forty Hours." The three-day spiritual exercise was organized as part of a yearlong commemoration of the Great Jubilee, in which Catholic dioceses and communities around the globe sought to revitalize and rekindle the faith of their members through a renewed focus on the person of Jesus Christ, Lord and Savior, the same "yesterday, today, forever." The Forty Hours Devotion, which has been less of a fixture in the devotional life of American parishes than in previous decades, was organized in every one of the archdiocese's 286 parishes to focus the attention of the faithful on the centrality of the Eucharist, and Christ's presence therein, as a cornerstone of Catholic life. The Cardinal noted in his homily that evening that the Eucharist "is not just a doctrine to be believed, it is a mystery to be lived. . . . In it and through it, the fullness of our Catholic faith and life unfold."[2] The archdiocesan-wide devotion, then, was not meant to serve merely as an historical curiosity, a relic of bygone days, but as a means to "inflame, especially among the young, the true devotion to our Lord present in the Blessed Sacrament, which we ourselves received from those who went before us."[3]

The cardinal's presence at St. Philip Neri Church that October evening was hardly accidental. For one of those very much in his mind that night, who had "gone before him" as bishop of Philadelphia, was St. John Neumann (1811-60), who had come to the very same church on 26 May 1853 to inaugurate the first diocesan-wide celebration of the Forty Hours in the history of the Catholic Church in America.[4] It was Neumann's decision to begin the devotion in the Church of St. Philip Neri,[5] a parallel not lost on those gathered in the same church almost 150 years later. Catherine Stutski, a parishioner, commented that this connection with the saintly bishop was "an honor and a pleasure," adding, "I think he would be very proud, as we are proud of him."[6]

Certainly Neumann would have been proud to know that the devotional exercise he introduced to his flock almost a century and a half ago is still celebrated in the archdiocese. Even more, he would no doubt be pleased to be told that the Catholic faith, and faithful, are flourishing in the archdiocese he once shepherded, for it was his one aim as bishop of Philadelphia to build up, nourish, and strengthen the Church by every means at his disposal. To further that end he founded parishes, established schools, and undertook countless visitations of his faithful. Yet along with the building of edifices and his pastoral exertions, Neumann did something some considered unusual at the time: he established the devotion of the Forty Hours as one of the first acts of his episcopal ministry. Despite the demurral of his diocesan clergy and advisors, he went ahead with plans to encourage prayer and adoration before the exposed Sacrament in every church in the diocese, seeing this as a vital way to nurture the faith among his burgeoning flock. An examination of Neumann's affection for the Blessed Sacrament, his reasons for introducing the devotion to the Church in Philadelphia, and its reception by the faithful will form the subject of the following study.

THE FORTY HOURS DEVOTION: ORIGINS AND HISTORICAL DEVELOPMENT

Before taking a look at Bishop Neumann's introduction of the Forty Hours, however, it would be helpful to pause for a moment to sketch the history of the devotion itself. That history is by no means without ambiguity, but it is possible to outline its basic growth and development. The roots of the practice of spending this set period of time—forty hours—in prayer and adoration in the presence of the Blessed Sacrament can be traced to the holiest time of the Christian year, the Easter Triduum, the three days from Holy (or Maundy) Thursday to Easter Sunday. After the Mass of the Lord's Supper on Holy Thursday evening, it was (and is) the practice of the Roman Catholic Church to remove the hosts that have been consecrated for distribution on Good Friday (the only day of the Christian year on which Mass is never celebrated) to a separate place of reservation, apart from the main body of the church. At least by the dawn of the second millennium, it was the custom in some regions for the subdeacons to watch and pray before the Eucharist, which was often reserved in the church sacristy.[7] Around the year 1177, the Croatian city of Zadar was given papal permission to conduct a forty-hour-long period of Eucharistic devotion coinciding with the days of the Easter Triduum. Records from the year 1380 indicate that a relay of watchers spent the hours from eight o'clock on Holy Thursday evening till twelve o'clock noon on Holy Saturday in prayer and adoration.[8]

By the fourteenth century, the practice known as the "Prayer [Supplication] of the Forty Hours" had spread throughout Europe. The Eucharist would be solemnly transferred to a sepulcher located within the church, and the faithful would "watch" and pray there in commemoration of the hours that Christ had spent in the tomb.[9] The liturgist Josef Jungmann believes this typically occurred from 3:00 P.M. Good Friday till 3:00-4:00 A.M. Easter Sunday.[10] The "rising" of the Eucharistic Lord from the sepulcher would then herald the resurrection. It was from this pious practice of Holy Week that the Forty Hours (or *Quarant' Ore*) emerged.

The first recorded evidence of the devotion's development beyond the liturgy of Holy Week can be found in Milan in 1527. Fr. John Anthony Bellotto, a priest of the Church of the Holy Sepulcher, scheduled forty hours of continuous prayer four times a year in the church, at Easter, Pentecost, Assumption of the Blessed Virgin Mary, and Christmas, in the presence of the reserved (but not exposed)

Sacrament. He recommended this devotion to the faithful especially for the cause of peace, as the troops of the Emperor Charles V were ravaging the Italian peninsula.[11] In 1529, as Charles's armies again seemed poised to overrun Milan, the Forty Hours was held in all the churches of the city, first upon the conclusion of the octave of the Feast of Corpus Christi, and then again in September.[12]

Further development occurred in 1537, again in Milan, when a Capuchin friar, Joseph of Fermo, arranged for a continuous, year-round celebration of the devotion. Under this arrangement, upon the conclusion of the Forty Hours in one city parish, the Eucharist would be carried in procession to another church for the inauguration of the observance there.[13] The intent was to provide for an uninterrupted exercise of the devotion throughout the city. St. Anthony Maria Zaccaria, founder of the Barnabite congregation, seems to have undertaken the role of enthusiastic promoter of the practice; hence he is often cited as the "originator" of the Forty Hours.[14]

The success of this spiritual exercise came to the attention of Pope Paul III in 1539. The Pope, intent on revitalizing the faith of the Church in the wake of the emerging Protestant Reformation, ardently endorsed the Forty Hours. He described it as the offering of "prayers and supplications" by night and by day, to "appease the anger of God aroused by the offenses of Christians," and to implore divine aid against the incursions of the Turks. He encouraged its promotion, granting an indulgence to the devotion.[15]

The Forty Hours enjoyed rapid growth from that time forward. St. Philip Neri, known as the "Apostle of Rome" for his tireless work in the evangelization of the city, prescribed it as an exercise for his confraternity of *Trinità dei Pellegrini* at some time prior to 1550, and St. Ignatius Loyola encouraged its use during the lawless days of the Roman Carnival.[16] It was introduced in France in 1574 (by the Jesuit Edmond Auger), and in Spain in 1577-84 (by the Capuchin Joseph de Rocaberti).[17] Pope Pius IV offered his approval of the devotion in 1560,[18] and by 1592 Pope Clement VIII would call for the practice of a perpetual Forty Hours in the churches of Rome along the lines of the Milanese model.[19] It was this latter pontiff who would attach a plenary indulgence to the devout undertaking of this quickly expanding, and popular, form of Eucharistic worship.[20] Left to a future bishop of Rome would be the establishment of exacting regulations and instructions for those charged with conducting the devotion; these would be issued by Pope Clement XIII in his *Instructio Clementina* of 1 September 1730.[21]

What then, according to these regulations, did a typical Forty Hours look like when celebrated in a parish church? First of all, the Blessed Sacrament was exposed upon the main altar of the church. At the time of the initial exposition, a Solemn High Mass of the Blessed Sacrament was celebrated, followed by a *Missa pro pace* on the second day. The Litany of Saints was chanted at the beginning and at the end of exposition. During the forty hours of prayer, a series of watchers would be scheduled including, at all times if possible, a priest or cleric (who would kneel within the sanctuary). Twenty candles would be kept burning day and night, and all statues or pictures in the vicinity of the altar were covered. Apart from the brief sermons that were delivered throughout the three-day period on subjects connected with the Eucharist, measures were taken to ensure constant silence and an atmosphere of recollection.[22]

The rubrics for the celebration of Forty Hours are, of course, far more detailed than the brief summary given above. With very few alterations, though, the guidelines offered by Pope Clement XIII would remain unchanged until the liturgical revisions that followed the Second Vatican Council. Nathan Mitchell has written: "the *Ceremonial for the Use of the Catholic Churches in the United States of America*, published by order of the First Council of Baltimore (1852), contains rites and rubrics for Forty Hours that are virtually indistinguishable from the ceremonies described in the *Instructio Clementina*."[23] Thus when Bishop Neumann introduced the devotion on a large scale in Philadelphia, the ceremonies would most likely not have appeared foreign to one familiar with the practices of Rome, Milan, or Catholic churches throughout continental Europe.[24]

The Theology and Spirituality
of the Forty Hours Devotion

We have spoken briefly about the rubrics, or the manner in which the Forty Hours was observed; perhaps a few comments would now be in order describing the theology or spirituality that informed the devotion. Mitchell characterizes its primary themes as "repentance and reparation."[25] Originally the Forty Hours had been rooted in the liturgy of Holy Week, when Christians call to mind in sorrow the Lord's suffering and abandonment at Gethsemane and Calvary, and meditate on the anguish that prepared the way for the joyful resurrection of Easter Sunday. Indeed, the "forty hours" of prayerful identification with the afflicted Lord in some way encapsulated the whole forty days of Lent, itself a penitential time when Christians intensified their prayer and mortification in preparation for Easter. In addition, Pope Pius IV, in giving his approbation to the practice in 1560, noted that the forty hours of prayer were a reflection of Jesus's fast of forty days, a dominical model of personal prayer and abnegation worthy of imitation.[26]

When this period of intense Eucharistic prayer was first detached from the liturgy of Holy Week, it was with a purpose. War was threatening the city of Milan, and the Forty Hours proposed by Fr. Bellotti was seen as a means of pleading for divine assistance. This theme would be an important one in the history of the devotion; it was often heralded as an effective means of securing the Lord's blessing in times of "serious social upheaval."[27] Hand in hand with the concept of intercession went the idea of reparation. Since societal traumas were often considered to be the result of personal or communal immorality, the Forty Hours was considered an effective way of making amends for one's own sins and the sins of one's community by offering up the gift of time spent in prayer before the Eucharistic Lord.

St. Ignatius Loyola was surely thinking of this aspect when he encouraged the scheduling of the Forty Hours during the season of Carnival, a time notorious for its dissolution and debauchery. But he must also have been aware, as was his contemporary and friend St. Philip Neri, that communal devotions were a good way of building up the life of the community. Not only would participants be spared the temptations of carnival bacchanalia and have an opportunity to make prayerful atonement for the sins of their neighbors, but they would also grow in their own faith through the sermons preached, and the shared experience of prayer and adoration. The Forty Hours "built community" and nourished the faith of those who took part in it. It encouraged a sense of *esprit de corps*, which the Counter-Reformation Church found valuable as it sought to revitalize the Catholic faith under the twin challenges of apathy and Protestant proselytism.

The Catholic Community in Philadelphia

These dual hazards were certainly operative in the youthful Church in the United States. As the nineteenth century reached its midpoint, the American Church found itself awash in a sea of immigrants (many of whom lacked a proper formation in their faith) and aggressively challenged by a culture that saw the newly arrived Catholics as a threat to American freedom and democracy. Philadelphia (the largest urban area in the country in 1830 with 188,000 citizens) was the port of entry for tens of thousands of Catholic immigrants, many of whom took up residence in the city or its environs.[28] Hostility grew up between the poor Irish Catholics and the equally disadvantaged "native" Americans, as well as with the many poor Scotch-Irish from the north of Ireland who, upon arrival in America, were nourished on the steady stream of anti-Catholic propaganda that was all the rage in the 1830s. This simmering tension exploded over the refusal of the Philadelphia public schools to permit Catholic children to use an approved Bible of their own choosing (as opposed to the standard King James Version). Catholics were accused of wanting to exclude the Bible from public schools, and it took little encouragement from the Nativist press and pulpit to fan the flames of violence. May and July of 1844 saw bloody riots in Philadelphia, during which the Church of St. Augustine was burned, St. Philip Neri Church was placed under siege, homes were looted, and unarmed Catholics found on the street were attacked.[29]

Bishop Francis Patrick Kenrick counseled calm and withdrawal from places of public assembly, and by summer's end peace had been restored, but Catholics in Philadelphia were left to wonder about their future in a society in which such outrages were possible. They needed encouragement to remain strong in their faith, to be sure, but where was such solace to be found?

A column in the *Catholic Herald* newspaper, published in Philadelphia, offered an interesting solution in its edition of 8 August 1844, only a few weeks after the violence had subsided. An anonymous author known only as "Vindex" presented to his readers, of all things, a history of the Forty Hours Devotion, describing it as follows:

> There is in Rome a church for every day of the year. Now these churches—at least all the large ones—have entered into an agreement, that each of them by turns will adopt throughout the whole year what is called the "Forty Hours" devotion; that thus, there may not be one day, nor even <u>one hour</u>, in the whole year, which, in some part of Rome, is not dedicated to God by the practice of this beautiful worship. The devotion consists in exposing, for the period of forty hours, the Holy Sacrament to the adoration of the people . . . . This perpetual adoration of Christ in the Holy Sacrament is rendered still more attractive by the Benediction which is given at stated intervals. Here is truly a perpetual prayer and adoration! Will you find this anywhere in all the dreary land of Protestantism?

Vindex went on to make a point more specific to his local readership:

> . . . an effort is now made in England to introduce this same devotion. Even in our own country—in Philadelphia, the city of "brotherly love," and of most <u>unbrotherly</u> persecution of Catholics, some attempt has been recently made to introduce it, at least on a limited scale. And we know of no devotion better calculated than this to cheer the persecuted and deeply outraged Catholics of that city; and to enable them to bear up under the

heavy trials, which have fallen to their lot. Nor do we know of any
more effectual means of staying the violence of persecution itself,
and softening the hearts of the persecutors, than fervent prayers
poured out for them before the holy altar of God, and in the
presence of that divine Victim of the expiation, who died for
sinners, and prayed, with His last breath, for His persecutors! The
Catholics of Philadelphia have done this, and they are yet disposed
cheerfully to do it. Their patience and silence under the most
galling and atrocious injuries which in this free (!!) country, have
ever fallen to the lot of any portion of our citizens, is, perhaps, the
brightest jewel in their crown.[30]

It is unclear in what church, or for how long, the devotion was celebrated in the summer of 1844, if it occurred at all. Certainly, the
practice was not unknown to Catholics in America.[31] It is noteworthy, however, that eight years before John Neumann's arrival in
Philadelphia, there was a move afoot to strengthen the distressed
Catholic community through the collective encouragement and
fervent prayer of the Forty Hours Devotion.

Neumann's Ardent Love for the Eucharist

When John Neumann arrived in Philadelphia as the diocese's
fourth bishop on 30 March 1852, he brought with him his own
understanding of the importance of the Eucharist in the life of the
faithful. As a young seminarian in Prague, he had an acute awareness of the centrality of the Eucharist in the Christian life, as his
Spiritual Journal reveals. A few excerpts will have to suffice:

I believe you are truly present in the Most Holy Sacrament of the
Altar, and I adore you with all my heart (1 Nov. 1834).[32]

I am a great sinner and I deserve your wrath. However, Your
graciousness, Your Real Presence in the Holy Eucharist through
which You give Yourself as my food —this enormous love makes
me forget Your justice and see only Your love (24 Nov. 1834).[33]

As a consequence of visiting those churches [in which the Eucharist was reserved in the Sepulcher during the Triduum] I was more disposed to pray today. The adoration of the Blessed Sacrament helped to ease the chagrin I felt occasionally at the thought of my friend Schmid[t]'s failure to write and of my uneasiness over the delicate situation with the Prefect (18 Apr. 1835).[34]

Even from the few lines cited above, it will be seen how deep a reverence Neumann had for Christ's presence in the Eucharist. Though at times overwhelmed by his own fragility and lack of resolve, the young saint-in-the-making was able to deepen his awareness of Christ's mercy and love through his devotion to the sacrament of the altar. Beyond that, his experience of finding solace at prayer in the Lord's Eucharistic presence no doubt convinced him of the importance of cultivating such piety among the faithful.

It surely was a matter of no little significance to Neumann the missionary that he set foot on the shores of his new homeland for the first time on 1 June 1836, the Feast of Corpus Christi, a day dedicated to the presence of the Lord in the Blessed Sacrament.[35] Quickly ordained for the Diocese of New York, the young priest was sent off to rural parishes in the vicinity of Buffalo, where he acquired a permanent parish house (though only a modest two-room cabin), and rejoiced that the Eucharist could henceforth be reserved where he dwelt. A visit to the Blessed Sacrament would now form part of his daily schedule.[36] While a Redemptorist novice in 1841, he would certainly have deepened his familiarity with the writings of the community's founder, St. Alphonsus Liguori, who had discerned his own call to the priesthood while at prayer before the Eucharist.[37] Liguori's spiritual works emphasized the love that was the foundation of Christ's gift of Himself in the Blessed Sacrament, and marveled at the accessibility of Christ in the Eucharist, such that rich and poor, weak and powerful, all had the same opportunity to converse with him in prayer.[38] Neumann the Redemptorist, faithful to the spirituality of his saintly founder, would encourage devotions to the Blessed Sacrament and societies dedicated to its honor, both at St. James and St. Alphonsus in Baltimore, and at St. Philomena in Pittsburgh.[39]

As bishop of Philadelphia, it was said by one religious superior that "As soon as he entered the house, his first visit was to the chapel, where, as he knelt before the altar, his whole soul seemed absorbed in God and that air of devout recollection, so habitual to him, became doubly intensified by his faith in the Sacramental Presence."[40]

The bishop's enthusiasm for Eucharistic devotions was not mere uninformed piety—he took a keen interest in the proper celebration of such exercises as well. So respected was he for his exacting approach to the proper celebration of all liturgical rites that, at the First Plenary Council of Baltimore in 1852, the newly consecrated Bishop Neumann would be placed on a committee working to revise a manual of church ceremonies.[41]

Neumann brought with him to Philadelphia, then, a love for the Blessed Sacrament and a conviction that devotion to it played an important role in Christian spirituality. In addition, he possessed a familiarity with the liturgical ceremonies that honored the Eucharist, including the devotion of the Forty Hours. Fostering this practice would be one of the first actions he undertook as bishop of Philadelphia.

NEUMANN'S INTRODUCTION OF THE FORTY HOURS TO THE DIOCESE OF PHILADELPHIA

The bishop's initial year in Philadelphia was taken up with pastoral visitations to the parishes of the diocese; he greatly enjoyed these opportunities to be with his flock, and minister to the spiritual needs of the people. What he saw on these visits convinced him of the need to build up the laity's knowledge of the faith, and foster the spiritual life of the people. He worked energetically for the rapid expansion and development of the Catholic school system, which he referred to as his "key project."[42] And he believed as well that a chief component in the spiritual renewal of the diocese should be the introduction of the Forty Hours Devotion. His nephew, the Redemptorist John Berger, writes:

> In the Blessed Sacrament Bishop Neumann found the sweet object of his lively faith, his firm hope, his tender love. His devotion to

Jesus hidden under the Eucharistic veils was earnest and edifying and intense was his desire to enkindle the same among his flock. He longed for them to share largely in the rich blessings flowing from this source of grace. The best means to accomplish this lay, as he thought, in the devotion of the Forty Hours; and the thought of introducing it into his diocese, of celebrating it with all possible pomp and splendor, was one that constantly recurred to his mind.[43]

A diocesan synod was planned for April of 1853, and the bishop was desirous that one or more of the clergy of the diocese would offer a proposal regarding the Forty Hours for the gathering to consider. His hopes, however, seemed sure to be disappointed. His friends among the clergy were unreceptive to his proposals, as they "were of the opinion that the time had not yet arrived for the worthy celebration of the devotion in this country; that the faithful were not ripe for it; that our Lord Jesus Christ would receive more dishonor than honor in those long hours of exposition."[44] Their first concern, though well intentioned, seems unwarranted given the subsequent popularity of the devotion. It is not impossible that, through his visitations, the bishop had come to know the spiritual state of the diocese more insightfully than his clergy. As to their second concern, however, even the bishop had to admit that the anti-Catholic violence of the last decade made the organization of so "Catholic" a display as the Forty Hours a risky proposition. There was the possibility that it could serve as a pretext for a violent Nativist rejoinder, and in such a situation there was always the danger that the Eucharist would be profaned—the very opposite of the fruit Neumann hoped to gain from the devotion.[45]

As he was pondering the course of action to adopt, wondering whether it would be wiser to postpone his plans for a more propitious time, the following incident occurred, which Berger does not hesitate to describe as miraculous. His portrayal of this unusual episode is best reproduced in full:

Late one evening, Bishop Neumann sat in his room busy inditing answers to innumerable letters that lay before him. Midnight sounded and found him still at work. The candle that he used in sealing his letters had well-nigh burned out, and he vainly tried to steady the only remaining piece at hand in the candlestick. Not being able to succeed, and preoccupied with the thought that had so long pursued him, that of the Forty Hours, he rather carelessly—we should perhaps say providentially—stood the piece of lighted candle on the table, placing around it as a support some letters and writing-paper. Wearied by so many hours of close application, he fell into a light sleep, from which he suddenly awoke in alarm to find the candle consumed and his table covered with smoldering paper. He gazed in astonishment at the glowing sheets, many of them burnt and charred, though the writing they contained remained untouched and legible. Overcome by what he saw, and heedless of quenching the glowing sparks, the servant of God sank on his knees. As he knelt in silent gratitude for this apparently miraculous interposition of Divine Providence, it seemed to him that he heard an interior voice saying: "As the flames are here burning without consuming or even injuring the writing, so shall I pour out My grace in the Blessed Sacrament without prejudice to My honor. Fear not profanation, therefore; hesitate no longer to carry out your designs for My glory."[46]

The incident had a profound effect on Neumann's deliberations. This was not the first time he had discerned the hand of Providence in his life; while on his journey to America he was one day standing alone in the prow of the ship as it made its way through storm-tossed waters. It is said that he "heard an interior voice telling him to move away. Scarcely had he left the spot when a mast came crashing down upon the place where he had stood, leaving him in admiration of the providence of God."[47] The good bishop was not one to distrust further wise counsel from the Lord, so he went ahead with his plans for the Forty Hours on his own, introducing the matter to the synod which he convoked in Philadelphia on 20 April 1853. The statutes of the synod, when subsequently published, would show that at the head of the decrees stood the following declaration:

> That the faithful may be afforded a better opportunity of eliciting acts of faith, hope and love towards the Lord Jesus in the Most Holy Mystery of the Eucharist, and in addition that greater satisfaction may be made Him for the many and great offenses committed against this Mystery; it has been decided to institute the pious devotion of the Forty Hours in those churches and chapels of this Diocese which shall be indicated by the Bishop annually together with the time at which it is to be celebrated in each church. Further, we instruct Pastors to observe diligently all the directions regarding this devotion which are given in the Baltimore *Ceremonial*.[48]

The bishop had achieved his goal, and it is interesting to note the reasons offered by the synod for the introduction of the Forty Hours: fostering an increase in faith among the Catholics of the diocese, and satisfaction for the offenses committed against the presence of Christ in the Eucharist. Both motivations echo the perennial themes that had characterized the devotion throughout history.

Scarcely had the synod concluded, when Neumann set to work making preparations for the inauguration of the Forty Hours. He composed a pamphlet containing "the history of the devotion, the manner of conducting it, and the prayers for the same ...,"[49] and drew up a schedule indicating the dates and churches in which it would be held.[50] He chose the Feast of Corpus Christi, Thursday, 26 May, as the opening day, and St. Philip Neri parish on Second and Queen Streets as the maiden church, in honor of that saint's efforts to propagate Eucharistic adoration. The *Catholic Herald* reported the momentous occasion as follows:

> We understand that on this day the Devotion of the Forty Hours will commence in St. Philip's church, Southwark. It will begin at six o'clock in the morning and will be continued through the remaining days of the week. The faithful are advised to visit that church to join in the devotion some time during its continuance.
>
> Solemn Pontifical Mass will be celebrated on the morning of Corpus Christi at 6 o'clock, by the Rt. Rev. Bishop Neumann,

which is to be the opening of the exercise. There will be a solemn High Mass on the same day at 10½ o'clock at which the Bishop is to preach. On the two succeeding days Solemn High Mass will be offered at 8½ o'clock, at which, as well as the evening service at 7½ o'clock, discourses suitable to the occasion will be delivered by clergymen specially invited. The Benediction of the Most Adorable Sacrament will be given each day after 8½ o'clock Mass, and after the evening discourse. Confessions will be heard every day, so as to afford an ample opportunity to the faithful of availing themselves of the benefit of a Plenary Indulgence, which is to be gained by all who, truly contrite, approach the Sacraments of Penance and Holy Communion, and pay a visit to the Most Adorable Sacrament within the time specified.[51]

Berger notes that the bishop "scarcely left the church during the three days of its continuance," and that "clergy and laity alike were deeply edified at his ardent love for Jesus in the Holy Eucharist."[52]

To augment the solemn and festive atmosphere of the devotions, Neumann would often lend his own vestments and monstrance, and whenever his schedule allowed, he would personally celebrate the opening Mass, or assist with the closing ceremonies.[53] The bishop continued to draw up the yearly schedules for the Forty Hours,[54] and contemporary accounts indicate that the exercises became a popular feature of Catholic life in the Diocese of Philadelphia. For example, a newspaper report from 1855 announced Neumann's presence at a Forty Hours in April, describing the devotion as "a religious practice which our holy Bishop first introduced into this diocese, and which is producing the most happy results in the renewed piety of our fellow Catholics."[55] Other prelates throughout the country took note of the success of the Forty Hours in Philadelphia, and soon followed Neumann's lead; first, his ecclesiastical patron, the archbishop of Baltimore, Francis Patrick Kenrick, in 1858, and shortly thereafter many more.[56] Soon there were few dioceses in America that did not celebrate this Eucharistic exercise as a popular and accustomed part of their devotional life.

THE MOTIVES FOR NEUMANN'S INITIATIVE

The Forty Hours was popular indeed, but it is important to see what lay behind Neumann's intention in making the devotion such a regular part of the spiritual life of his diocese, and by extension, the Catholic Church in the United States. One scholar has noted that "The importance of devotional expressions in the immigrant experience of community rested on three basic principles: devotions grew from a base of social co-operation; they became the symbolic meeting ground of doctrine, instruction and life; they provided for both institutional cohesion and ethnic diversity."[57] These three themes of social cooperation, doctrinal instruction, and institutional cohesion are all key to the introduction of the Forty Hours in Philadelphia. For example, Alfred Rush, C.Ss.R. observes: "To Neumann the Forty Hours was not merely the pious practice of making visits. To him it was the way of seeing that Catholic life in Philadelphia was rooted in the Eucharist; it was a parish mission on a small scale. It involved deeper instruction in Christian teaching by sermons, the frequentation of the sacraments, Mass and visits."[58] An important phrase in Rush's observation is "a parish mission on a small scale." For, in Neumann's eyes, the real challenges to the faith in Philadelphia consisted of a lack of catechesis, a poor record of sacramental participation, and a spirit that had been demoralized by what Vindex had called "unbrotherly persecution." Parish missions, which "provided a period of intense preaching, the possibility of receiving the sacraments of Penance and the Eucharist and the opportunity of getting religion and setting oneself straight with God as the Church had traditionally instructed" were growing in popularity as a response to the vast number of religiously lukewarm immigrants arriving on America's shores.[59] The bishop longed to give his people better instruction in the faith, to see them immersed in the sacramental life of the Church, and united by a bond of charity and perseverance that could withstand the challenges of poverty and persecution in a land that was still foreign to so many of them. The Forty Hours Devotion, no doubt, seemed tailored to his needs, and his genius consisted in giving the traditional Catholic devotion an enhanced evangelical thrust. It was, first of all, an entreaty for divine assistance, which Neumann valued above all—to put it somewhat crudely, it got people praying, in church, on their knees, asking for divine guidance. That was a good start. But in addition, it also exposed the faithful to sermons and instructions and encouraged their frequentation of the sacraments, especially the sacrament of Penance, the gateway to renewed participation in the life of the Church.[60] What Jay Dolan has written about the parish mission could just as well be said of the Forty Hours: "As an organizing force it strengthened the parish community; as a spiritual agent it not only awakened the piety of the people, but channeled this renewed enthusiasm into the local church...."[61] In short, the Forty Hours, with its emphasis on prayer and reparation, its tendency to build up the community and counteract the twin dangers of apathy and proselytism, seemed an appropriate response to the challenges that confronted Neumann as he began his episcopacy in Philadelphia.

Joseph Chinnici has remarked: "By 1884, due in some measure to the efforts of Neumann, eucharistic devotions had become staple elements in Catholic spiritual life, and national, provincial, and diocesan legislation would insure that they would remain a structural part of Catholic piety for generations to come. Neumann's fostering of eucharistic devotions and their consequent popularity may be taken as symbolic of the close link that emerged in the mid-nineteenth century between immigrant religion and devotional expressions."[62] Neumann's institution of the diocesan-wide Forty Hours was an attempt to arrive at a pastoral technique by which the faith could be nurtured among an immigrant flock both diverse and swelling, and he rightly surmised that the venerable devotion of the Forty Hours would achieve his purpose. In 1921, Pope Benedict XV observed, with regard to the bishop's life and work, that "wonderful results can spring from simple deeds. . . ." He went on "Ven. Neumann's activity was indeed admirable, not so much for the good he effected in the fleeting hour of the present, as for that which assured the benefit for future ages . . . . Even today the diocese which was so fortunate to have him as shepherd enjoys the fruits of his activity."[63] Which brings us back to that evening on 10 October 2000, and another (arch)bishop's visit to St. Philip Neri Church.

Cardinal Bevilacqua and the faithful gathered for that Jubilee Forty Hours could rejoice in the fact that, not only was the devotion introduced by St. John Neumann still being celebrated in the diocese in which he inaugurated it so many years before, but even more than that, the faith which he worked so hard to plant was alive and flourishing.

NOTES

1. *The Catholic Herald*, 8 Aug. 1844, 251.
2. Quoted by Christie L. Chicoine in "Forty Hours—A Mystery to Be Lived," *The Catholic Standard and Times*, 19 Oct. 2000, 3; reprint, *The National Catholic Register*, 12 Nov. 2000, 3.
3. Ibid.
4. *The Catholic Herald*, 26 May 1853, 82. The best biography of Neumann in English is Michael J. Curley, C.Ss.R, *Venerable John Neumann, C.Ss.R., Fourth Bishop of Philadelphia* (New York: Crusader Press, 1952).
5. Curley, 220. It was St. Philip Neri, as we shall learn in due course, who helped popularize the Forty Hours Devotion in Rome.
6. Chicoine, 3.
7. James Monti, in Benedict J. Groeschel, C.F.R., and James Monti, *In the Presence of Our Lord: The History, Theology, and Psychology of Eucharistic Devotion* (Huntington, In.: Our Sunday Visitor Press, 1996), 203.
8. Ibid.
9. Herbert Thurston, S.J., "Forty Hours Devotion" in *The Catholic Encyclopedia* (1909), vol. 6, 152.
10. Cited in Nathan Mitchell, O.S.B., *Cult and Controversy: The Worship of the Eucharist Outside Mass* (New York: Pueblo, 1982), 316. Jungmann noted that occasionally the cross was "buried" in the sepulcher instead of the Eucharist.
11. Mitchell, 312. For details of the Emperor Charles's depredations in Italy, especially the Sack of Rome, see Ludwig Pastor, *The History of the Popes from the Close of the Middle Ages*, ed. Ralph Francis Kerr, vol. 9 (St. Louis: Herder, 1950), 306-466. Also see E. R. Chamberlin, *The Sack of Rome* (London: B. T. Batsford, 1979).
12. Monti, 244.
13. Ibid; Mitchell, 312; Thurston, 151.
14. For further details on St. Anthony Zaccaria and the Barnabites, see Richard L. DeMolen, "The First Centenary of the Barnabites," in *Religious Orders*

of the Catholic Reformation: In Honor of John C. Olin on His Seventy-Fifth Birthday, ed. Richard L. DeMolen (New York: Fordham University Press, 1994), 58-96.

15. Thurston, 151. This concession of an indulgence to the Forty Hours is the first on record.

16. Ibid., 152. Also see Thurston's *Lent and Holy Week: Chapters on Catholic Observance and Ritual* (London: Longmans, Green & Co., 1914), 110-14.

17. Monti, 244.

18. *Divina disponente clementia* (17 Nov. 1560), quoted in Mitchell, 314.

19. *Graves et diuturnae* (25 Nov. 1592), noted in Monti, 245. Also see Thurston, "Forty Hours," 152. Clement would inaugurate the continuous cycle of observance on the First Sunday of Advent in the chapel of the Apostolic Palace.

20. Mitchell, 314.

21. *Manual for Forty Hours*, ed. Walter J. Schmitz, S.S. (Washington, D.C.: Catholic University of America Press, 1961), 5.

22. Summarized by Thurston, "Forty Hours," 152-53, who comments that the *Instructio Clementina* "stands almost alone among rubrical documents in the minuteness of detail into which it enters."

23. Mitchell, 316. Thurston observes that the Clementine guidelines were the foundation for nearly all future practices associated with Benediction and Exposition. "For example, the incensing of the Blessed Sacrament at the words "*Genitori Genitoque*" of the *Tantum Ergo*, the use of the humeral veil, and the giving of the Blessing with monstance, etc., are all exactly prescribed in section thirty-one of the same document" ("Forty Hours," 153).

24. For example, the 1577 Milanese regulations of St. Charles Borromeo are similar to the *Instructio Clementina* in numerous instances, e.g., exposition on the main altar, watchers, the use of candles, recitation of litanies, etc. (Monti, 245).

25. Mitchell, 317.

26. Ibid., 314.

27. Ibid., 313. Hence the Mass for Peace to be offered on the second day of the devotion.

28. Hugh J. Nolan, "Francis Patrick Kenrick, First Coadjutor-Bishop," in *The History of the Archdiocese of Philadelphia*, ed. James F. Connelly (Philadelphia: Archdiocese of Philadelphia, 1976), 127-31.

29. Nolan, 173-86. Also see Michael Feldberg, *The Philadelphia Riots of 1844: A Study in Ethnic Conflict* (Westport, Ct.: Greenwood Press, 1975), and Ray Allen Billington, *The Protestant Crusade, 1800-1860: A Study of the*

Origins of American Nativism (New York: Macmillan, 1938), 220-37.

30. *Catholic Herald*, 8 Aug. 1844, 251.

31. Alfred Rush notes that "the Forty Hours Devotion had been held in individual churches in Philadelphia as well as in other places of the United States before that time [the arrival in the city of Bishop Neumann]...." (Alfred C. Rush, C.Ss.R. and Thomas J. Donaghy, F.S.C., "The Saintly John Neumann and his Coadjutor Archbishop Wood," in *History of the Archdiocese of Philadelphia*, 209-70, at 216). The First Provincial Council of Baltimore (1829) had mandated that a *Book of Ceremonies* be issued; it appeared in 1833, and included the rubrics for the Forty Hours Devotion (Mitchell, 324). Ann Taves notes, in *The Household of Faith: Roman Catholic Devotions in Mid-Nineteenth Century America* (Notre Dame: University of Notre Dame Press, 1986), 25, that although no Catholic prayer books *prior* to 1840 included the Forty Hours Devotion, 63% of those printed *after* 1840 did.

32. "John Nepomucene Neumann's *Spiritual Journal*, Part I (1 Oct.–31 Dec. 1834)," ed. and trans. William Nayden, C.Ss.R., *Spicilegium Historicum Congregationis SSmi Redemptoris* 25 (1977): 321-418, at 349.

33. Ibid., 373.

34. "John Nepomucene Neumann's *Spiritual Journal*, Part III (1 Mar.–4 May 1835)," ed. and trans. William Nayden, C.Ss.R., *Spicilegium Historicum Congregationis SSmi. Redemptoris* 26 (1978): 291-352, at 338. For more information on Neumann's relationship with his friend Adalbert Schmidt, see Curley, 20, 23, 34-35, 41-43; for his dealings with the Prefect at the Prague Seminary, see Curley, 28.

35. Curley, 53.

36. Ibid., 73, 76.

37. W. Frean, C.Ss.R., *Blessed John Neumann: The Helper of the Afflicted* (Ballarat, Aus.: Majellan Press, 1963), 164.

38. Alphonsus Liguori, *Meditations on the Eucharist*, ed. Thomas M. Santa, C.Ss.R. (St. Louis: Liguori Press, 1997), 5, 7.

39. Curley, 97, 132.

40. Mother St. John Fournier of the Sisters of St. Joseph, writing to Neumann's nephew John Berger, quoted in Curley, 371.

41. Ibid., 204.

42. Ibid., 209. Within two years of Neumann's arrival in Philadelphia, schools were flourishing; enrollment grew from 500 students in 1852, to 5,000 by 1853, and 9,000 in 1856.

43. John A. Berger, C.Ss.R., *Life of Right Rev. John N. Neumann, D.D.*, trans.

Eugene Grimm, C.Ss.R., 2nd ed. (New York: Benziger, 1884), 373.

44. Ibid.

45. Curley, 220. Neumann had personal experience that exposition of the Blessed Sacrament offered opportunities for blasphemy. As a seminarian in Prague, he was present when a certain Count Levebrun "committed a sacrilege in full sight of the devout pilgrims" at a Forty Hours Devotion. The horrified Neumann notes that the "monster of debauchery" was arrested, but does not provide details on the nature of the profanation. See "John Neumann's *Spiritual Journal*, Part IV (5 May-21 July 1838)," ed. and trans. William Nayden, C.Ss.R., *Spicilegium Historicum Congregationis SSmi Redemptoris* 27 (1979): 81-152, esp. 91.

46. Berger, 373-74. Taves notes that the Forty Hours was "a means of expressing veneration for the Blessed Sacrament in the face of attacks on it by the church's 'enemies'" (31).

47. Curley, 52.

48. Archives of the Archdiocese of Philadelphia, *Statutes of the Fourth Diocesan Synod of Philadelphia, April 20-21, 1853*, No. 1 [English translation provided by the Archives].

49. Berger, 374.

50. Curley, 220. The author was unable to locate any extant copies of this manual.

51. *Catholic Herald*, 26 May 1853, 82.

52. Berger, 375.

53. Ibid.

54. The schedule for 1854 begins at St. Malachy's Church in the city of Philadelphia on New Year's Day, and continues throughout the year, including locations both near and far, such as Easton, Pottsville, Lebanon, and Carbondale (*Catholic Herald*, 29 Dec. 1853, 322).

55. *Catholic Instructor*, vol. 10 (31 March 1855). I thank the staff at the Philadelphia Archdiocesan Historical Research Center for locating a copy of this rare, and hitherto uncatalogued, periodical. Also see Berger, 375.

56. Cf. *American Catholic Historical Researches*, new series, 8, no. 3 (July 1911), 341, and Berger, 375.

57. Joseph Chinnici, O.F.M., *Living Stones: The History and Structure of Catholic Spiritual Life in the United States* (New York: Macmillan, 1989), 78.

58. Epilogue to his translation of *The Autobiography of St. John Neumann, C.Ss.R.* (Boston: St. Paul Books & Media, 1977), 45.

59. Jay P. Dolan, *Catholic Revivalism: The American Experience, 1830-1900*

(Notre Dame: Notre Dame University Press, 1978), 15. Neumann's own religious community, the Redemptorists, were enthusiastic proponents of the parish mission in Europe and the United States.

60. It is noteworthy in this regard to observe the stress laid by the *Catholic Herald* (29 Dec. 1853, 322) on the availability of confessors at the Forty Hours Devotions scheduled for 1854.

61. Dolan, 197.

62. *Living Stones*, 68-69.

63. Quoted in Curley, 400.

PART III

THEOLOGY AND SPIRITUALITY

"NO MORE POWERFUL FRIEND HAVE WE WITH GOD":[1]

THE MARIAN DEVOTION OF ST. JOHN NEUMANN

THOMAS A. THOMPSON, S.M.

In the Prayer for the Mass of St. John Neumann, we thank God for calling the saint "to a life of service, zeal, and compassion for the guidance of your people in the new world." Neumann's "service, zeal, and compassion" stemmed from his commitment to Christ and the Church and from his confidence in the intercession of the Virgin Mary and the saints. There are no writings by Neumann exclusively devoted to the Virgin Mary, and he never promoted one specific Marian title or devotion. However, his *Spiritual Journal*, written as a seminarian and during his early years of priestly ministry, reveals a confidence in Mary's intercession and in her assistance in his efforts to attain holiness. Similarly, his catechetical works contain distinctive references to Mary's intercession. As bishop of Philadelphia, he issued two pastoral letters (1854, 1855) on Pope Pius IX's proclamation of the doctrine of the Immaculate Conception; both speak of his devotion to Mary, and also tell of the reception of the definition and the consequences of that pronouncement in the lives of the faithful.

Before examining Neumann's writings, his expressions of devotion to the Virgin Mary and to the saints, as well as the zeal with which he promoted the devotion, should be viewed within the context of post-Tridentine Marian spirituality which was revived at the beginning of the nineteenth century. After the Enlightenment, elements of Tridentine spirituality took on new meaning in the nineteenth-century Catholic Restoration, the period that formed Neumann's theological and spiritual outlook.

I. POST-TRIDENTINE MARIAN DEVOTION

Events immediately after the Council of Trent (1545-63) encouraged a deep confidence in the Virgin Mary's powerful intercession on behalf of the Church. When Pope Pius V approved and granted indulgences to the rosary in 1569, he noted that the "Virgin Mary alone had crushed all heresies and the head of the serpent," and where the rosary was promoted, "the darkness of heresy receded and the light of faith reappeared."[2] The image of the Virgin Mary who had "crushed the head of the cunning serpent" (a reference to which Neumann alludes in his 1855 pastoral letter) instilled confidence in her victory over evil and was a forceful reminder that Marian devotion had both an apologetic and evangelizing role. The Church's confidence in Mary's power was strengthened by the victories of the Christian forces at Lepanto (1570) and at Vienna (1663), which were attributed to Mary, *Auxilium Christianorum*. After Lepanto, Pius V added *Auxilium Christianorum* to the Litany of Loreto and instituted the Feast of Our Lady of the Victory, later changed to Our Lady of the Rosary.[3]

Mary's intercessory power was prominently featured in the "official" Marian prayers–that is, those recommended and indulgenced by the Church. In 1569, the text for the *Ave Maria* appeared in the Roman Breviary; it became the principal and almost exclusive Marian prayer in the Western Church. The phrases in the second part of the prayer, the Church's addition to the Scriptural verses, well expressed Neumann's devotion: "Holy Mary, Mother of God" spoke of her privileged position before God; "pray for us" referred to Mary's intercessory power; "us, sinners" established the identity of those praying; "at the hour of our death" highlighted the most important moment of human existence. Similarly, Mary's intercessory power was highlighted in the Litany of Loreto (to which Neumann made frequent reference); its every invocation was followed by the request, "pray for us." The collects for the Commons of the Blessed Virgin

Mary invoked God's blessing "through the intercession of the Blessed Virgin Mary."

With the Virgin Mary, the saints were also intercessors with God. Celebration of the feasts of saints and other public displays of devotion became, especially in German-speaking countries close to Protestant areas, a distinguishing trait of post-Tridentine Catholicism. The Tridentine calendar of saints' days, which contained commemorations for about half of the days of the year, was quickly filled. To the 182 feast days in the Calendar of 1568, an additional 145 were added by 1900, with almost all of the new feasts taking precedence over Sunday.[4]

Missionary zeal, not unrelated to Marian devotion's evangelizing dimension, was another characteristic of Tridentine spirituality evident in Neumann's life. Although the Council of Trent said nothing about the missions, the post-Tridentine Church witnessed an outburst of missionary activity, so striking that one historian has termed it a *Missionskirche*.[5] The sixteenth and seventeenth centuries were the period of exploration and colonization of America and parts of Asia; this "first evangelization" (contrasted with the new evangelization) was spearheaded largely by the religious orders, especially the Franciscans and Jesuits. Created in 1622 to coordinate these activities, the Congregation for the Propagation of the Faith had jurisdiction over foreign lands as well as lands influenced by heresy.[6] Throughout the nineteenth century, the United States was considered a "mission territory," and Neumann was ordained for "the American mission."

By the nineteenth century, the Enlightenment and the events surrounding the French Revolution had taken their toll on many expressions of popular devotion. Natural religion and forms of rationalism weakened belief in revelation and fostered an attitude of indifference to religion. Strong forces of nationalism conspired to remove the Catholic community from the influence and authority of the papacy. In the Hapsburg empire, Josephinism,[7] which included elements of Gallicanism and Jansenism, promoted a "reform Catholicism" which advocated a liturgy based on that of the early Church and purged of devotional excrescence. The bonds with the

Church of Rome were weakened by, among other means, the elimination of monasteries and religious orders (the Jesuits were suppressed in 1773). In that "reform," practices associated with devotion to Mary and the saints disappeared in many places.

After the French Revolution, the Napoleonic wars, and the Congress of Vienna, the Church's task was to restore the bonds uniting the local churches with the papacy, to reestablish the monasteries and religious congregations that had been suppressed, and to revive the devotional life of the Church that in many areas had been uprooted. In Austria, the Jesuits were reestablished in 1819. There was a Marian character to the Restoration, especially evident in the number of Marian religious congregations founded in the nineteenth century.[8] Upon his return to Rome from exile on 24 May 1815, Pope Pius VII inserted *Auxilium Christianorum* into the liturgical calendar of the papal states. St. Clement Marie Hofbauer, "the Apostle of Vienna," who was instrumental in the restoration of the Redemptorists in 1820 in Austria, astonished the people of Vienna by reintroducing a practice that had fallen into desuetude—the rosary. In the words of his biographer, "he would warmly recommend the invocation of her powerful aid together with confidence in her intercession."[9]

The revival of the missionary spirit in nineteenth-century European Catholicism influenced Neumann's missionary vocation. In 1822, Pauline Jaricot founded the Pontifical Work for the Propagation of the Faith, which in Germany was known as the Francis Xavier Missions (Aachen) or Ludwig-Missionsverein (Munich). (John Neumann regarded St. Francis Xavier as one of his patrons). The Leopold Association was founded in Vienna in 1829 through the efforts of Frederick Résé (later Bishop of Detroit) to support the missions in Asia and to help the German Catholics in the United States. Neumann was attracted to the missions in America through the writings of Fr. Frederic Baraga, the one-time penitent of St. Clement Hofbauer.

In the nineteenth-century Catholic Restoration, there was a return to reading the works of an earlier period. Neumann records his efforts to acquire the works of Peter Canisius, Robert Bellarmine, Teresa of

Ávila, Lorenzo Scupoli, and Jean Croiset. The nineteenth century gave new importance to these "heroes" of the Counter-Reformation, and Neumann included them in his list of "patron saints."[10]

Popular devotions—to the Blessed Sacrament, to Mary and the saints—occupied a significant role in the nineteenth-century Church. They were not "private" nor in a peripheral position, as is the case since Vatican II where the liturgy is central. They were highly recommended and encouraged by the Church in various ways, especially through the granting of indulgences. They were regularly scheduled parish events, promoted through a network of confraternities, sodalities, "third orders," and religious congregations. These organizations provided support and identity with the parish community. Popular devotions had many advantages: they were flexible, participative, easily adapted to different occasions. They also provided an opportunity where one could perform good works on behalf of another individual. For example, the rosary could be prayed for the protection and health of the family, for the conversion of specific individuals, etc.

Neumann's life and ministry give evidence of a variety of different devotional practices. In his autobiography, written before he became a bishop, he spoke of the deep impression his parents' example made on him: "We were brought up in the old-fashioned school. Our parents were deeply Christian. . . . In my case there was needed at times the promise of a penny and something similar to bring me to Mass, rosary and Stations of the Cross."[11] As a youth, he went on pilgrimage to Marian shrines and visited churches dedicated to Mary.[12] He made a daily visit to the Blessed Sacrament, and as bishop of Philadelphia, he instituted, through the diocesan synod of 1853, the Forty Hours devotion throughout the diocese. His notes record his resolve to be faithful to the rosary, and, on the day he received the subdiaconate in New York, he promised to say the rosary daily in honor of Mary, "to secure her assistance in the discharge of my duties, and to ask her protection over my dear ones at home."[13] He also prayed the rosary for the conversion of sinners. "The recitation of the rosary for my stray sheep is always productive of abundant fruit."[14] He regularly prayed the Litany of Loreto, and, through the 1853 diocesan synod, he encouraged the singing of the Litany on Sunday and feast days before the principal Mass in all the churches of the diocese. Throughout his ministry, he was devoted to establishing confraternities—of the Blessed Sacrament, the Scapular, the Rosary, the Immaculate Heart of Mary. He believed that these organizations fostered "true piety among the faithful."[15] Of the ninety-two churches built while he was bishop of Philadelphia, twenty-seven were dedicated to the Virgin Mary, and three to the Immaculate Conception.[16] These practices sprang from deep convictions and sincere devotion to Mary and the saints, as can be seen in Neumann's writings.

II. THE *CATECHISM* AND THE *SPIRITUAL JOURNAL*

Throughout his ministry, Neumann promoted religious education. He was an energetic and successful catechist. His lifelong interest in catechetics stemmed from the example of teachers in his early schooling at Budweis and also in Prague. He acquired a copy of Peter Canisius's *Summa of Christian Doctrine*, Robert Bellarmine's catechism, as well as the *Catechism of the Council of Trent*.[17] Before leaving for America, he made a resolution to read daily from the Scriptures, from the *Imitation of Christ*, and from a catechetical work.

During the 1840s as a Redemptorist in Baltimore and Pittsburgh, in accord with the classical catechetical tradition, he wrote two versions of the catechism—the small and the large—for his German-speaking parishioners. The catechisms were reprinted many times. (By 1882, the "small Catechism" reached a thirtieth edition, and the intermediate or "large Catechism" reached eighteen editions.) At first, the catechisms appeared without his name. It was not until 1853 that the tenth edition of the *Katholischer Katechismus*—the large or "intermediate" catechism (hereafter *Catechism*)—bore his name, together with the notice that it had been approved by the Plenary Council of Baltimore in 1852.[18]

The divisions of Neumann's *Catechism* are similar to those of Canisius: 1. Faith (the Creed); 2. Hope (Commentary on the Our

Father and Hail Mary); 3. Charity (The Ten Commandments);
4. Christian Justification and the Four Last Things. Newman's
Catechism also had an appendix of prayers. In both Canisius's and
Neuman's catechism, the section on the Virgin Mary is found prin-
cipally in the explanation of the Creed and of the Hail Mary. In
Neumann's *Catechism*, the classical Marian doctrines of the divine
motherhood, perpetual virginity, and the Immaculate Conception
are clearly stated and strongly affirmed. But in addition, there are
several times when Neumann points to the intercession of Mary and
the saints, with original references that reveal his deep confidence in
such intercession.

Neumann's *Spiritual Journal* is a different type of religious
literature and was never intended for publication. It covers the period
1834-39, Neumann's last year of study in Prague, his journey to
America, and the first five years of his ministry as a priest. The work
is a "record of his interior life, an account of his spiritual and
emotional condition"[19] The form is a private diary, an account before
God of his efforts to attain humility, truthfulness, purity of soul—in
a word, to attain perfection. "Give me the graces which will aid me to
obtain the perfection you desire."[20] Virtually every entry concludes
with an invocation to the Virgin Mary, his patron saints, and guardian
angel. This record of constant struggle for virtue may be difficult to
understand in the twenty-first century where spirituality does not
usually stress the pursuit of virtue and perfection. However, earlier
works of spirituality were imbued with moral considerations.
Neumann had the works of the French Jesuit Jean Croiset (1656-
1738), who composed meditations for every day of the year. Each
meditation concluded with an "Exercise of Piety" in which the reader
was typically urged to enter into the way of humility, to renounce self-
love, to practice mortification.[21] The spiritual life was a struggle to
resist the world, to acquire virtue, all to be judged in the light of
death. He was also guided by Lorenzo Scupoli's *The Spiritual Combat*
in which the spiritual life was presented as a constant struggle against
the forces of evil within onself. Another spiritual guide was the *Life* of
St. Teresa of Ávila, whom he asked to be his "advocate in this
important matter of my devotions and reflections, in acquiring a

genuine sense of contrition for my sins."

Here follow assembled references to Mary and the saints as found first in the *Catechism* and then in the *Spiritual Journal*. They deal with the intercession of Mary, the intercession of the saints, the virtues of Mary, and, lastly, the titles and the way Neumann expressed his relation to Mary. This comparison of his public works—the *Catechism*—with his private diary—the *Spiritual Journal*— reveal a great consistency between what Neumann taught and what he strived to attain in his personal life. That Neumann so sincerely practiced what he preached is no small sign of his holiness.

1. THE INTERCESSION OF MARY

Nineteenth-century moral treatises contained an exhortation to invoke Mary's intercession to overcome sin and acquire virtue. In a work of moral theology, possibly known by Neumann, there is a significant reference to the power of Mary's intercession to attain virtue: "The Church urges and preaches devotion and filial invocation of the Virgin Mary as the most efficacious way to perfection. . . . Who could possibly think that the intercession which she offers to her son on our behalf could be rejected or made void?"[22] In the *Catechism*, Neumann's confidence in Mary's intercession appears in his comments on the *Hail Mary*. It is, he said, both a "prayer of praise, and a prayer of petition." Why, he asks, did the Church add the second part to the prayer (the invocation after the verses from Scripture)? "To implore her, as the *powerful intercessor*, for the conversion of sinners, for the dying, because these most need the grace of God to be saved."[23] When explaining the virtue of hope, he asks: "On whom, after God, can we place our hope?" The response: "On the Blessed Virgin Mary, because, through her intercession, she can obtain all things from God."[24] The appendix of prayers in the *Catechism* contains several references to Mary's intercessory role. Neumann's version of the ancient Marian prayer *Sub tuum praesidium* concluded with an ending common to German-speaking countries: "Deliver us from all evil, O Glorious and Blessed Virgin. O Lady, our Advocate, our intercessor. Reconcile us to your Son; recommend us to your Son; place us before your Son."

This confidence in Mary's intercession was also evident in the *Spiritual Journal.*

> Holy Mother of God, Mary my Patroness, do not refuse to intercede for me. My self-centeredness, my apathy, my conceit befoul my prayers. Yours, on the contrary are humble, fervent and conform to God's will. Put yours in the place of mine (30 Nov. 1834).

> May heaven grant me the grace of an ardent devotion to Our Blessed Mother. . . . Help me, Queen of Angels and Heaven! I shall always pray to You since You are all-powerful with my Lord. I shall turn to you today and every day of my life until I die (4 Oct.1834).

> I have prayed to Our Blessed Mother for that grace and She did not fail me (5 Oct. 1834).

> Holy Mary, pray for me, for you are blessed among all in heaven and on earth. Your blessed Son, my Savior, never ignores your prayers (28 Nov. 1834).

> Holy Mary, most powerful patroness, bid Your Son to hear my pleas. Amend them, should they be marred by my sins; You whose every prayer is perfect! I offer Him all that I have, all I have received from Him, no matter how soiled and damaged by my sins. Cleanse my soul and will and present them both to Him (13 Dec. 1834).

Mary's assistance is invoked when receiving the sacraments of Penance and Holy Communion. The *Catechism* states that, in the preparation for confession, "we should especially recommend ourselves . . . to the Blessed Virgin, who is the mother of mercy and the refuge of sinners, to the angel guardian and to our patron saints." After Communion, "We should ask him [Jesus] for his love, for great devotion to the Blessed Virgin, and for final perseverance."[25] Similarly, in the *Spiritual Journal,* Neumann frequently asks Mary's assistance when receiving these two sacraments:

You know how we should best prepare ourselves for holy Communion (20 Dec. 1834).

Mary, mother of grace, . . . I want to give you the devotion you granted me that I might receive these two sacraments worthily (23 Nov. 1834).

Holy Mary, tomorrow [Saturday] is the day dedicated to you by our Church and I shall go to confession. Intercede for me so that in your honor I may properly receive that sacrament (17 Nov. 1834).

Holy Mary, Mother of God, intercede for me that God may forgive the sins I have committed today, and those of my past and of my future (13 Nov. 1834).

2. THE INTERCESSION OF THE SAINTS

In the *Spiritual Journal*, Mary is invoked frequently together with Neumann's guardian angel and patron saints. Neumann's belief was that we are joined to the angels and the saints in a vivid and strong communion, and they are our patrons, intercessors, protectors, friends before God. The *Catechism* says that God created the angels, so "that they might worship, love, and serve Him and *protect* us."[26] In turn, "We owe them respect on account of their presence, gratitude on account of their benefits, and confidence in their protection."[27]

In the explanation of the Creed, Neumann speaks of the Church and the Communion of Saints. The Church (9th article) is defined in post-Tridentine style as "the gathering of justified Christians, who, under their visible head, the Roman pontiff, confess one faith and celebrate the sacraments."[28] This definition is balanced by an organic and relational concept of the Communion of Saints (10th article), which in some respects anticipates twentieth-century descriptions of the Church. "All the members of the Communion of Saints—the saints, the souls in purgatory, and those on earth—form 'one mystical body, with Jesus Christ as head.'" We are bound to the saints in a loving relationship: "The saints love and pray for us to God that He may be gracious to us in body and soul, and we honor and love them as friends of God and ask their intercession for us."[29] The celebration of Holy Mass includes the saints in heaven, the souls in purgatory, the Church on earth. "We show our friendship with the souls in purgatory as we pray to God for them, and offer good works, especially the Holy Sacrifice of the Mass."[30] Far from detracting from God's worship, devotion to the saints is pleasing to God who also regards the saints as friends: "we honor them [the saints] not with the highest honor which is due to God alone, but we honor and love them on account of their sanctity and because God himself honors them as his friends." We invoke the saints for their help and intercession, not directly from them alone, but that "as friends of God, they would pray for us poor sinners before God that he might help us."[31]

In the *Spiritual Journal*, there are many references to the intercession of Mary and the saints and to his "patron saints."

> O Mary, Mother of my Lord Jesus Christ, in union with all the saints and angels, pray for me that I may become a perfect disciple of Jesus (23 Dec. 1834).

> My God, help me through the intercession of Mary and all the saints.[32]

Neumann frequently refers to the intercession of his patron saints.

> How I long to be like the saints I have chosen to be my patrons. You teach me, divine Master, what I ought to do in every case. . . . My holy patrons, heavenly brothers of mine, pray constantly for me and for all the faithful, living and dead (26 Dec. 1834).

> St. John [Nepomucene], give me the virtues I need to be a worthy priest. St. Francis Xavier, intercede with your Lord that He may grant me the strength of soul to be a missionary. St. Ignatius, pray

for me that God may give me the wisdom I need. St. Aloysius, keep me from all sin. St. Teresa, intercede for me that I may receive from God the grace of true interior devotion, of recollection, of spiritual union and vision. St. Joseph, obtain for me the gift of God's love (2 Jan. 1835).

3. THE VIRGIN MARY, MODEL OF VIRTUES

Moral theology referred to Mary as the "eminent model of virtues," but cultural factors have influenced the listing of virtues. Eighteenth-century moral and devotional treatises gave prime importance to humility and purity. In the *Catechism*, after listing the theological and moral virtues, Neumann lists the "seven principal virtues, those opposed to the seven vices." The first was humility, followed by generosity, purity, love, moderation, patience, zeal. These seven virtues are principal in the sense that they are opposed to the capital sins and contain all the other virtues.[33] In that spirit, Neumann viewed humility as Mary's principal virtue. To the *Catechism*'s question "Why does the Catholic Church honor Mary more than the other saints and angels?," Neumann replied: "Because the Blessed Virgin Mary exceeded all in her humility and holiness, and because Jesus Christ has elevated her as His mother above the angels and saints."[34]

In the *Spiritual Journal*, Newman frequently alluded to the humility of Mary in relation to his own desire to acquire humility and other virtues.

Mother of God, perfect exemplar of humility, I beg you to plead my cause (22 Dec. 1834).

O Mary, Mother of mercy, whose help I so sensibly experienced today, pray to thy Divine Son for me, a poor sinner; beg Him to make me humble! Oh, how humble thou wast! Behold, my dear heavenly Mother, how gladly I would devote myself to thy Divine Son that His will may also be mine. But my pride, my self-esteem, my vanity, are always against me.[35]

My heavenly Mother, intercede for me with your Son that He may grant me the grace of humility and purity, that He may strengthen me in my struggle with intemperance (25 Dec. 1834).

Holy Mary, I implore you, guide me along the path of humility. Intercede for me that the Holy Spirit may fill me with an ardent love for Jesus, my Savior, so that this most important business succeed for me (19 Dec. 1834).

Dear Mother of God, pray for me. I would be your humble servant all the days of my life (14 Oct. 1834).

In the *Spiritual Journal*, Neumann called upon Mary under a number of different titles, drawn in large measure from the Litany of Loreto or from liturgical hymns: Mother of God and my Mother, Purest of Virgins, Holy Mother, Mother of Divine Grace, Mother of Grace, Queen of all Saints, Queen of Angels and Saints, Queen of the Universe, Consolation of Sinners, Comforter of the Afflicted, Mirror of Justice, Star of the Sea, my patroness, Holy Mary, Mother of God, Spouse of the Holy Spirit, Daughter of the Heavenly Father. However, rarely did Neumann describe his relation to Mary in terms of a mother-child relation. In his own humility, and in imitation of Mary who designated herself as servant, he referred to his relation to Mary as that of a servant or slave.

Dearest Mother Mary, you are the sturdy pillar that supports me in my prayers. For all that you ask of your Son, He will most swiftly grant you. Should then my prayers deserve to be placed before Him, do not reject your slave who would love you as much as you deserve (15 Nov. 1834).

My dearest Mother Mary, I make bold to place before you once more my resolution: to be your slave (3 Dec. 1834).

Two invocations that have great importance in Neumann's writings are Mother of Mercy and Refuge of Sinners. Mother of

Mercy is found in the prayer "Hail, Holy Queen." (The *Catechism* contains an amplified version of this prayer "to obtain Mary's powerful protection," attributed to St. Alphonsus de Liguori.) The second invocation, "Refuge of Sinners," evokes a tradition, widespread in German Marian piety, of "seeking refuge" in the Virgin Mary.[36] In the *Catechism*, the Marian invocation at Morning Prayer is "Most Blessed Virgin Mary, guard me under your protective mantle, Holy Guardian Angel, all my patron saints, stay by me." Similarly, the last words of Evening Prayer were: "Mary, my mother, bless me and take me under your protection. My holy patrons, pray for me." Included in the prayers is the inscription on the Miraculous Medal (1830), which, in the German version, refers to the "seeking refuge": "O Mary conceived without sin, pray for us who take refuge in you." The *Catechism* states that, before confession, we should seek God's enlightenment, assistance, and grace, and also the help of the Virgin Mary, "who is the Mother of Mercy and the Refuge of Sinners."[37] The two invocations appear in the *Spiritual Journal*.

Holy Mother Church calls you refuge of sinners (20 Dec. 1834).

Holy Mother of my Lord, Refuge of Sinners, Mother of God, intercede once more for me with your Son . . . (14 Jan. 1835).

Mother of Mercy, my conscience bothers me because of all the sins I have committed (25 Nov. 1834).

Our holy Church, established on earth by your Son, calls you the Refuge of Sinners, and she is infallible (1 Feb. 1835).

III. THE PASTORAL LETTERS ON THE IMMACULATE CONCEPTION (1854-55)

In 1846, the American bishops had chosen the Virgin Mary under the title of the Immaculate Conception as the patroness of the United States, and in 1849 had petitioned Pope Pius IX to proclaim the Immaculate Conception as a dogma of faith. Bishop Neumann was one of the five American bishops invited to attend the proclamation of the doctrine of the Immaculate Conception in 1854. It was, as he later wrote, "an honor and a happiness which my words cannot describe, but for which I return and forever will return humble thanks to our Lord Jesus Christ."[38] Before leaving for Rome, he issued a pastoral letter to the people of Philadelphia on the upcoming proclamation, and on returning in 1855, he issued another letter.[39] The letters are formal ecclesial documents, containing long passages of Scripture and lacking in the personal style of the *Catechism* or the *Spiritual Journal*. They do reflect the same confidence in Mary's intercession as found in earlier writings, now expressed in a pastoral exhortation. The letters reveal Neumann's joy that the "pious belief" would now be among the doctrines of the Church, and, at the same time, they indicate how the proclamation was received, the role of dogmatic pronouncements on the Church's life, and their role in fostering Marian devotion.

Both pastoral letters, in addition to explaining the significance of the proclamation, also have a strong moral tone; they were an opportunity to exhort the people to accept their Christian responsibilities. The 1854 letter announced the Jubilee which Pope Pius IX declared, and Neumann invited the diocese "to join the faithful in every part of the world, to unite their supplications before the throne of God by prayer, fasting, alms, and deeds and other good works to obtain from Him . . . those temporal and heavenly succors of which the Church was seldom, if ever, more in need." The provisions for gaining the Jubilee indulgence were given: the reception of the sacraments of Penance and the Holy Eucharist, fasting, and the giving of alms, visits to churches to pray for the Church, the pope, "for the extirpation of heresy, for peace and concord among Christian princes, for the peace and unity of the whole Christian people." The provisions were generous, especially those related to the visiting of churches, and reflect Neumann's own devotional practice of paying visits to the Blessed Sacrament in different churches. At the same time, Neumann reminded the people of Philadelphia that the fulfilling of the conditions of the indulgence avail nothing, if not accompanied by conversion: "Fly from evil company. . . . Beware of secret societies. Trust not their agents; too often only false brethren in disguise. . . . Frequent the church and not the taverns. Banish from your homes dangerous books. Teach your children to pray, and never to be ashamed of their religion." Similarly, in the letter of 1855, after the proclamation of the doctrine of the Immaculate Conception, Neumann noted that since the doctrine referred to Mary's freedom from original sin, it was opportune to speak of the importance of the sacrament of baptism, the means by which original sin is remitted, and the "contemporary disregard for sin."

The letters also include indications of Neumann's understanding of the process leading to the dogmatic definition. The 1854 letter relates that one of the purposes of the Jubilee was "to obtain the grace of the Holy Spirit in giving a decision on the subject of the Immaculate Conception." He continued, that, although not yet a doctrine of faith, the Immaculate Conception was being investigated with "a zeal probably never surpassed in former ages . . . by many of the most gifted and holy men now living . . . with such a magnificent outlay of ancient and modern learning, of profound arguments, and soul stirring eloquence . . . as to leave not only the most devout clients of Mary, but every unbiased mind, convinced" of the truth of this "ancient and beautiful belief." The letter of 1855 speaks of the great joy that the declaration has brought to the Church. The doctrine was first investigated by individuals who were "learned, scholarly, wise," and their decision was then ratified by the certitude which alone the Lord Jesus can give. "We have humanly speaking the strongest guarantee imaginable for the most sure truth of any and every decree issued in the name and by the authority of him who is the Chief Pastor."

Similar to many post-Tridentine documents, the pastoral letters described the dire situation in which the Church found itself and exhorted the faithful to pray for Mary's intercession and assistance. In the world, there are "calamities of every kind that afflict His [Christ's] Church, the Vicar of Christ partaking in the sufferings of his beloved Master." Yet, despite the sufferings, the Church continues, even thrives. The missions and the "glorious example of conversions" are given as indications of its success (1854). The hostility of the forces of evil are described in apocalyptic terms: "Should the Dragon of Impiety . . . still continue to make war on God and on His Church . . . to whom can we turn with more confidence than to His 'divine' mother whom the Church has never invoked in vain" (1854). The next year's letter contained the same exhortation to turn to Mary. "To whom, with more reason, propriety, confidence and veneration can we turn than to a being, whom, from all eternity God has so loved and honored—the advocate of Eve, and therefore the Refuge of all her children. . . . At the same time, the compassionate protector of all his descendents . . . no more powerful friend have we with God."

The actual explanation of the Immaculate Conception occupies a relatively small place in the two letters. There are strong, unequivocal statements on Mary's absolute sinlessness, drawn from the Church's tradition and the universal testimony of the Catholic world. St. Augustine's words on never associating Mary with sin are cited as the reason the Council of Trent did not wish to include Mary under the universal condemnation of original sin. Significant sources include the verse adapted from the Canticle of Canticles, found in the Roman Breviary, which Neumann cites with an additional phrase apparently intended to strengthen its force: "You are all beautiful, O Virgin Mary, and no stain of sin is in thee, *and no stain of sin was ever nor will be in thee.*" Neumann attributes to St. Augustine the words, "The flesh of Jesus is the flesh of Mary." (The words have now been identified as coming from a medieval manuscript on the Assumption by Pseudo-Augustine.[40]) Another quotation is from St. Cyril: "Who ever heard that an architect built a glorious dwelling for himself, and at once gave it over to be possessed by his most cruel and hated enemy." Neumann concludes with a strong affirmation of Mary's freedom from sin, followed by a series of invocations to Mary (reminiscent of the style of St. Cyril's Marian Homily at Ephesus). "How can it be that the God of all purity, to whom even the least shadow of sin is an object of eternal abhorrence, would have suffered His Virgin Mother to be, even for an instant, such an object in His Sight. Mary could never be subject to sin: she who was the Spouse of the Holy Spirit, the Ark of the New Covenant, the Mediatrix of

Mankind, the Terror of the Powers of Darkness, the Queen of all the heavenly hosts."

Neumann's purpose in outlining the process by which the declaration was made was to instill a certitude leading to a "confidence which none but the true children of the Church can experience or even conceive." This confidence should make one more devoted to the Church and should result in a "filial obedience" to the Church, a growth in charity (Jn 14). The sense of confidence was increased by uniting oneself to the universal testimony of the Church throughout the ages. It was also an invitation to draw strength from the testimony of the apostles, the evangelists, the martyrs, the heroic confessors of the faith, the Fathers and Doctors, to more closely identify oneself with this band of witnesses. This affirmation and identification should instill a pride "never to be ashamed," and "always ready to reply in the spirit of St. Hilary to the Emperor Constantius, 'I am a Catholic; I am a Christian; I will not be a heretic.'"

Neumann's pastoral letters reflect a stance common in the nineteenth century towards the Church's definition of doctrine. It is not so much the particular content of the doctrine that was being proclaimed which touched the lives of the believer. Rather, the Church's definitive pronouncement of a doctrine, after consultation and investigation, strengthened the Catholic's belief in "objective, immutable truths" and in the "sacraments and the sacrifice of the Mass, as well as in the keeping of the Commandments."[41]

Lastly, the letters were a call for devotion to Mary, and an exhortation to parents to "first devoutly learn, and then teach your children from their earliest years, to cultivate true, filial piety towards her [Mary], letting no day pass without repeating the Archangel's salutation (1854). To the confraternities and religious societies, he recommended the cultivation of this spirit of filial love and reverence for Mary, the Immaculate, whom says St. Anselm, God has made His Mother that she should be the Mother of all" (1855).

⁂

Expressions of Marian devotion do not exist in a vacuum. They are embedded in a theological outlook and a culture of devotion, and they reflect that culture's strengths and weaknesses. Counter-Reformation and nineteenth-century Catholicism presented an image of Mary almost exclusively as powerful intercessor, but, in many respects, a person who was distant and lofty, characterized by great humility and purity.[42] These images are reflected in Neumann.

Neumann's early writings were simple, direct, and unaffected, and they reflect the deep intensity and seriousness with which he invoked Mary for assistance in living the Christian life, and with which he proposed Marian devotion as an integral part of Catholic life. The pastoral letters of 1854 and 1855 offered an occasion to explain the Immaculate Conception, but were also an exhortation to have confidence in all the Church's teaching, to take more seriously one's Christian responsibilities, and adopt some practice of Marian devotion. Today when some expressions of Marian devotion seem to be unrelated to daily conduct, Neuman's example is instructive.

Neumann's image of Mary stresses the power of Mary's intercession. However, this intercession was not invoked for material advantage; rather it was sought as part of the life of Christian virtue. His pastoral recommendations to invoke Mary's powerful intercession were intended to help his people in living their commitment to Christian holiness. His devotion was ecclesial, in the sense that it was based on the prayers and practices recommended by the Church. Marian devotion gave hope in an atmosphere that spoke of the pervasiveness of sin and emphasized constant striving. Mary's victory over sin and evil was the source of evangelical zeal. His presentation of Mary and the saints as intercessors and friends before God communicated a sense of the Communion of Saints. The sincerity of his Marian dedication is evident in his practices of devotion, in his writings, and, most convincingly, in his own life. To the people of Philadelphia, he recommended the virtues of Mary's Magnificat—humility, faith, and obedience. These, he said, were the "foundation of her glory," the way in which she repaired the "pride, unbelief, and disobedience" which brought about the downfall of our first parents. Humility, faith, and obedience were also the virtues so apparent in his own life.

NOTES

1. From Neumann's "Pastoral Letter on the Immaculate Conception of 1 May 1855." This was the second of two pastoral letters that Neumann wrote on the Immaculate Conception, the first being that of 4 Nov. 1854. First published in *The Catholic Herald*, 9 Nov. 1854, and 3 May 1855, and in *The Catholic Instructor*, 5 May 1855, these letters have been reprinted, and are now most readily accessible, in *Social Justice Review* 76 (Mar.-Apr. 1985): 60-64, and (May-June 1985): 86-90.

2. Pius V, 17 Sept. 1569, "Consueverunt" in *Le saint rosaire: les enseignements pontificaux et conciliaires* (Paris: Desclée, 1960), app. I, p. 4.

3. "Rosaire," in *Dictionnaire de spiritualité*, vol. 13, col. 960.

4. P. Jounel, "The Veneration of the Saints," in *The Liturgy and Time: The Church at Prayer*, vol. 4 (Collegeville: Liturgical Press, 1986), 125.

5. Hubert Jedin's term. Cf. John W. O'Malley, *Trent and All That: Renaming Catholicism in the Early Modern Era* (Cambridge, Ma.: Harvard University Press, 2000), 66.

6. Cf. Alfred C. Rush, "Saint John Neumann, Catechist," *Spicilegium Historicum Congregationis SSmi Redemptoris* 32, no. 1 (1984): 210; hereafter Rush.

7. In his autobiography, Neumann noted his rejection of the Josephinist views of some of his teachers at Prague: see *The Autobiography of St. John Neumann, C.Ss.R.*, ed. and trans. Alfred C. Rush (Boston: St. Paul Books and media, 1977) 28; hereafter *Autobiography*.

8. The church historian Roger Aubert wrote: "The intensity of the piety connnected with Mary in the nineteenth century was also demonstrated by the names which religious congregations adopted when they were founded in this period. Between 1802 and 1898, not a single year passed that did not witness the founding of one or more congregations devoted to the Virgin Mary, with especially numerous foundations in the decades 1830-40 and 1850-60" ("The Growth of Piety," ch. 15 in *The Church in the Age of Liberalism*, vol. 8 of *The History of the Church*, eds. H. Jedin and J. Dolan [New York: Crossroad, 1981], 225-26).

9. "He had nothing more at heart than to diffuse this devotion to the Blessed Virgin; and so, in the pulpit as in the confessional, he would warmly recommend the invocation of her powerful aid together with confidence in her intercession" (Michael Haringer, *Life of Clement Marie Hofbauer* [Baltimore: Pustet, 1883], 188).

10. The nineteenth-century church historian Ludwig von Pastor, in his *History of the Popes*, singled out four representatives of the Catholic Reformation: Ignatius Loyola, Charles Borromeo, Philip Neri, and Teresa of Ávila. Cf. Ludwig von Pastor, *Charakterbilder katholischer Reformatoren des XVI Jahrhunderts* (Freiburg im Breisgau: Herder, 1924).

11. *Autobiography*, 22.

12. As a student, he traveled to the Marian churches at Pisek, and in 1835, by way of clarifying his decision to go America, he made a pilgrimage to the Marian shrine in Strakonitz. After the visit, Newman wrote in his diary, "To thee, O my Mother, Our Lady of Podsrp and Skocic, I owe much. I love thee with my whole heart" (Johann Berger, *The Life of the Right Rev. John N. Neumann*, 2nd ed. [New York: Benziger, 1884], 102; hereafter Berger). While in Europe for the proclamation of the dogma of the Immaculate Conception, he visited the Marian shrines of Loreto and Altötting: see "Neumann, Johann," in *Marienlexikon*, eds. R. Baumer and L. Scheffczyk (St. Ottilien: EOS Verlag, 1992), 4:603.

13. Berger, 152.

14. Berger, 197.

15. Berger, 163, 218, 376.

16. "Neumann, Johann," in *Marienlexikon*, 4:603.

17. Rush, 191.

18. Johann Nep. Neumann, *Katholischer Katechismus, Verfasst von Johann Nep. Neumann, Bischof von Philadelphia, Zehnte Auflage, Mit Genehmigung des National Conciliums von Baltimore* (Baltimore: Murphy, 1853); hereafter *Katechismus*. All quotations from this work are the author's translations.

19. An English translation by William Nayden of the French entries of "John Nepomucene Neumann's Spiritual Journal" is published in four parts in *Spicilegium Historicum Congregationis SSmi Redemptoris* 25(1977): 321-418 (Part 1 Oct.1-Dec. 31, 1834); 26 (1978): 9-74 (Part 2: Jan.1-Feb. 28, 1835), 291-352 (Part 3: Mar. 1-May 4, 1835); 27 (1979): 81-152 (Part 4: May 5, 1835-July 21, 1838). The quote is from Nayden's introduction to Part I of the *Spiritual Journal*, 322.

20. Michael J. Curley, *Venerable John Neumann, C.Ss.R., Fourth Bishop of Philadelphia* (Washington, D.C.: Catholic University of America Press, 1952), 33; hereafter Curley.

21. Paul Mech, "Croiset, Jean," *Dictionnaire de Spiritualité*, vol. 2, part 2, cols. 2557-60.

22. Joseph Stapf, *Epitome theologiae moralis* (Innsbruck, 1842-43), vol. 2, 424.

23. *Katechismus*, 47.

24. Ibid., 40.

25. *Katechismus*, 100.

26. Ibid., 13.

27. From a later edition of the *Katechismus*, translated and "re-arranged and enlarged by a member of the Congregation of the Most Holy Redeemer." John Nepomucene Neumann, *Intermediate Catechism of the Catholic Religion* (Baltimore, Kreuzer, 1884).

28. *Katechismus*, 30.

29. Ibid., 34.

30. Ibid.

31. Ibid., 56.

32. Berger, 209.

33. *Katechismus*, 137.

34. Ibid., 46.

35. From the *Spiritual Journal*, as cited in Berger, 24.

36. Moral theologians, such as Johann Michael Sailer (1751-1832), J. B. Hirscher (1788-1865), and Ferdinand Probst (1816-99), stressed Mary's role as Refuge of Sinners as an antidote against the natural theology of the Enlightenment. See Johannes B. Torelló, "Die Anrufung 'Refugium peccatorum' in der Literatures des XIX Jhdt.," in *De Cultu Mariano Saeculis XIX-XX* ([Kevalaer, 1987] Rome: Pontificia Academia Mariana Internationalis, 1991), 2:501-13.

37. *Katechismus*, 105.

38. Curley, 239.

39. See note 1 above.

40. Cf. "Pseudo-Augustinus," in *Marienlexikon* 5:367. It is found in a work that Neumann may have possessed: Jean Croiset, *La Vie de la Vierge*, 25, in *La Vie de Notre Seigneur . . . .et Celle de la Très Sainte Vierge Marie* (Lyon: Bruyset, 1732).

41. Robert Appleton, "Dogma," *The Catholic Encyclopedia* (1909), vol. 5, 91.

42. A description of the image of Mary in Counter-Reformation spirituality, not written with Neumann in mind, but applicable, is the following: "the typical figure of the Counter-Reformation, that is militant and victorious, as well as the image Queen of Heaven elevated into glory and endowed with god-like privileges. This victorious and militant image expresses tension and controversy in the wake of the Protestant Reformation, and the hope to overcome it victoriously. Mary is victorious over evil and all attacks against the true believers. Her ultimate qualification in the combat is her role as Queen of Heaven. This combination of a militant, victorious and queenly woman again makes of Mary a powerful figure, remote as person but very present as helper, intercessor and mediator" (Johann G. Roten, S.M., "Woman Made Culture: Mary between Religion and Culture," *Ephemerides Mariologicae* 51, no. 4 (Oct.-Dec. 2001): 325-44, at 337-38. At the end of the nineteenth century, St. Thérèse of Lisieux complained of sermons on Mary which presented her removed from daily life: "They [sermons] show her to us as unapproachable, but they should present her as imitable, bringing out her virtues, saying that she lived by faith just like ourselves. . . . It's good to speak about her privileges, but it's necessary, above all, that we can imitate her" (*Derniers Entretiens* 23.8.6; 23.8.7).

"ST. TERESA SAYS SHE NEVER FAILED TO RECEIVE WHATEVER SHE ASKED OF YOU!":[1]
ST. JOSEPH IN THE LIFE AND MINISTRY OF JOHN N. NEUMANN, C.SS.R.

JOSEPH F. CHORPENNING, O.S.F.S.

It is a commonplace in the history of Catholic devotional life that St. Teresa of Ávila (1515-82) played a pivotal role in the popularization of veneration of St. Joseph, both in the Hispanic world and in Western Europe, in the period following the Council of Trent (1545-63). Teresa disseminated devotion to St. Joseph by her encomium of the saint in her autobiography, *The Book of Her Life* (begun in 1562 and completed in 1565), by naming for him twelve of the seventeen monasteries she founded in Spain during her lifetime, and by popularizing his image by installing paintings and sculptures of the saint in all her foundations. These initiatives, as well as the continuation—after Teresa's death in 1582—of her apostolate of propagating devotion to St. Joseph by her Discalced Carmelite nuns and friars, are well documented.[2] There is, however, an instance of Teresa's influence, from the nineteenth century, in promoting veneration of St. Joseph that has been overlooked: the decisive role that her testimony to the saint's powerful intercession had in sparking the warm devotion to St. Joseph of St. John Nepomucene Neumann, C.Ss.R. (1811-60), fourth bishop of Philadelphia, during his seminary days in Prague.

Neumann's *Spiritual Journal* (*Mon Journal*), begun in 1834 during the final year of his theological studies at Prague, and continued almost until he became a Redemptorist novice in 1840, offers ample testimony to the significant place that Teresa occupied in his spiritual life and development. Neumann turned to Teresa for guidance and friendship at a critical moment during his seminary formation: he carefully read and outlined her autobiography, appropriated her teaching on loving communion with God in prayer and good works done in His service, and invoked her heavenly intercession for assistance on his spiritual journey. This paper chronicles a further—and heretofore neglected—aspect of Teresa's impact on Neumann by examining his discovery of the person and mission of St. Joseph in Teresa's *Life*, chapter 6, his subsequent veneration of St. Joseph and its principal themes, and the evident presence of St. Joseph from this point forward in Neumann's life and ministry. In the *Spiritual Journal*, Neumann testifies as to the origin, and offers the fullest expression, of his devotion to St. Joseph, and, for this reason, it is the most important primary source for the present study.

Neumann and the Teresian Paradigm of Devotion to St. Joseph

Neumann found his final two years of preparation for priesthood ordination (1833-35) at the archdiocesan seminary associated with the theological faculty at the University of Prague to be very difficult for various reasons.[3] One of the major challenges with which Neumann wrestled at Prague was the lack of a good spiritual director. Perhaps for this reason he began, in October 1834, to write his *Spiritual Journal*. "This remarkable day-to-day account of the soul of John Neumann is sometimes called a diary, though it is far more than that; it was what ascetics call an examination of conscience, undertaken for ascetical purposes to enable him to keep account of his spiritual progress as the days wore on. Nowhere in his writings is there such a remarkable close-up of the mind and heart and spirit of this man as in these pages."[4] In the absence of a director, Neumann looked for spiritual guidance, as his *Journal* witnesses, from the writings of the great spiritual masters. Primary among these was St. Teresa's *Life*, which Neumann refers to as her *Confessions*, and which he, as a gifted linguist, read in Spanish.[5] In the manuscript of his handwritten theological notes, there are seventy-four pages outlining the great reformer of Carmel's spiritual doctrine.[6]

The first reference to Teresa in Neumann's *Journal* is found early on, on 5 November 1834. The greater portion of this entry is addressed to Teresa, whom Neumann adopts as his "dear patroness": "I enjoy reading the life of St. Teresa. When shall I reach her degree of virtue? St. Teresa, since God has deigned to bless you with so many graces and visits here on earth, you too be my patroness in the court of our mutual Father. I shall bend all my efforts to be like you. Ask God to give me a devout, wise and strict spiritual director who can lead me to Himself." Neumann usually concludes each journal entry by invoking the assistance of his particular heavenly patrons. At the end of this entry, we discover Neumann's first invocation of St. Joseph, which originates in his reading of Teresa's *Life*, chapter 6: "O Holy Virgin Mary, Queen of Apostles, help me! And you, St. Joseph, of whom St. Teresa declares she never requested anything but that she received it, help me also. My holy patrons, and you, my Guardian Angel, pray for me. So be it." Teresa's testimony to her devotion to St. Joseph not only inspires, but also serves as the paradigm for Neumann's own. Consequently, this portion of her text deserves close examination.

The context for Teresa's reflections on St. Joseph is her discussion of the difficulties that she confronted during her early days in the convent, including lack of good spiritual direction—something that must have resonated deeply with Neumann's own experience. Teresa's point of entry into her exposition of the mystery of the person and mission of St. Joseph is the crippling illness, brought on by excessive austerities and the absence of well-balanced spiritual direction, that afflicted her shortly after she entered Carmel at the age of twenty-one—within the range of Neumann's age when he began reading Teresa's *Life*. The "doctors of earth" were "helpless" in this instance, and so she turned to the "doctors of heaven."[7] Among the latter, "it was the figure of Christ's foster-father that [Teresa] saw standing out from among the other saints, for he, too, had once not known which way to turn."[8]

Teresa's synopsis of her situation at this moment of her life and her concluding statement that St. Joseph "brought it about that I could rise and walk and not be crippled" frame what might be described as her "deposition" concerning the remarkable power of this saint's intercession. Teresa supports each statement that she makes by specifying her firsthand experience of St. Joseph's intercessory power. She then corroborates her testimony by appealing to the comparable experience of others. Teresa's "deposition" also proffers a veritable "litany" of St. Joseph's titles.

Teresa commences her testimony with the declaration: "I took for my advocate and lord the glorious St. Joseph and earnestly recommended myself to him." "[T]his father and lord of mine," the former invocation being unprecedented in Christian history,[9] came to Teresa's "rescue" not only in her need for physical healing, but also in "other greater" spiritual needs "in better ways than I knew how to ask for." This assistance is underscored by a statement suggesting another appellation, although she does not use this word as such: a mediator—a term more often employed to speak of the role of Jesus and the Virgin Mary—who secures Teresa's deliverance from physical and spiritual dangers: "I don't recall up to this day ever having petitioned [St. Joseph] for anything that he failed to grant. It is an amazing thing the great many favors God has granted me through the mediation of this blessed saint, the dangers I was freed from both of body and soul." Teresa further develops the point by identifying the source of the extraordinary efficacy of St. Joseph's heavenly intercession, mentioning more of the saint's titles in the process: "For with other saints it seems the Lord has given them grace to be of help in one need, whereas with this glorious saint I have experience that he helps in all our needs and that the Lord wants us to understand that just as He was subject to St. Joseph on earth—for since bearing the title of father, being the Lord's tutor, Joseph could give the Child commands—so in heaven God does whatever he commands."

Teresa avers that her experience of St. Joseph's all-powerful intercession is by no means unique, but is corroborated by that of others who, like her, have appealed to him: "This has been observed by other persons, also through experience, whom I have told to recommend themselves to him. And so there are many who in experiencing this truth renew their devotion to him." Teresa tries to reciprocate her "impressive experience of the goods this glorious saint obtains from God" by striving to persuade "all to be devoted to him." For his part, St. Joseph repays veneration accorded him by bestowing great spiritual benefits: "I have not known anyone truly devoted to him and rendering him special services who have not advanced more in virtue. For in a powerful way he benefits souls who recommend themselves to him." And with characteristic Teresian humor, she explains: "It seems to me that for some years now I have asked him for something on his feast day, and my petition is always granted. If the request is somewhat out of line, he rectifies it for my greater good."

In addition to providing protection or rescue from physical and spiritual danger, unfailing assistance in every need, and growth in virtue, St. Joseph models how to serve Jesus and Mary and to pray, suggesting further titles that may be attributed to the saint. "Especially persons of prayer should always be attached to him. For I don't know how one can think about the Queen of Angels and about when she went through so much with the Infant Jesus without giving thanks to St. Joseph for the good assistance he then provided them both with. Anyone who cannot find a master to teach him prayer should take this glorious saint for his master, and he will not go astray."

Today many otherwise careful readers of Teresa's *Life* miss or pass over this key section of her text, unless they are already attuned to the many important roles that St. Joseph plays in her life and Carmelite reform.[10] By contrast, Neumann seems to have immediately noted, grasped, and appropriated Teresa's warm appreciation of St. Joseph. Teresa's effusive recommendation of St. Joseph may have made such a strong impression upon Neumann possibly because he stood in need of some of the same spiritual benefits that she obtained from St. Joseph in a situation that the future bishop of Philadelphia may have perceived as similar to his own. In any event, this testimony of his "dear patroness" introduced him to her own beloved patron, heavenly protector, and spiritual father, to whom Neumann would also entrust himself. Throughout the remainder of the *Journal*, Neumann invokes St. Joseph more than any other saint, his appeals being modeled for the most part on the paradigm of Teresa's own veneration.

ST. JOSEPH AS NEUMANN'S
INTERCESSOR, ADVOCATE, PROTECTOR, FATHER

Like Teresa, Neumann has unlimited confidence in St. Joseph's intercessory power, acknowledging too that its source is the saint's unique relationship with the Son of God: "Beloved foster-father of Jesus, your intercession has got to be all-powerful. St. Teresa says she never failed to receive whatever she asked of you!" (9 Mar. 1835). Ten days later, on the Feast of St. Joseph, Neumann adds his own testimony to Teresa's: "St. Joseph, it must have been your intercession that won for me such delightful graces. Poor sinner that I am, how can I properly thank you? Ah! pray to my Jesus that He may grant me His love which taught you so many virtues" (19 Mar. 1835). A few weeks earlier, struggling with discouragement, tepidity, and pride, Neumann turned, as Teresa had, to St. Joseph as his spiritual father: "St. Joseph, pray that my love for the Child Jesus may increase. Be a father to me! My holy patron saint (help me!)" (24 Feb. 1835).

These quotations bring to the fore another overlooked aspect of Neumann's spirituality that is inseparable from his veneration of St. Joseph: his devotion to the Infant Jesus, to whom Teresa and the nuns of her Carmelite reform were similarly greatly devoted.[11] Neumann's focus on the Christ of the public ministry and passion—the latter summed up in his episcopal motto "Passion of Christ strengthen me," a verse from the celebrated medieval prayer, quoted and recommended by St. Ignatius Loyola (1491-1556) in his *Spiritual Exercises*, and a favorite of Neumann from early childhood—is well known.[12] But in the pages of his diary, Neumann's Christ is equally the Jesus of the Infancy Narratives, perhaps foreshadowing a similar dual emphasis by another nineteenth-century saint, Thérèse of the Child Jesus and the Holy Face (1873-97).

Neumann often addresses and speaks of the Infant Jesus. The tone of these passages is affectionate and intimate. For example, he writes: "The thought of holding the Infant in my arms is very good for me. . . . I would so like to be able to gaze upon You always and to hug You and yes, I am even tempted to kiss You. You have become a human being, my Savior" (19 Dec. 1834). Another time Neumann confesses with characteristic candor and self-awareness: "I have tried several times to recall the presence of the Infant in the manger, for that is very beneficial for me. Would that this practice were more deeply rooted in my heart, then I wouldn't sin so frequently" (21 Jan. 1835). And more positively: "I did succeed fairly often in picturing the Infant Jesus in my arms and that kept me from any more grievous sins" (25 Dec. 1834).

For Neumann, St. Joseph's love for Jesus, expressed by his physical care and protection of Him during infancy and childhood, is of paramount importance. St. Joseph's gift of self in the service of the redemptive Incarnation models for the young seminarian the generosity and selflessness that are to be the hallmarks of his living out his Christian and priestly vocation. Likewise, it is the basis for Neumann's frequent appeal to St. Joseph to intercede with the Savior both to shower His love upon and to grant him a greater love of the divine Infant.

> I would like St. Joseph's intercession tomorrow that the Infant Jesus may bestow upon me the grace of His love (28 Jan. 1835).

> St. Joseph, I beseech you to obtain for me a perfect love of the Infant Jesus for whom you yourself exercised such a fatherly care (29 Jan. 1835).

> St. Joseph, foster father of my Jesus, teach me the proper way to love Our Savior. I still know nothing about this, and I will be docile towards you. O, hear my prayer! . . . You plead my cause with Christ. Your holy spouse, my Mother, will join you. How fortunate I am to be able to call upon you who on earth took care of Jesus despite His omnipotence (9 Feb. 1835).

> St. Joseph, obtain for me the love of my Jesus (25 Feb. 1835).

St. Joseph, you who were so conscientious about providing for the physical health of my Lord, please intercede for me that I may find joy in the performance of my duties, so that I may know how to provide for the Christian souls God may confide to my care. . . . I turn to you because your holiness will make my lowly prayers acceptable to our Lord (9 Mar. 1835).

St. Joseph, you obtain for me perfect resignation to the will of God (11 Apr. 1835).

St. Joseph, whose feast we shall celebrate tomorrow, obtain for me the graces I need to be a priest (18 Mar. 1835).

St. Joseph, ask the Divine Infant, to kindle ever more intensely the fire of His love in my heart (1 June 1835).

Neumann's *Journal* also echoes another primary theme of Teresa's theology of St. Joseph, namely, that his person and mission have no meaning apart from Jesus and Mary—the Holy Family.[13] Neumann regards St. Joseph not only in relation to Jesus as His earthly guardian, but also to Mary as her divinely ordained husband.[14] For example, on 19 January 1835, Neumann writes: "St. Joseph, may you and your immaculate spouse assist me in the final struggle." And three weeks later: "O holy Virgin, pray for me together with Your saintly husband, that God may forgive my sins despite the imperfections in my confession." Neumann rarely refers to St. Joseph apart from either Jesus or Mary; sometimes he refers to all three together. "Jesus, Mary, and Joseph . . . be with me always" (13 Feb. 1835); "Jesus, Mary, and Joseph, help this weak, desolate creature" (26 Feb. 1835). Veneration of the Holy Family thus flows organically from Neumann's devotion to St. Joseph.

Veneration of St. Joseph, as found in Neumann's *Journal*, also focuses on one of the saint's most popular advocations: patron of a good death (*bona mors*) or the dying. Teresa had testified to the unfailing efficacy of St. Joseph's protection in every need, especially physical and spiritual danger. During the Counter-Reformation, the need for which St. Joseph's patronage came to be most often invoked was the hour of death because his death in the company of Jesus and Mary made him the most efficacious protector of the dying.[15] This rationale was further elaborated by, among others, St. Alphonsus Ligouri (1696-1787), founder of the Redemptorists and doctor of the Church, who avers: "We should especially be devout to Saint Joseph, in order that the Saint may obtain us a good death. He, on account of having saved the infant Jesus from the snares of Herod, has the special privilege of delivering dying persons from the snares of the devil. Moreover, on account of the services which he rendered for so many years to Jesus and Mary, having by his labours provided them a dwelling and food, he has the privilege of obtaining the special assistance of Jesus and Mary for his devout clients at death."[16]

St. Joseph was thus most widely known as a companion who could guide the dying through the last rite of passage. Pious associations and confraternities that prayed for the dying took him as their patron, and images of the saint's death became commonplace in Catholic churches and homes, offering comfort particularly to those about to face the same fate.[17] Neumann's invocation of St. Joseph's protection and assistance in his final hour reflects the currency of this facet of the saint's cult. For example, "St. Joseph, protect me at the hour of my death that Satan may not conquer me" (19 Nov. 1834); "St. Joseph . . . Assist me in my final struggle" (18 Jan. 1835); "St. Joseph, guide my soul in all the circumstances of my life so that I may be worthy of your assistance in my last hour" (21 Jan. 1835).

St. Joseph's Continuing Presence

The *Journal* is unique in its documentation of Neumann's expression of his appreciation of, and affection for, St. Joseph. There are, however, indications that St. Joseph continued, after a fashion, to be a palpable presence in Neumann's life after he discontinued making entries in his spiritual diary. The "fervor" that Neumann "observed at St. Joseph's parish in Rochester" was the ideal that he sought to replicate in his own priestly ministry, as well as an important factor in his decision to enter the Redemptorist order.[18]

Neumann would have found his fervent devotion to both St. Joseph and Teresa affirmed in the Redemptorists, as their founder, Alphonsus Ligouri, was also greatly devoted to these two saints. In fact, one of the pillars of Alphonsus's appreciation of St. Joseph is also Teresa's encomium in her *Life*, almost the whole of which he quotes at the beginning of the section on "Devotion to St. Joseph" in his *Mission Book of the Congregation of the Most Holy Redeemer*.[19]

A treasured material testament to this aspect of Neumann's life is the holy card of St. Joseph and the Christ Child found among his possessions at his death and now displayed at the Neumann Center, St. John Neumann Shrine, St. Peter the Apostle Church, Philadelphia (Plate 15). This image was given to Neumann by the Venerable Joseph Passerat, C.Ss.R., who for twenty-eight years was Vicar General of the North European Redemptorists (1820-48). With one hand, Joseph holds his attribute of a flowering staff of lilies, symbolic of his divine election as the husband of Mary, as well as of his chastity; with the other, the saint holds the left hand of the Christ Child, who blesses the viewer with His right hand. The inscription beneath the image reads: *Ecce fidelis servus & prudens, quem constituit Dominus super familiam suam*, "Behold the faithful and prudent servant, whom the Lord placed over His family."

Archbishop Kenrick received the papal bull appointing Neumann as bishop of Philadelphia on the evening of the Feast of St. Joseph, 1852.[20] When Neumann came to compose the running account of his life that he wrote, under obedience, immediately before his episcopal ordination, he penned the abbreviations "J.M.J.A.Th." at the top of the first page. These stood for "Jesus, Mary, Joseph, Alphonsus, Theresa." In so doing, Neumann followed Alphonsus's custom of using "J.M.J.T." at the head of his letters, a practice that Alphonsus likely appropriated from the Carmelite nuns of the Teresian reform to whom he was greatly devoted.[21] Neumann added to these abbreviations, as many Redemptorists did, Alphonsus's own initial.[22] "J.M.J." appears at the top of Neumann's letters as well, witnessing to his devotion to the Holy Family of Nazareth.

The first Catholic church founded in Philadelphia was Old St. Joseph's (1733), and, significantly, Neumann's first parish visitation, upon his arrival in the city of brotherly love, was to St. Joseph's, where he preached a sermon that was highly praised by many in the large audience in attendance.[23] In the autumn preceding Neumann's appointment, the Jesuits had opened Saint Joseph's College (1851). One of Neumann's outstanding accomplishments in Philadelphia was the establishment of the first diocesan school system in the United States. In view of this initiative and his own strong intellectual orientation, it is hardly surprising that he likewise took a special interest in Catholic higher education, particularly the fledgling Saint Joseph's, which "gave promise of supplying the need of a long-desired Catholic college in the city of Philadelphia itself."[24] As bishop of Philadelphia, Neumann also named several foundations that he established for Jesus's earthly father, including St. Joseph's church in Ashland (1857) and St. Joseph's College for young men in Susquehanna County (1852).[25]

Among the manifold roles that St. Joseph had in Teresa's life and Carmelite reform was the guardian of her foundations, to whom she turned in times of financial difficulty since he provided for the temporal needs of Jesus and Mary.[26] This appeal to the saint for assistance finds a resonance too in Neumann's episcopate, according to an incident recorded by his first biographer, his nephew John Berger. Writing to allay the anxiety of the superior of a religious community of nuns about finances, Neumann counsels: "Let us trust in God and St. Joseph. In God's own good time things will come right. Procure what is necessary. Be satisfied with what is needed for the present day, and confide the future to God."[27]

During this same period, Neumann's veneration of St. Joseph and the Holy Family of Nazareth entrusted to his care and protection, so exalted by Teresa and Alphonsus, is expressed in yet another way. During his sojourn in Europe in 1854-55, to attend the solemn declaration of the dogma of the Immaculate Conception, Neumann visited and celebrated Mass at the Holy House of Loreto. According to tradition, this is the house of the Virgin Mary in Nazareth where the Annunciation took place and where Jesus, Mary, and Joseph lived after returning from Egypt.[28]

Neumann's Place in the "Century of St. Joseph"

The nineteenth century has been characterized as a Marian Age because of the tremendous popular and official veneration of Mary.[29] But it was also the century of St. Joseph. As one of the best-selling devotional authors of the period in the English-speaking world explains: "Devotions in honour of St. Joseph . . . were reserved by God, for His own wise end, to the 19th century . . . . to secure in heaven a new Protector for the Church in the days of bitter and protracted trials; to hold up our Saint as a model to every Christian of a holy, hidden, and active life, and as Patron of a happy death."[30] As with Mary, the papacy approved and promoted the honor accorded St. Joseph.

On 10 September 1847, Pope Pius IX extended to the whole Church, in addition to the Feast of St. Joseph traditionally celebrated on 19 March, the Feast of the Patronage of St. Joseph. The latter had been observed by the Discalced Carmelites (who officially chose St. Joseph as patron of the Order at the General Chapter of 1621) since the late seventeenth century. Celebrated on the Third Sunday after Easter, the Feast of the Patronage was extended to the Augustinians in 1700, the Discalced Mercedarians in 1702, Mexico in 1703, and soon thereafter to many other religious orders and dioceses. By the middle of the nineteenth century, it was so widespread that it was easily extended to the whole Church. Twenty-three years later, on 8 December 1870, at the conclusion of the First Vatican Council, the same pontiff solemnly proclaimed St. Joseph "Patron of the Universal Church," thus giving theological recognition to the reality already celebrated in the Feast of the Patronage.[31] His successor, Pope Leo XIII, in 1889 devoted an encyclical to this saint, further reflecting on the theological foundation for his patronage of the Church and the devotion due him, as well as urging his veneration among the faithful.

Neumann's strong affection for and solid appreciation of St. Joseph unfolds against this larger ecclesial backdrop of his age. Although since 1655 St. Joseph had been the special patron of Neumann's native Bohemia, being so proclaimed by King Ferdinand II,[32] the inspiration and model for the fourth bishop of Philadelphia's veneration of this saint was Teresa of Ávila's declaration that "she never requested anything [of St. Joseph] but that she received it." Moreover, just as Teresa ascribed many roles to St. Joseph, so too does Neumann: faithful advocate, spiritual father, all-powerful intercessor, guide in all life's circumstances, protector at the hour of death, model of perfect resignation to the will of God, and teacher of the perfect love of the Infant Jesus. And for Neumann, as for Teresa, these roles and the graces obtained through St. Joseph flow from his faithful, conscientious, and loving fulfillment of his God-given mission as the chaste and beloved spouse of Mary and the earthly father and guardian of Jesus. In short, in chronicling the evolution of the cult of St. Joseph during the nineteenth century, St. John Nepomucene Neumann clearly merits a place alongside the Little Flower and Bernadette Soubirous (1844-79), other great saints of his century who were also lovingly devoted to St. Joseph.[33]

Notes

1. This quotation is from the entry for 9 Mar. 1835 in Neumann's *Spiritual Journal*. This and subsequent references are to the date of the journal entry in William Nayden's English translation of the French text of "John Nepomucene Neumann's *Spiritual Journal*," published in four parts in *Spicilegium Historicum Congregationis SSmi Redemptoris* 25 (1977): 321-418 (Part 1: Oct. 1-Dec. 31, 1834); 26 (1978): 9-74 (Part 2: Jan. 1-Feb. 28, 1835), 291-352 (Part 3: Mar. 1-May 4, 1835); 27 (1979): 81-152 (Part 4: May 5, 1835-July 21, 1838). There are actually two diaries: one in German (Neumann's native language), which begins with 22 Mar. 1835 and ends with 27 Nov. 1839, and another in French (a language that Neumann was learning), which begins with 1 Oct. 1834 and ends, after an interruption of several years, with 21 July 1838. Neumann often made entries concurrently in both texts. Another version of the present essay was published in *Saint Joseph Studies: Papers in English from the Seventh and Eighth International St. Joseph Symposia, Malta 1997 and El Salvador 2001*, ed. Larry Toschi, O.S.J. (Santa Cruz, Ca.: Guardian of the Redeemer Books, 2002), 121-41.

2. There is an enormous bibliography on this subject. See, e.g., León de San Joaquín, *El culto de San José y la Orden del Carmen*, trans. from the French

ed., with corrections and additional material (Barcelona: Juan Gili, 1905); Fortunato de Jesús Sacramentado, O.C.D., "Santa Teresa de Jesús y su espíritu josefino," *Estudios Josefinos* 7 (1953): 9-54; the special double issue of *Estudios Josefinos*, entitled "San José y Santa Teresa," 18 (1963-64); Simeón de la Sagrada Familia, "San José en Santa Teresita," *Estudios Josefinos* 32 (1978): 201-34; Christopher C. Wilson, "St. Teresa of Ávila's Holy Patron: Teresian Sources for the Image of St. Joseph in Spanish American Colonial Art," in *Patron Saint of the New World: Spanish American Colonial Images of St. Joseph*, exh. cat., ed. Joseph F. Chorpenning, O.S.F.S. (Philadelphia: Saint Joseph's University Press, 1992), 5-17; *Just Man, Husband of Mary, Guardian of Christ: An Anthology of Readings from Jerónimo Gracián's "Summary of the Excellencies of St. Joseph"* (1597), trans. and ed. with an introductory essay and commentary by Joseph F. Chorpenning, O.S.F.S. (Philadelphia: Saint Joseph's University Press, 1993); Julen Urkiza, "Beata Ana de San Bartolomé, heredera del josefinismo teresiano," *Estudios Josefinos* 51 (1997): 223-42; José de Jesús María, O.C.D. (Teófanes Egido), *Présence de saint Joseph chez Thérèse de Lisieux*, Lumière sur la Montagne, no. 11 (Montreal: Centre de recherche et de documentation, Oratoire Saint-Joseph, 1999).

3. For Neumann's own unfavorable assessment of the seminary program at Prague, see *The Autobiography of St. John Neumann, C.Ss.R.*, with introduction, translation, commentary, and epilogue by Alfred C. Rush, C.Ss.R. (Boston: St. Paul Books & Media, 1977) (hereafter *Autobiography*), 22-23. Also see Augustinus Kurt Huber's indispensable study of this period of Neumann's life: "John N. Neumann's Student Years in Prague, 1833-1835," trans. from German by Raymond H. Schmandt, *Records of the American Catholic Historical Society of Philadelphia* 89 (1978): 3-32. An English translation of Neumann's autobiography is also appended to Huber's article (Appendix I, 14-22). Neumann's brief "autobiography" was written, "under obedience," and is dated 27 Mar. 1852, the eve of his episcopal ordination.

4. Michael J. Curley, C.Ss.R., *Venerable John Neumann, C.Ss.R., Fourth Bishop of Philadelphia* (Washington, D.C.: Catholic University of America Press, 1952), 29.

5. Neumann's mother tongue was German; he mastered Latin, Greek, Czech, Italian, French, Spanish, English, and, later as a bishop enough Gaelic to hear confessions. In fact, the reason why Neumann wanted to study in Prague was because he believed that it would afford him the opportunity to learn French and English. Neumann was so proficient in languages that the Austrian government offered him the post of an official secretary: see *Autobiography*, 22, 76-77, note 49.

6. Curley, 29.
7. All quotations in this paragraph and in what follows from ch. 6 of Teresa's autobiography are from *The Collected Works of St. Teresa of Ávila, I: The Book of Her Life, Spiritual Testimonies, Soliloquies*, trans. Kieran Kavanaugh, O.C.D., and Otilio Rodríguez, O.C.D. (Washington, D.C.: Institute of Carmelite Studies Publications, 1976), 53-54, and are otherwise not noted.
8. Joseph Weiger, *Mary, Mother of Faith*, trans. Ruth Bethell, with a special introduction to the English trans. by Romano Guardini (Chicago: Regenery, 1959), 15.
9. Andrew Doze, *St. Joseph: Shadow of the Father*, trans. Florestine Audett, R.J.M. (New York; Alba House, 1992), 16.
10. For example, Carole Slade, *St. Teresa of Ávila: Author of a Heroic Life* (Berkeley: University of California Press, 1995), 73-74, mentions Teresa's adoption of the Virgin Mary as her mother, but overlooks the saint's unique relationship with St. Joseph.
11. For an overview of devotion to the Infant Jesus, see Irénée Noye, "Enfance de Jésus (Dévotion à l')," *Dictionnaire de spiritualité*, vol. 4, part 1 (Paris: Beauchesne, 1960), 652-82, and Michele Dolz, *Il Dio Bambino: La devozione a Gesù Bambino dai Vangeli dell'infanzia a Edith Stein* (Milan: Mondadori Editore, 2001). On the place of this devotion in the Teresian Carmel, see, in addition to the aforementioned references, *L'Art du XVIIe siècle dans les Carmels de France*, ed. Yves Rocher, exh. cat. (Paris: Musée du Petit Palais, 1982), 130-31, 136-37.
12. See Alfred C. Rush, C.Ss.R., and Thomas J. Donaghy, F.S.C. , "The Saintly John Neumann and his Coadjutor Archbishop Wood," in *The History of the Archdiocese of Philadelphia*, ed. James F. Connelly (Philadelphia: Archdiocese of Philadelphia, 1976), 209-70, esp. 212, and Michael Walsh, *Dictionary of Catholic Devotions* (San Francisco: Harper, 1993), 25-26. In the *Journal*, Neumann repeatedly appeals to Christ as his Good Shepherd, Beloved Physician, Heavenly Teacher, Most Holy Redeemer, and Divine Master. Neumann identifies with Bartimeus, confident that Jesus will take pity on, help, and heal him as He did this blind man (Mk 10:46) (1 Dec. 1834). He also meditates on Christ during His passion, as He was crowned with thorns and as He hung on the cross, His arms open in invitation for the sinner, for Neumann, to return to Him (31 Oct. 1835; Part 4, 151 [undated final entry]).
13. Others in the Christian tradition who concur with this conviction about the inseparability of Jesus, Mary, and Joseph include Jean Gerson, St. Francis de Sales, the French Ursuline missionary to Canada Blessed Marie of the Incarnation, and Pope John Paul II: see Joseph F. Chorpenning,

O.S.F.S., "Icon of Family and Religious Life: The Historical Development of the Holy Family Devotion," in *The Holy Family as Prototype of the Civilization of Love: Images from the Viceregal Amercias*, exh. cat. , ed. Joseph F. Chorpenning, O.S.F.S. (Philadelphia: Saint Joseph's University Press, 1996), 3-39, esp. 5, 10, 17, 21, 28.

14. Neumann's *Journal* attests to the large role Mary played in his life. As he would explain by quoting St. Augustine in one of his later Marian pastoral letters: "*Caro Jesu! Caro Mariae!*, The flesh of Jesus is the flesh of Mary!" ("Pastoral Letter of St. John Neumann on the Immaculate Conception of the Mother of God [4 Nov. 1854]," *Social Justice Review* 76 [May-June 1985]: 86-90, at 88). Neumann invokes Mary's intercession, compassion, and protection in virtually every diary entry. The many titles under which he addresses her constitute a veritable Marian litany, e.g., Queen of Angels and Heaven, Mother of Mercy, Mother of Divine Grace, Mother of Divine Consolation, Refuge of Sinners, Immaculate Mother of Heaven, Comfortress of the Afflicted, Mirror of Justice, Mother of my God, Spouse of the Holy Spirit, Daughter of the Heavenly Father, my holy Mother and Mistress. Neumann calls upon Mary to recommend him to the Infant Jesus "that He may enlighten and stir my heart and urge me on by His grace," and to intercede for him "with [her] Infant Son Whom [she] so often held in [her] motherly arms." He pleads as well that mindful of "the enormous affliction [Mary] suffered looking upon [her] Son on the Cross . . . [she] ask Him to have compassion on my poor soul" (25 Feb. 1835; 31 May 1835; 17 June 1835). As bishop of Philadelphia, Neumann wanted Mary to have a comparable role in the lives of his people. One of the principal ways he sought to achieve this goal was by his pastoral letters on Mary that urged his flock "to cultivate a tender devotion to the Immaculate Mother of Jesus Christ," for "no more powerful friend have we with God" ("Pastoral Letter on the Immaculate Conception of 1 May 1855," *Social Justice Review* 76 [March-April 1985]: 59-64, at 63). Also see Thomas A. Thompson, S.M., "'No More Powerful Friend Have We with God': The Marian Devotion of St. John Neumann," in this volume, 143-64.

15. St. Joseph's protection of Teresa continued to her last hour on earth. In the canonical proceedings for her beatification and canonization, eyewitnesses testified that Teresa's death was accompanied by various supernatural phenomena, including an apparition of Christ with the Virgin Mary and St. Joseph. Moreover, after Teresa's death, one of her nuns in Burgos had a vision of Teresa ascending to heaven in the company of Jesus and St. Joseph. See Irving Lavin, *Bernini and the Unity of the Visual Arts*, 2 vols. (New York: Pierpont Morgan Library and Oxford University Press, 1980),

1:114, and Carlos M. N. Eire, *From Madrid to Purgatory: The Art & Craft of Dying in Sixteenth-Century Spain* (New York: Cambridge University Press, 1995), 416.

16. St. Alphonsus Ligouri, "Meditation for the Feast of St. Joseph," in *The Glories of Mary,* trans. from the Italian, rev. by Robert A. Coffin (1852; Rockford, Ill.: Tan Books, 1982), 645-46.

17. Keith P. Luria, "The Counter-Reformation and Popular Spirituality," in *Christian Spirituality: Post-Reformation and Modern,* eds. Louis Dupré and Don E. Saliers, in collaboration with John Meyendorff, World Spirituality: An Encyclopedic History of the Religious Quest, vol. 18 (New York: Crossroad, 1989), 93-120, esp. 114. For examples of the kinds of images of the Death of St. Joseph that were often displayed in Catholic homes during the nineteenth century, see *The Holy Family as Prototype of the Civilization of Love,* 135-36.

18. *Autobiography,* 31.

19. See, e.g., in addition to Alphonsus's "Meditation for the Feast of St. Joseph" (as in note 16 above), his "Sermon for the Feast of St. Joseph," in *Glories of Mary,* 605-16, and *The Mission Book of the Congregation of the Most Holy Redeemer, The American Catholic Tradition* (reprint of the new, revised and enlarged edition published in 1862 by Kelly & Piet, Baltimore; New York: Arno Press, 1978), 177-81 Also see Roberto Koch, C.Ss.R., "San Giuseppe nell'opera di S. Alfonso," *Cahiers de Joséphologie* 39 (1991): 331-45, and Ángel Luis, C.Ss.R., "San Alfonso María de Ligorio, tributario de Santa Teresa en su devoción a San José," *Estudios Josefinos* 37 (1983): 55-72.

20. *Autobiography,* 36.

21. On Alphonsus's affection for Teresa and dedication to her Carmelite nuns, see Frederick M. Jones, *Alphonsus de Liguori: Saint of Bourbon Naples and Founder of the Redemptorists 1696-1787* (1992; Ligouri, Mo.: Ligouri Publications, 1999), 94, 339, 348, 370.

22. *Autobiography,* 16, 66 (note 1), and Luis, 58.

23. Curley, 198-99.

24. Curley, 212. Also see Curley, 262, 285, 379; Rush and Donaghy, 225-29; David R. Contosta, *Saint Joseph's: Philadelphia's Jesuit University, 150 Years* (Philadelphia: Saint Joseph's University Press, 2000), 32, 36.

25. Curley, 212, 263.

26. *Just Man,* 242-43.

27. John A. Berger, C.Ss.R., *Life of Right Rev. John N. Neumann, D.D., of the Congregation of the Most Holy Redeemer, Fourth Bishop of Philadelphia,* trans. Eugene Grimm (New York: Benziger, 1884), 369.

28. *Our Sunday Visitor's Catholic Encyclopedia,* ed. Peter M. J. Stravinskas

(Huntingdon, Ind.: Our Sunday Visitor Publishing Division, 1991), 603, and Marcello Montanari, O.F.M.Cap., "Il Santuario di Loreto e la devozione alla Sacra Famiglia," in *La Sagrada Familia en el siglo XVII: Actas del Segundo Congreso Internacional sobre la Sagrada Familia*, Barcelona/Begues, 7-11 septiembre de 1994 (Barcelona: Hijos de la Sagrada Familia/Nazarenum, 1995), 117-34.

29. See Hilda Graef, *Mary: A History of Doctrine and Devotion*, 2 vols. (London: Sheed & Ward, 1963-65), 2:79, and Barbara Corrado Pope, "Immaculate and Powerful: The Marian Revival in the Nineteenth Century," in *Immaculate and Powerful: The Female in Sacred Image and Social Reality*, eds. Clarissa W. Atkinson, Constance H. Buchanan, and Margaret R. Miles, The Harvard Women's Studies in Religion Series (Boston: Beacon Press, 1985), 173-200.

30. Thomas H. Kinane, *St. Joseph: His Life, His Virtues, His Privileges, His Power*, 3rd ed. (Dublin: H. Gill & Son, 1884), 249. This book went through at least eight further editions between 1885 and 1908 by Gill in Dublin, and by Benziger and The Catholic Publication Society in the United States. See Roland Gauthier, C.S.C., *Bibliographie sur saint Joseph et la sainte Famille* (Montreal: Centre de recherche et de documentation, Oratoire Saint-Joseph du Mont-Royal, 1999), 617.

31. Francis L. Filas, S.J., *The Man Closest to Jesus: The Complete Life, Theology and Devotional History of St. Joseph* (Boston: St. Paul Editions, 1962), 572, 577-96, and Larry Toschi, O.S.J., "Feast of the Patronage of Saint Joseph," *Guardian of the Redeemer* 7, no. 1 (Mar.-May 2001): 12-13. Pope St. Pius X, in the years 1911-13, changed the name of the Feast of the Patronage of St. Joseph to "Solemnity," transferred it to the third Wednesday after Easter, and assigned it an octave, which Joseph's feast on March 19 could not have on account of Lent. In 1955 Pope Pius XII suppressed the Solemnity and instituted the Feast of St. Joseph the Worker that was to be celebrated annually on 1 May, in order to christianize May Day.

32. Filas, 551-52.

33. On Thérèse of Lisieux's devotion to St. Joseph, see the bibliography cited in note 2 above; on Bernadette, see Doze, 59-76, and *Presence of St. Joseph in the Life of Bernadette of Lourdes*, texts of René Laurentin and of André Doze, trans. from the French by Francine Britnell, rev. by Roméo Jean, C.S.C., Lumière sur la Montagne, no. 10 (Montreal: Centre de recherche et de documentation, Oratoire Saint-Joseph, 1998).

THE SECOND VATICAN COUNCIL,
1962-1965, AND BISHOP NEUMANN

ALFRED C. RUSH, C.SS.R.

The title of this article may come as a surprise. We have heard a great deal about Vatican II. Are we aware that Bishop Neumann finds his way into the *Acta* of the Council? He does. And when the Council introduces him, it is making a very important point; it cites a document that was a turning point in his Cause, a document that is a milestone in the history of holiness because of its clarity and balance in determining what constitutes heroic virtue. This material, like Neumann himself, is quiet and unobtrusive; it is contained in a footnote. The reference is found in paragraph 50 of the Constitution on the Church, *Lumen Gentium*.[1] Paragraph 50 is part of the seventh chapter that is entitled: "The Eschatological Nature of the Pilgrim Church and its Union with the Church in Heaven."

Describing the union of the Church on earth with the Church in heaven, the Constitution speaks of various types of saints. It speaks of the first group, the Apostles and martyrs, who gave the supreme witness of faith and charity by the shedding of their blood. The Council points out that the Church has always venerated them with special devotion. When the classical age of martyrdom came to an end, another type of saint appeared in the Church, the Confessors, men and women who had consecrated themselves to Christ by the vows. Because martyrdom was regarded as the ideal of holiness, these saints were often called spiritual martyrs, white martyrs or daily martyrs. It was axiomatic to say that "the Monk was the brother of the Martyr."[2] The Council is also mindful of these saints in heavenly glory. Not all Christians are martyrs; neither are all living under the vows of poverty, chastity and obedience. Nevertheless, all are called to holiness. It is here that the Council speaks of all the other saints "whom the outstanding practice of the Christian virtues and the divine charisms recommended to the pious devotion and imitation of the faithful." As soon as the Council spoke about "the outstanding practice of the Christian virtues," it gave as its reference the decree of the Congregation of Rites on the heroicity of the virtues of Bishop Neumann.

To understand the decree and its importance, some background is necessary. On June 29, 1905, Pope Leo XIII declared valid all the Ordinary and Apostolic Processes of Neumann's Cause.[3] This opened the way for the next step, the proof of the exercise of heroic virtue. It was here that the Cause ran into extremely difficult, almost insurmountable and—as will be seen—unnecessary obstacles. The *Antepreparatory* meeting of the Congregation of Rites was held on May 16, 1911.[4] At the end of this, there were grave difficulties that still awaited a solution. It was decided to leave them until the next meeting. The *preparatory* meeting took place on April 16, 1912.[5] Because of the serious difficulties still remaining, it was prudently decided not to proceed to the *general* meeting, the meeting to be held in the presence of the Holy Father.

At this stage it seemed that sufficient proofs were lacking by which the exercise of heroic virtue could be demonstrated. There are various reasons for this. Even when he was living, Neumann was quiet and unobtrusive; he did not stand out in a crowd. These qualities seemed to hover about him when dead. Furthermore, his life seemed so ordinary, one kept asking: what is heroic or special about it? The write-up of his Cause did not help. His achievements are written up in a style that is described as dry, jejune and laconic. This was not much of a help in winning the court over. Lastly, the norms then in vogue in the Congregation of Rites are described as very strict.[6] More will be said on this when we hear from Pope Benedict XV.

All was not lost. The Redemptorist Postulator of the Cause was Father Claudius Benedetti. He was also the Postulator of the Cause of Bishop Anthony Gianelli, the bishop of Bobbio. This Cause also was running into similar difficulties. By dint of hard work he saw Gianelli's virtue declared heroic by Benedict XV.[7] Other causes were going along more smoothly because less rigid norms were being used to judge heroic virtue. Consequently, Father Benedetti requested a second *preparatory* meeting in the Cause of Neumann. This was held on April 8, 1919.[8] At the end of this, there was good hope that a successful conclusion would take place in the *general* meeting in the presence of the Pope. Even at that time, one of the Consultors could not bring himself to favor the Cause; actually, he openly opposed it. The general meeting of the Congregation of Rites took place in the presence of Pope Benedict XV on November 29, 1921. As the members were gathering, the news arrived that the Consultor, just mentioned, died suddenly when he dropped into a barber shop on his way to the Vatican.[9] At that scheduled meeting, the Congregation of Rites approved the heroicity of Neumann's virtues.

The decree of Neumann's holiness was solemnly proclaimed by Benedict XV on December 11, 1921. He was surrounded by the Cardinals, Bishops and Prelates, members of the Redemptorist Congregation and representatives from America, Germany and Bohemia. The decree speaks of the successful ending of a remarkable Cause that seemed extremely difficult to settle, that looked as though it would not advance further, a Cause that was bogged down for ten years or more by discussion, difficulties and dissensions about heroic virtue.

Two reasons are given for the successful outcome of this phase of the Cause. The first is its own intrinsic goodness. After that, credit for the decree on Neumann's heroic virtue is given to Pope Benedict XV. Other Causes dealing with heroicity were being discussed before the Congregation. The same problems regarding heroic virtue were surfacing. The constant problem was: in what does heroicity of the Christian virtues consist? Benedict XV kept pursuing this problem, studying the teaching of St. Thomas Aquinas and Pope Benedict XIV.[10] With regard to the various elements that enter into heroic virtue, he asked what is to be regarded as the principal one, the one without which there would be no heroicity. He unravelled the question and taught openly that the one norm for heroic virtue is the faithful, perpetual and constant carrying out of the duties and obligations of one's proper state in life. When that norm was used and applied to every phase of Neumann's life, it was patently clear that his virtue was heroic. This showed clearly how Neumann advanced on the way of Christian holiness from day to day and from virtue to virtue. Towards the end the decree notes how, with God's help, the discussion about holiness and Neumann's holiness that went on for years was successfully settled in the *general* meeting held in the presence of the Holy Father.[11]

After the decree was read, the Most Reverend Patrick Murray, the Superior General of the Redemptorists, expressed the thanks of all to the Holy Father.[12] Benedict XV responded with a rather lengthy talk. The talk has two main themes. The first is a more detailed description of heroic virtue; the second is the justification for ascribing heroic holiness to Neumann. It is from these two themes of the Pope that we have a summary of the objections raised in the course of the Cause, against ascribing heroic virtue to Neumann. The first objection is summed up in the Latin phrase: *labor communis*; in English, this means his life was made up of actions that were common, average, ordinary, every day. The second objection is summed up in the Latin phrase: *res simplex*; in English, this means that his life and holiness were very simple. There was nothing singular, unusual or exceptional about them.

With regard to the charge based on the ordinariness of Neumann's life, Benedict XV points out that his life was not without difficulties and he lists the great many achievements carried out in the midst of difficulties and setbacks. He then insists that he cannot understand how all this could be regarded as ordinary. On the charge of simplicity levelled at Neumann's life and holiness, he says:

> Perhaps the simplicity of this type of holiness has been exaggerated by those who thought that they could not recognize a heroic degree of virtue in the Servant of God because—in their opinion—the good and holy works performed by Neumann were the good and holy works that every pious religious, every

missionary zealous for the salvation of souls, and every good bishop is supposed to do. There is no need to repeat that the most simple of works, if carried out with constant perfection in the midst of inevitable difficulties, can bring every Servant of God to the attainment of a heroic degree of virtue. Rather, precisely in the simplicity of these works we find a great argument on the basis of which we can say to the faithful of every age: "You are all obliged to venerate Venerable Neumann."[13]

After pointing out the obvious fact that he does not mean that everyone has to be a cleric, missionary, religious, pastor or bishop, he states: "Only this one thing is required of all, namely, that each one be a man of his own state in life."[14] The Holy Father keeps returning to his theme and speaks of his wish to arrive at a universal verdict on the true character of the virtues of Venerable Neumann in order to be able to tell all that no one can remain indifferent to the imitation of these simple works. The Pope knew that he had pleaded his case well and he brings this section to a close with these words:

> If, in spite of this, there should be some who still seem surprised and cannot picture him to themselves as a hero apart from great undertakings, We hasten to add that wonderful results can come from simple deeds when they are graced with perfection and carried out with unremitting constancy.[15]

The precision given to heroic virtue and the illustration of this in Neumann's holiness meant a great deal to Benedict XV in his role of "the Father of Christendom" who is concerned with interests that are universal. It was pointed out that the decree on Neumann was a source of great joy to the Church in America, Germany and Bohemia, to religious, priests and bishops. Benedict XV admitted this but he insisted that the import of the decree was not to be limited to particular local churches, to specific groups or classes; rather, its significance extended to the entire Church, to all the faithful without exception. We just saw how the Pope could say to all the faithful of every age, sex and state: "You are all obliged to venerate

Venerable Neumann." This is the theme that runs all through the address. As a matter of fact, he repeats it at least six times: the lesson of the decree is meant for all the faithful; there is not a single individual who is not to draw profit from it. Twice, as he was bringing his talk to a close, he returned to his favorite theme. The final words in the Pope's talk on Neumann read:

> By the power of God's holy blessing, may the import of the decree that proclaims the heroic virtue of the Bishop of Philadelphia, spread out beyond the groups of people who are united with him by special bonds. Yes, may the result be that no one remains untouched by this declaration, since all should imitate him in whom the simplicity of works did not hinder a life of wonderful activity.[16]

Benedict XV wanted to teach the entire Church about heroic holiness; the holiness of Venerable Neumann was his way of doing it.

The Second Vatican Council continues Benedict's teaching and method. In its Constitution on the Church, the fifth chapter deals with the universal call to holiness. After pointing out that "the Lord Jesus, the Divine Teacher, Model of all perfection, preached holiness of life to each and every one of His disciples of every condition," it goes on to say:

> Thus it is evident to everyone, that all the faithful of Christ of whatever rank or status, are called to the fullness of the Christian life and to the perfection of charity; by this holiness as such a more human manner of living is promoted in this earthly society. In order that the faithful may reach this perfection, they must use their strength accordingly as they have received it, as a gift from Christ. They must follow in His footsteps and conform themselves to His image seeking the will of the Father in all things. They must devote themselves with all their being to the glory of God and the service of their neighbor. In this way, the holiness of the People of God will grow into an abundant harvest of good, as is admirably shown by the life of so many saints in Church history.[17]

In the seventh chapter the document looks to those who attained this holiness; it looks to the Saints in heaven as models and seeks their intercession for its weakness. It recalls the martyrs, the confessors and the others who attained holiness through "the outstanding practice of the Christian virtues." As noted, this is where the document quotes the decree on Neumann's heroicity. As in the past, so all down the ages throughout the rest of history, the Church will proclaim its message of heroic virtue. It is fitting that Neumann, the one about whose heroicity so many difficulties were raised, the one whose Cause occasioned the clarification of this doctrine, should be the one singled out by the Church in a document from an ecumenical council to proclaim the balanced, consoling and encouraging doctrine about heroic holiness.

NOTES

1. Vatican II, *Lumen Gentium*, 50: Acta Apostolicae Sedis = AAS 57 (1965) 56, n. 155. See W. Abbott, S.J., *The Documents of Vatican II* (Paperback ed., New York, 1966) 68.

2. E. Malone, O.S.B., *The Monk and the Martyr*, Washington, D.C., 1950.

3. See Acta Sanctae Sedis 29 (1896-97) 443. Fine summaries of Neumann's Cause are found in *Analecta Congregationis Sanctissimi Redemptoris = Analecta 5* (1926) 194-197; 35 (1963) 198-201.

4. AAS 3 (1911) 254. Curiously, the index of the volume spells his name Newman. See also Joseph Wuest, C.SS.R, *Annales Congregationis SS. Redemptoris Provinciae Americanae* 4/1 (Boston, 1914) 153.

5. AAS 4 (1912) 336. On the various stages of the process leading to canonization, see F. Molinari, S.J. "Canonization of Saints, History and Procedure," *New Catholic Encyclopedia* 3 (1967) 55-59.

6. *Analecta 5* (1926) 195f.

7. AAS 12 (1920) 170-174. For an account of Father Benedetti's life, see *Analecta 5* (1926) 183-187.

8. AAS II (1919) 61, 205.

9. *Analecta 5* (1926) 196.

10. Benedict XIV, *De Servorium Dei Beatificazione et Beatorum Canonizatione*, 2 vols. fol. Bologna 1734-1735.

11. AAS 14 (1922) 23-26.

12. *Analecta 1* (1922) 14-15.

13. *Ibid.*, 15-22; *L'Osservatore Romano*, Dec, 12, 1921.

14. *Analecta* 1 (1922) 16.

15. *Ibid.* 18.

16. *Ibid.* 22.

17. Vatican II, *Lumen Gentium* 40: AAS 57 (1965) 45.

PLATES

Plate 1. Matyás Rauchmiller, Jan Brokoff, and Jeroným Heroldt, *St. John Nepomuk*. 1683. Prague, Charles Bridge.

Plate 2. Jan Brockoff, *St. John Nepomuk*. 1709-1710. Prague, Radniční steps in the Malá Strana.

Plate 3. Odoardo Vicinelli, *The Apotheosis of St. John Nepomuk*. 1729. Oil on linen painted on both sides. Prague, St. Vitus's Cathedral.

Plate 4. Woodcut of St. John Nepomuk in the hymnbook of Georgius Barthold Pontan von Breitenberg, *Hymnorum Sacrorum de beatissima Virgine Maria et S. Patronis S. R. Bohemiae libri tres* (1602). In the foreground Nepomuk receives the confession of the Queen; in the background his death is represented, on the right through the window the Greater Church of the Cross, where Nepomuk was first buried, and on the left his grave with ironwork enclosure in St. Vitus's cathedral.

Plate 5. *St. John Nepomuk Hearing Queen Sophia's Confession.* Engraving from
*Der Neu=eröffnet=Joannäishcen Ehr=und Gnaden=Pforte...des Heiligen Joannis
von Nepomuk* (1721), 143. Courtesy Pius Library, St. Louis Room—Rare Books
and Archives, Saint Louis University.

Plate 6. *St. John Nepomuk Preaching*. Engraving from *Der Neu=eröffnet=Joannäishcen Ehr=und Gnaden=Pforte…des Heiligen Joannis von Nepomuk* (1721), 7. Courtesy Pius Library, St. Louis Room—Rare Books and Archives, Saint Louis University.

Plate 7. *St. John Nepomuk Places His Finger to His Lips in the Presence of King Václav.* Engraving from *Der Neu=eröffnet=Joannäishcen Ehr=und Gnaden=Pforte...des Heiligen Joannis von Nepomuk* (1721), 11. Courtesy Pius Library, St. Louis Room—Rare Books and Archives, Saint Louis University.

Plate 8. *The Triumph of St. John Nepomuk.* Engraving from *Der Neu=eröffnet=Joannäishcen Ehr=und Gnaden=Pforte...des Heiligen Joannis von Nepomuk* (1721), 7. Courtesy Pius Library, St. Louis Room—Rare Books and Archives, Saint Louis University.

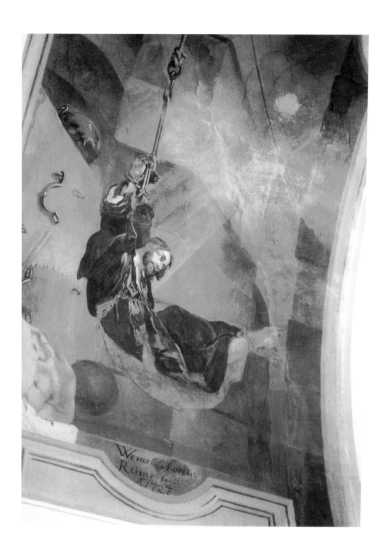

Plate 9. Fresco by Wenceslas Laurence Reiner (1727) in the Church of St. John Nepomuk on Hradčany Hill, Prague, showing the casting of John Nepomuk into the river. Photo by Milan Poselt.

Plate 10. Portrait of John Neumann as young boy. Redemptorist Provincial
Archives, Baltimore Province, Brooklyn, New York.

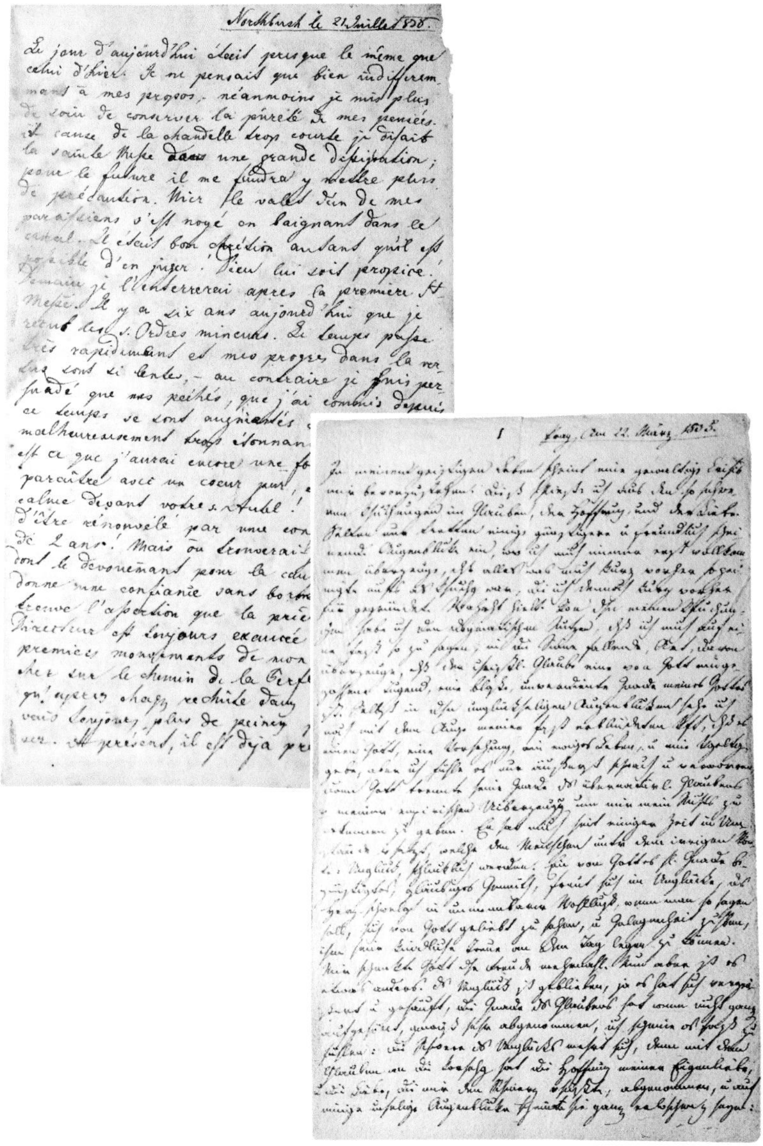

Plate 11. Handwritten pages in French and in German of Neumann's *Spiritual Journal*, which covers the period 1834-39, his final year of theological studies in the seminary at Prague, his journey to America, and the first five years of his ministry as a priest. Redemptorist Provincial Archives, Baltimore Province, Brooklyn, New York.

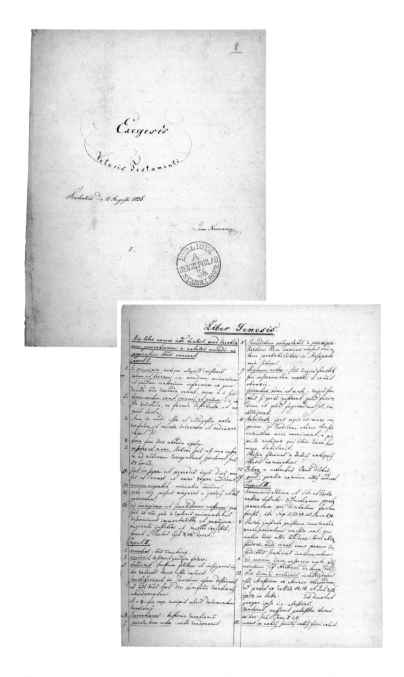

Plate 12. Handwritten title and text pages of Neumann's *Exegesis of the Old Testament*. Philadelphia Archdiocesan Historical Research Center.

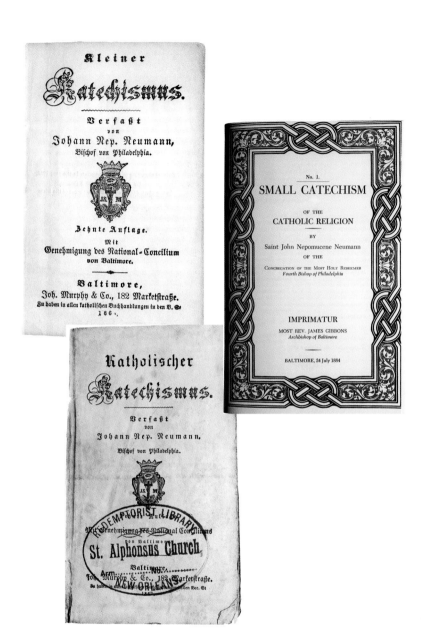

Plate 13. Neumann's *Small* and *Large Catechisms* were his most well-known published works during his lifetime. They were prepared in connection with his pastoral ministry in Pittsburgh and Baltimore, and were used extensively in German-speaking communities in the United States during the mid- and late 1800s. Redemptorist Provincial Archives, Baltimore Province, Brooklyn, New York.

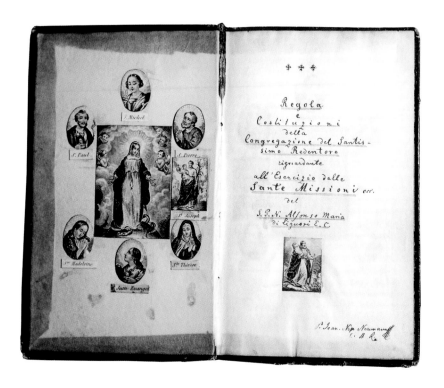

Plate 14. A booklet that Neumann made for himself of the section of the Redemptorist Rule having to do with preaching missions. The frontispiece shows the Immaculate Conception surrounded by images of a number of Neumann's "patrons" that were not printed on the page, but were cut out and pasted in by Neumann himself. From clockwise, the saints are: St. Michael the Archangel, St. Peter the Apostle, St. Joseph, St. Teresa of Ávila, St. John the Evangelist, St. Mary Magdalen, and St. Paul. The Good Shepherd is illustrated on the title page. Redemptorist Provincial Archives, Baltimore Province, Brooklyn, New York.

Plate 15. Holy card of St. Joseph and the Christ Child given to Neumann by
Venerable Joseph Passerat, C.Ss.R., who for twenty-eight years was Vicar
General of the North European Redemptorists (1820-48). With one hand,
Joseph holds his attribute of a flowering staff of lilies, symbolic of his divine election as the husband of Mary, as well as of his chastity; with the other, the saint
holds the left hand of the Christ Child, who blesses the viewer with His right
hand. The inscription beneath the image reads: *Ecce fidelis servus & prudens,
quem constituit Dominus super familiam suam*, "Behold the faithful and prudent
servant, whom the Lord placed over His family." Neumann Center, St. John
Neumann Shrine, St. Peter the Apostle Church, Philadelphia.

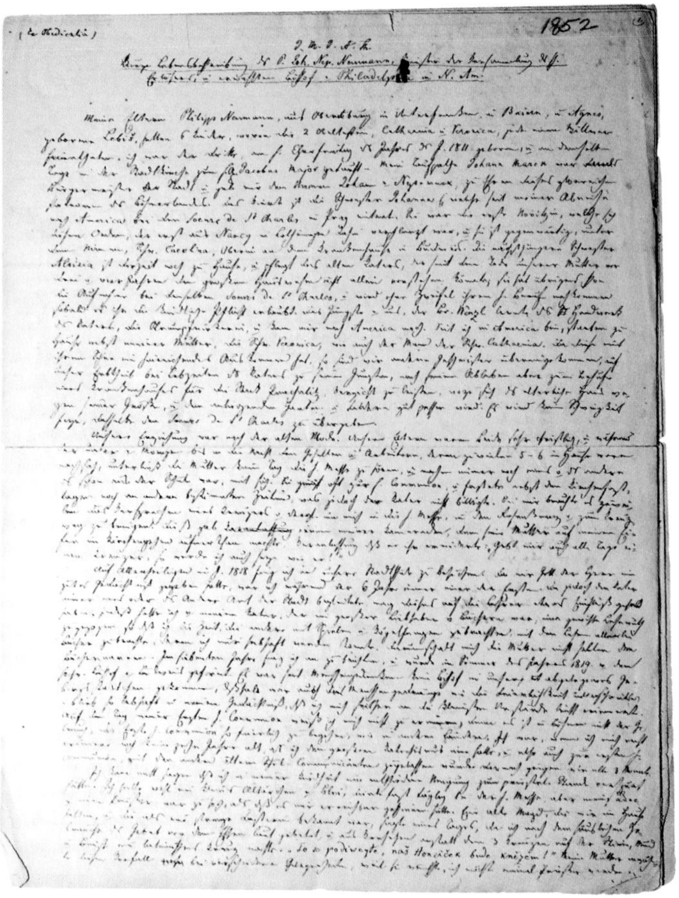

Plate 16. Handwritten page of Neumann's *Autobiography*, with "J.M.J.A.Th.," i.e., the abbreviations for "Jesus, Mary, Joseph, Alphonsus, Theresa," at the top of the page. Neumann thus followed the custom of St. Alphonsus Ligouri, founder of the Redemptorists, who wrote "J.M.J.T." at the head of his letters, a practice probably borrowed from the Carmelite nuns of the Teresian reform, to whom he was greatly devoted. Neumann added to these abbreviations, as many Redemptorists did, Alphonsus's own initial. Redemptorist Provincial Archives, Baltimore Province, Brooklyn, New York.

CONSTITUTIONES
Synodi Philadelphiensis Quartæ.

1. Ut Christi-Fideles magis opportunam nasciscantur occasionem eliciendi actus fidei, adorationis, spei, et amoris, erga Dominum *JESUM* in SS. Eucharistiæ Mysterio, ut præterea eidem amplius satisfieret pro tot tantisque, quæ contra illud committuntur reatus; constitutum fuit, ut piissimum exercitium *Quadraginta Horarum*, in iis Ecclesiis et Capellis hujus Diœceseos habeatur, quæ ab Episcopo quolibet anno una cum tempore indicabuntur, quo in qualibet Ecclesia celebrandum sit. Monentur tamen Pastores, ut omnia stricte observare curent, quo circa hoc exercitium in Ceremoniali Baltimorensi traduntur.

2. Cum Beatissima Virgo Maria, sub titulo Immaculatæ Conceptionis, rogantibus Patribus Concilii Baltimorensis III. Principalis Patrona Ecclesiæ Catholicæ in Fœderatis Nostris Statibus, a Summo Pontifice concessa sit, et ideo a fidelibus Nostræ curæ concredetis speciali veneratione et cultu veneranda sit: commendamus ad normam statuti Diœcesis Baltimorensis, A. D. 1791. habitæ, ut diebus Dominicis, et Festis de Præcepto, ante Missam Principalem, cantentur Litaniæ Lauretanæ, addita loco suo invocatione, "Regina, sine labe originali concepta, ora pro nobis." Ubi vero non sunt, qui eas cantare sciant, recitentur quinque Decades Rosarii cum eisdem Litaniis.

Plate 17. *Constitutions of the 1853 Synod of the Diocese of Philadelphia.* Among the statutes enacted by this synod were (no. 1) the establishment of the Forty Hours Devotion in the Diocese of Philadelphia and (no. 2) the promotion of the singing of the Litany of Loreto on Sundays and feast days before the principal Mass in all churches of the diocese. Philadelphia Archdiocesan Historical Research Center, Pamphlet 812.

St. Joseph's Church.

We had this week, the consolation of assisting at the Devotions in honor of the Blessed Sacrament, usually termed "The Forty Hours," in the abovementioned Church. It was but recently that the Churches of Philadelphia commenced this method of honoring the adorable sacrament of love: its good effects cannot but be visible to even the most indifferent observer. Each respective church has, in its turn, used every exertion to prepare a becoming resting-place for the Heavenly Guest. Amongst others we cannot but notice the admirable success which has crowned the untiring and zealous efforts of the friends of St. Joseph's sanctuary. The devotions in this Church commenced at 5 o'clock on Sunday, the 9th, and concluded on Tuesday, the 11th. It was truly a consolation to the Christian heart to observe with what eagerness the pious worshippers crowded about the brilliantly illuminated sanctuary; there, in humble sincerity of heart endeavoring to make amends to the amiable Jesus for the many indignities offered to him by an ungrateful and unthinking people. The able and feeling discourses delivered by the Very Rev. Drs. Moriarty and O'Hara, as also by the Very Rev. E. J. Sourin and Fr. John A. McGuigan, S. J., tended not a little to nourish and increase the flame of piety which Divine Grace had enkindled in the hearts of His devoted servants.

A new and interesting spectacle was presented to us on our first entrance into the Church, in the tasteful arrangement of gaslights encircling the golden Remonstrance lately received from Europe. This exquisite piece of workmanship is the gift of the friends of St. Joseph's to the devoted Pastor, the Rev. F. J. Barbelin. It is more than three feet high, resting upon a highly ornamented throne of about the same height, the two thus forming a most gorgeous repository wherein our loving Saviour, concealed under the Eucharistic veil, deigns to make His abode with the children of men.

Plate 18. Article from the 15 Oct. 1853 issue of *The Catholic Instructor* describing the Forty Hours devotion held at Old St. Joseph's Church on 9-11 Oct. 1853. Of special interest is the mention of the new monstrance that was used for the first time on this occasion and that had been presented as a gift to the pastor, Father Felix J. Barbelin, S.J., who was also the founder and first president of Saint Joseph's College. Philadelphia Archdiocesan Historical Research Center.

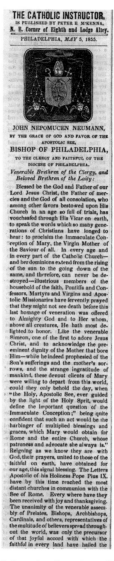

THE CATHOLIC INSTRUCTOR,
IS PUBLISHED BY PETER E M'KENNA,
N. E. Corner of Eighth and Lodge Alley.
PHILADELPHIA, MAY 5, 1855.

JOHN NEPOMUCEN NEUMANN,
BY THE GRACE OF GOD AND FAVOR OF THE
APOSTOLIC SEE,
BISHOP OF PHILADELPHIA,
TO THE CLERGY AND FAITHFUL OF THE
DIOCESE OF PHILADELPHIA.

*Venerable Brethren of the Clergy, and
Beloved Brethren of the Laity:*

Blessed be the God and Father of our
Lord Jesus Christ, the Father of mer-
cies and the God of all consolation, who
among other favors bestowed upon His
Church in an age so full of trials, has
vouchsafed through His Vicar on earth,
to speak the words which so many generations of Christians have longed to
hear: to proclaim the Immaculate Conception of Mary, the Virgin Mother of
the Saviour of all. In every age and
in every part of the Catholic Church—
and her dominions extend from the rising
of the sun to the going down of the
same, and therefore, can never be de-
stroyed—illustrious members of the
household of the faith, Pontiffs and Confessors, Martyrs and Virgins and Apostolic Missionaries have fervently prayed
that they might not see death before this
last homage of veneration was offered
to Almighty God and to Her whom,
above all creatures, He hath most delighted to honor. Like the venerable
Simeon, one of the first to adore Jesus
Christ, and to acknowledge the pre-
eminent dignity of the Mother that bore
Him—while he indeed prophesied of the
Son's sufferings and the mother's sor-
rows, and the strange ingratitude of
mankind, these devout clients of Mary
were willing to depart from this world,
could they only behold the day, when
"the Holy, Apostolic See, ever guided
by the light of the Holy Sprit, would
define the important question of the
Immaculate Conception;" being quite
confident that such an act would be the
harbinger of multiplied blessings and
graces, which Mary would obtain for
Rome and the entire Church, whose
patroness and advocate she always is."
Reigning as we know they are with
God, their prayers, united to those of the
faithful on earth, have obtained for
our age, this signal blessing. The Letters
Apostolic of his Holiness Pope Pius IX.
have by this time reached the most
distant churches in communion with the
See of Rome. Every where have they
been received with joy and thanksgiving.
The unanimity of the venerable assembly of Prelates, Bishops, Archbishops,
Cardinals, and others, representatives of
the multitude of believers spread throughout the world, was only the precursor
of that joyful accord with which the
faithful in every land have hailed the

Plate 19. Initial section of the printed version of Neumann's Second Pastoral Letter on the Immaculate Conception, published in *The Catholic Instructor,* 5 May 1855. Neumann's episcopal coat of arms, with his motto *Passio Christi conforta me,* "Passion of Christ comfort me," adopted from the prayer *Anima Christi,* appears above the letter's text. Philadelphia Archdiocesan Historical Research Center.

Plate 20. Giovanni Gagliardi, *St. John Neumann and Catholic School Children.* Ca. 1880. Oil on canvas. As the founder of the diocesan school system in the United States, Neumann will always have a place of great prominence in the history of Catholic education. Neumann once referred to the development and expansion of the Catholic school system in Philadelphia as his "key project." Office of Catholic Schools, Archdiocese of Philadelphia.

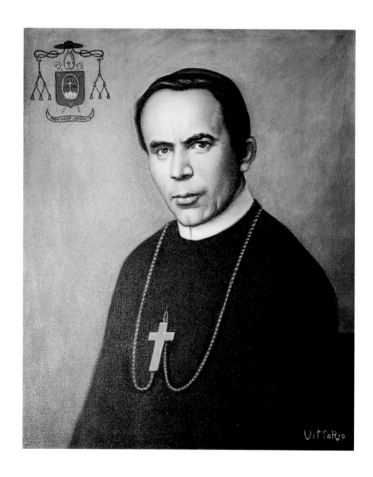

Plate 21. Vittorio, *St. John Neumann*. 1968-81. Oil on canvas. This portrait was commissioned by Bro. Barnabas Hipkins, C.Ss.R., during his tenure as Archivist. Unfortunately, there is no information in Bro. Barnabas's papers on the portrait's history or the artist, who, it is believed, was in New York City between 1968 and 1981. This painting of Neumman was to be the first of a series of portraits of former Redemptorist Provincials, but no others were ever done. Redemptorist Provincial Archives, Baltimore Province, Brooklyn, New York.

Plate 22. Alessandro Kokociski, *St. John N. Neumann.* 1977. Cover of program for Neumann's canonization. Saint Joseph's University Archives. Gift of Mr. & Mrs. John Puppo.

NOTES ON CONTRIBUTORS

Richard A. Boever, C.Ss.R., is Director of Formation at St. John Neumann House in St. Louis, Missouri, and a faculty member at Saint Louis University. He has served as an editor, and later publisher and president, at Ligouri Publications. His Ph.D. thesis at Saint Louis University was on "The Spirituality of St. John Neumann, C.Ss.R.." He is the author of more than fifty essays, articles, and booklets.

Mary Charles Bryce, O.S.B., was Associate Professor of Religion and Religious Education at The Catholic University of America. In recognition of her contribution to religious studies, Catholic University established the Mary Charles Bryce Lectureship in the Christian Education Trust. Her publications includes articles and reviews in journals, such as *Worship, American Benedictine Review*, and *The Living Light*, as well as the books *Come Let Us Eat: Preparing for First Communion* (New York: Herder & Herder, 1964) and *Pride of Place: The Role of the Bishops in the Development of Catechesis in the United States* (Washington, D.C.: Catholic University of America Press, 1984).

Joseph F. Chorpenning, O.S.F.S., is Editorial Director of Saint Joseph's University Press. He is the author of numerous articles and essays published in a wide variety of scholarly journals and books (*acta, festschriften*, and exhibition catalogues). His books include *The Divine Romance: Teresa of Ávila's Narrative Theology* (Chicago: Loyola University Press, 1992), and a critical edition and translation, with commentary, of Francis de Sales, *Sermon Texts on Saint Joseph* (Toronto: Peregrina Publishing Co., 2000).

Michael J. Curley, C.Ss.R., was Research Historian and Archivist of the New York Province of the Redemptorists. He is the author of Neumann's definitive biography (Washington, D.C.: Catholic University of America Press, 1952, with numerous reprints thereafter), as well as many other publications, including *The Provincial Story: A History of the Baltimore Province of the Congregation of the Most Holy Redeemer* (1963), and *Cheerful Ascetic: The Life of Francis Xavier Seelos, C.Ss.R.* (1969).

Augustinus Kurt Huber was editor of, and a frequent contributor to, the *Archiv für Kirchengeschichte von Böhmen-Mähren-Schlesien*, published by the Königsteiner Institut für Kirchen- und Geistesgeschichte der Sudetenländer.

Joseph C. Linck, a priest of the Diocese of Bridgeport, is an instructor at Saint John Fisher Seminary and its Permanent Diaconate Formation Program. He is the author of *"Fully Instructed and Vehemently Influenced": Catholic Preaching in Anglo-Catholic America* (Philadelphia: Saint Joseph's University Press, 2002), as well as articles on the spirituality of Colonial Catholicism, and the Catholic Church in Pennsylvania.

Alfred C. Rush, C.Ss.R., was a faculty member at The Catholic University of America for forty years (1941-81). His doctoral thesis, *Death and Burial in Christian Antiquity*, directed by Johannes Quasten, was published as the inaugural volume of the series "Studies in Christian Antiquity" (1941). Fr. Rush published many articles in learned journals, such as *Catholic Biblical Quarterly, Catholic Historical Review, The Jurist, Theological Studies, Traditio,* and *Vigiliae Christianae*. He is also the author of numerous articles on Neumann, as well as the translator and annotator of Neumann's *Autobiography* (Boston: St. Paul Books & Media, 1977).

Paul Shore is Professor of Educational Studies at Saint Louis University. His recent publications include *The Eagle and the Cross: Jesuits in Late Baroque Bohemia* (St. Louis: Institute of Jesuit Sources, 2002), "Cluj, A Jesuit Outpost in Translyvania" (*Catholic Education* 5/1, 2001, 55-71), and (with Paul Reinert, S.J.) *Seasons of Change:*

Reflections on a Half a Century at Saint Louis University (St. Louis: Saint Louis University Press, 1996).

Thomas A. Thompson, S.M., is Director of the Marian Library and a faculty member in the International Marian Research Institute of the University of Dayton. His articles have appeared in *Marian Studies, Ephemerides Mariologicae, The Josephinum Review of Theology, Liturgical Ministry*, and in various collections of essays.

INDEX